W9-AQZ-170

PAWNEE, BLACKFOOT
AND CHEYENNE

PAWNEE,

Selected and with an introduction by
DEE BROWN

BLACKFOOT

AND CHEYENNE

History and Folklore of the Plains
from the writings of

GEORGE BIRD GRINNELL

CHARLES SCRIBNER'S SONS
New York

COPYRIGHT © 1961 CHARLES SCRIBNER'S SONS

Selections from *Beyond the Old Frontier* and *Blackfeet Indian Stories* by George Bird Grinnell. Copyright 1913 Charles Scribner's Sons; renewal copyright 1941 Elisabeth C. Grinnell; and from *Blackfoot Lodge Tales* and *Pawnee Hero Stories*. Published by Charles Scribner's Sons.

Special acknowledgement is made to the following who have granted permission for the reprinting of material from the works of George Bird Grinnell as indicated:

Appleton-Century-Crofts, Inc. for selections from *The Story of the Indian*.

The American Museum of Natural History for "An Old-Time Bone Hunt" from JOURNAL OF NATURAL HISTORY, Volume 23, 1932 (pp. 329-336).

University of Oklahoma Press for selections from *The Cheyenne Indians* (Copyright 1956 by the University of Oklahoma Press) and *The Fighting Cheyennes* (Copyright 1915 Charles Scribner's Sons; renewal copyright 1943 Elisabeth C. Grinnell. Copyright 1956 by the University of Oklahoma Press).

Yale University Press for selections from *By Cheyenne Campfires*. Copyright 1926 Yale University Press.

This book published simultaneously in the United States of America and in Canada Copyright under the Berne Convention
All rights reserved. No part of this book may be reproduced in any form without the permission of Charles Scribner's Sons.

A-3.61 [v]

PRINTED IN THE UNITED STATES OF AMERICA

Library of Congress Catalog Card Number: 61-7217

CONTENTS

INTRODUCTION

George Bird Grinnell was a man interested in all the wonders of the world, but like his good friend, Theodore Roosevelt, his zest was keenest for things of the out-of-doors. During his long career he was a naturalist, sportsman, conservationist, cowboy, explorer, geographer, zoologist, ornithologist, mountain climber, editor, publisher, and author. In a brief autobiographical note written for *American Men of Science*, he listed himself only as an anthropologist, his main interests being the history and habits of Plains Indians.

Most of Grinnell's writings were about the Indians and their place in the history of the American West, and it is to his three favorite tribes, Pawnee, Blackfoot, and Cheyenne that this collection is mainly devoted.

He met the Pawnees first, when he made his memorable grand tour of the West in 1870 with Professor Othniel C. Marsh's geological expedition. Grinnell was only twenty years old, a senior at Yale, his head filled with Mayne Reid's tales of the Wild West, when he learned of Marsh's proposed expedition. "I felt that I had no qualifications for a position on such an expedition," he wrote afterward. "However, after much pondering I mustered up courage, called on Professor Marsh, and asked if I could in any way attach myself to his party. I found him far less formidable than I had feared."

Marsh not only accepted Grinnell for his party but asked his help in securing other young men. "Probably none of them except the leader had any motives for going other than the hope of adventures with wild game or wild Indians." For Grinnell it was a romantic journey, the hardships only challenges which he met with the same zeal as the hero of Joseph Conrad's *Youth*.

This was the beginning of a sixty-year spiritual liaison between a Brooklyn-born easterner and the Great West. Much as he loved the West, Grinnell never gave up his Eastern base. He seemed to do his best writing away from his subject, yet scarcely a summer passed

Introduction

after the 1870 geological jaunt through Nebraska, Wyoming, Utah, and Kansas, that did not find him somewhere in the Plains and the Rockies. He was interested in everything he found there—vertebrate fossils, rocks and minerals, trees and flowers, birds and big game animals, but most of all in the Indians, their way of life and their rich store of unrecorded history and folk legends.

During the 1870 tour through western Nebraska, the Yale geological group was escorted by Major Frank North and two Pawnees from the major's famed military scouting company. When Grinnell returned to the West in 1872, he joined Luther North for a long buffalo hunt with the Pawnees. Through the North brothers he won ready acceptance by the tribe, and later spent several summers studying Pawnee customs and listening to folktales told by old chiefs around campfires.

After his first expedition with Marsh, Grinnell worked under the professor's direction, preparing osteological materials for the Peabody Museum. Early in 1874, Marsh appointed him to the regular staff as assistant in paleontology, and a few months later showed his high confidence in his young aide by offering him an opportunity to accompany General George Custer on an expedition to the Black Hills.

For a young man in his mid-twenties this was high adventure indeed. He arranged to meet Luther North early in the summer at St. Paul and they went together to Fort Abraham Lincoln to join Custer. Grinnell was listed as official naturalist of the Black Hills expedition but received no salary, in fact had to agree to pay his own expenses and probably those of North who accompanied him by invitation as his assistant. During the march Custer was at his most flamboyant, riding at the head of about a thousand men, including a regimental band mounted on white horses. The band played the troops out of camp each morning and performed concerts in the evenings. President Grant's son, Lieutenant Frederick Grant, was on the general's staff. Chief guide was Charley Reynolds, who would die with Custer at Little Big Horn two years later.

Heading the scientific staff was Captain William Ludlow of the Army's Corps of Engineers. Grinnell's work in the Black Hills must have pleased Ludlow; the following year he asked the young man

Introduction

from Yale to accompany him as naturalist on a reconnaissance of Yellowstone National Park.

During this 1875 survey through Montana and Wyoming, Grinnell first became concerned over wanton destruction of game on the frontier. In his report to Ludlow he wrote: "It may not be out of place here, to call your attention to the terrible destruction of large game, for the hides alone, which is constantly going on in those portions of Montana and Wyoming through which we passed. Buffalo, elk, mule-deer, and antelope are being slaughtered by thousands each year, without regard to age or sex, and at all seasons. Of the vast majority of animals killed, the hide only is taken. Females of all these species are as eagerly pursued in the spring, when just about to bring forth their young, as at any other time.

"It is estimated that during the winter of 1874–75 not less than 3,000 elk were killed for their hides alone . . . Buffalo and mule-deer suffer even more severely than the elk, and antelope nearly as much. The Territories referred to have game laws, but, of course, they are imperfect, and cannot, in the present condition of the country, be enforced. Much, however, might be done to prevent the reckless destruction of the animals to which I have referred, by the officers stationed on the frontier, and a little exertion in this direction would be well repaid by the increase of large game in the vicinity of the posts where it was not unnecessarily and wantonly destroyed . . . The general feeling of the better class of frontiersmen, guides, hunters, and settlers, is strongly against those who are engaged in this work of butchery, and all, I think, would be glad to have this wholesale and short-sighted slaughter put a stop to. But it is needless to enlarge upon this abuse. The facts concerning it are well known to most Army officers and to all inhabitants of the Territory. It is certain that, unless in some way the destruction of these animals can be checked, the large game still so abundant in some localities will ere long be exterminated."

Thus was formulated Grinnell's philosophy of conservation. He loved hunting, or outdoor sportsmanship as he called it, but he detested useless slaughter of wild game.

In 1876 he was so busy with work on his doctor's degree, his regu-

Introduction

lar duties at the Peabody Museum, and some writing he was doing for *Forest and Stream*, that he passed up an opportunity to make another western jaunt with the Army. Perhaps it was just as well. The man who invited him was George Custer. Had Grinnell accepted he probably would have been a victim of the grand massacre, which would have been a double tragedy—the Indians would have killed off the young man who was to become their stanchest defender over the next half century. The nation also would have lost a first-rate historian and folklorist, as well as an outspoken advocate of the national parks system and protector of wildlife.

Grinnell was born in Brooklyn, September 20, 1849, and from the age of seven to manhood lived in Audubon Park on Manhattan Island. For a time he was a pupil of Lucy Audubon, widow of the artist-naturalist, and in 1886 when he founded a bird-protection organization, he named it in memory of the Audubons. Within a few years there were many state Audubon societies, and in 1905 the national association was founded with Grinnell as a trustee. In 1887 he joined with Theodore Roosevelt to form the Boone and Crockett Club, an association of sportsmen interested in game conservation. From 1891 until 1910 he fought for the establishment of Glacier National Park. He was one of the early explorers of the region, discovering its glaciers, and had he not been so modest the park might have borne his name. Grinnell Glacier, Grinnell Mountain, and Grinnell Lake remind tourists today of the man responsible for the preservation of this great wilderness area which he called "the crown of the continent."

His interest in the Blackfoot Indians began in 1885 when he made his first hunting and exploring trip into northwestern Montana. Each summer from 1887 for a number of years he made subsequent journeys to the Blackfoot country. After his marriage in 1902 he was often accompanied by his wife, an enthusiastic amateur photographer, and they camped with the Blackfeet, living in a tepee, studying the Indians' customs, listening to their stories. That Grinnell did not neglect his hunting or exploring for his anthropological researches is indicated in a remark made by his friend, James Willard Schultz: "On the day we discovered Grinnell Glacier, Grinnell killed a fine bighorn ram upon it, and we had a great feast that night."

Introduction

The Blackfeet named him "Fisher Hat," and not only adopted him into the tribe but eventually made him a head chief. Grinnell recalled the ceremony in a letter some years after the event: "At the Medicine Lodge in the ceremonial at which all the chiefs were present, he [Chief White Calf] made me stand up by his side and told me that he now transferred to me the care of the people, and henceforth I should be the head chief of the tribe. I have tried hard to deserve the confidence he put in me then and later, but I have often failed." The last sentence is characteristic of Grinnell's almost painful reserve. Another characteristic was his love of obstacles. "The conquering of difficulties is one of the chief joys of life," he once wrote to a friend.

In 1925 when President Coolidge presented him with the Theodore Roosevelt medal for promotion of outdoor life, the laconic New Englander summed up Grinnell's career in a single paragraph: "You were with General Custer in the Black Hills and with Colonel Ludlow in the Yellowstone. You lived among the Indians; you became a member of the Blackfoot tribe. Your studies of their language and customs are authoritative. Few have done so much as you, none has done more, to preserve vast areas of picturesque wilderness for the eyes of posterity in the simple majesty in which you and your fellow pioneers first beheld them. In the Yellowstone Park you prevented the exploitation and, therefore, the destruction of the natural beauty. The Glacier National Park is peculiarly your monument. As editor for thirty-five years of a journal devoted to outdoor life, you have done a noteworthy service in bringing to the men and women of a hurried and harried age the relaxation and revitalization which comes from contact with Nature. I am glad to have a part in the public recognition which your self-effacing and effective life has won."

His writing career began in 1876 when *Forest and Stream*, a weekly devoted to outdoor life, offered him a post as natural history editor. After receiving his Ph.D. in 1880, he returned to New York to become editor and eventually owner of the periodical, a career which he followed until 1911. In the 1880's he began publishing in *Forest and Stream* some of the folktales he had heard from the Pawnees. In 1889 he issued under the magazine's imprint a collection of these pieces, *Pawnee Hero Stories and Folk-Tales*, later republished by Scribner's in 1912. Scribner's published *Blackfoot Lodge Tales* in

Introduction

1892, and over the next thirty years Grinnell produced more than a score of volumes on Indians, Western history, hunting, camping, and conservation. He also was a frequent contributor to *The Journal of American Folklore, American Anthropologist, Harpers' Magazine,* and *Scribner's Magazine,* his articles ranging from Plains Indian myths to studies of tribal customs and traditions.

Among his most popular books were several juveniles, *Jack Among the Indians; Jack, the Young Cowboy; Jack in the Rockies,* etc. These were written nostalgically perhaps (he said they were meant primarily for his nephews and nieces) when Grinnell was in his fifties, the hero being an eastern boy who visited the West for adventure as the author had done in his youth.

Grinnell's most important contributions to the record of American Indian civilization are his works on the Cheyennes, *The Fighting Cheyennes* (published by Scribner's in 1915 and reprinted by University of Oklahoma Press in 1956), a two-volume work, *The Cheyenne Indians* (Yale, 1923) and *By Cheyenne Campfires* (Yale, 1926). These books are the products of a lifetime of observation, personal interviews and research into one tribe's way of life before and after it collided with the white man's settlement of the West. So extensive are details of dress, courtship, the place of women in the tribe, implements of war, hunting methods, games and amusements, religion, accounts of battles, they have long been favorite source books for everyone interested in Plains Indians.

Few other tribes could match the Cheyennes in story-telling abilities, the form of their tales often approaching that of our modern shaggy-dog stories. "Some of the stories were short, others were long, sometimes told in great detail, and even in sections," Grinnell said. "A short story might be told, and when it was finished the narrator stopped, and, after a pause, said, 'I will tie another one to it.' Then there was a long pause; the pipe was perhaps lighted and smoked, and a little conversation had; then the story teller began again and told another section of the tale, ending as before. Such stories were often told in groups of four or six, and might last all night. At formal gatherings a man might tell a story and when it was finished might say: 'The story is ended. Can anyone tie another to it?' Another man might then relate one, ending it with the same words, and so stories might be told all about the lodge. Or a story might end with the words, 'This cuts it off.' "

His last major work, *Two Great Scouts and Their Pawnee Battalion*, published in 1928, was a salute to the two brothers, Frank and Luther North, who had first introduced him to the Indians. He died ten years later, April 11, 1938, at the age of 88.

The following selections from Grinnell's writings are arranged by tribes—Pawnee, Blackfoot, and Cheyenne—with an added section devoted mainly to Indian relations with the white man. In a way the arrangement follows the chronology of the author's associations with these tribes. Each of the Indian sections opens with an account of his personal experiences with the tribe, followed by one or more pieces on tribal history or social organization, and then closing with selections of folktales collected from that tribe. The concluding section contains an account of first impressions made upon the Indians by the European intruders, a history of Bent's Fort (which Grinnell considered a symbol of Indian-frontiersman relationships), and the article which he wrote as a sort of keynote for his long campaign to create Glacier National Park.

DEE BROWN

THE PAWNEES

FROM YALE TO THE WILD WEST

(*An Old-Time Bone Hunt*; AN ACCOUNT OF THE EXPEDITION UNDERTAKEN BY PROF. O. C. MARSH IN 1870 TO THE THEN WILD WEST)

IN THE spring of the year 1870 it became known to members of the senior class at Yale that Prof. O. C. Marsh contemplated making a geological expedition to the Far West, for the purpose of collecting vertebrate fossils. Marsh, although then professor of palæontology at Yale, did not conduct courses and was personally known to few undergraduates. The students knew little about palæontology and were not greatly interested in geology.

From boyhood I had read the books of Capt. Mayne Reid, which told of the western country in the forties, and that country and its wildness had taken strong hold on my imagination. When I heard of the proposed expedition by Professor Marsh, I determined that, if possible, I would accompany it, but I felt that I had no qualification for a position on such an expedition.

However, after much pondering I mustered up courage, called on Professor Marsh, and asked if I could in any way attach myself to his party. I found him far less formidable than I had feared. He said that he would consider my application, and later told me that he would be glad to have me go. He discussed with me the composition of the party, and after a little it developed that I was the only member as yet chosen. His consultations with me enabled me to suggest to him names of men I knew well and whom I wished to be of the party.

Marsh was possessed of considerable means and had a wide acquaintance. He had interested General P. H. Sheridan in his project and from him had obtained orders directed to military posts in the West to provide the party with transportation and escorts needed in passing through dangerous Indian country. Besides that, some

3

well-to-do business men had contributed funds to defray the expenses of the trip, and I have always suspected that some of these, being railroad men, had given Marsh either free transportation for his party or at least rates much lower than those usually in force.

In the light of later events the personnel of the expedition is more or less interesting. Among its members were James W. Wadsworth (the father of the present senator from New York) who left Yale in 1864 to join the Union forces and who subsequently for twenty years represented one of the districts of northern New York in Congress; C. McC. Reeve, who later did good service in many directions for his fellow men, was a general in the Spanish War, and served effectively in the Philippines; Eli Whitney and Henry B. Sargent, who in later years were members of the corporation of Yale University; J. R. Nicholson, who subsequently served as chancellor of the State of Delaware; and a number of others, who became successful business men. All these finally left New Haven, June 30, on their start for a West that was then actually wild. Probably none of them except the leader had any motive for going other than the hope of adventure with wild game or wild Indians.

Except through what they had read Professor Marsh and his party knew nothing about the West. It was an entirely innocent party of "pilgrims," starting out to face dangers of which they were wholly ignorant. At this time the Sioux and Cheyenne Indians occupied the country of western Nebraska and that to the north and northwest, and they objected strongly to the passage of people through their territory, and when they could do so—that is, when they believed they had the advantage,—attacked such parties.

We crossed the Missouri River in one of the old-fashioned sternwheel ferry boats and spent a day or two in Omaha, where some of us tried our rifles, which up to then we had not fired, at targets in what is now the fashionable residential section of the town, but which was then bare—and, of course, uncultivated—prairie. Professor Marsh and Jim Wadsworth went on ahead to Fort McPherson on the Platte River, then the headquarters of the Fifth Cavalry, where General Emory was in command. The rest of us followed a day or two later.

The day we reached the post a party of two or three antelope hunters out from the fort had been attacked by a dozen Indians who had swooped down upon them. One of the Indians, bearing in mind the injunction often given him by his elders that it is no disgrace to be killed in battle, rode up close to one of the antelope hunters and sent an arrow through his arm. The hunter responded with a well-directed rifle ball and the Indian rode away, falling from his horse before he got out of sight, whereupon the antelope hunters returned to the post.

A troop of cavalry sent out to overtake the Indians, of course failed in their purpose but found the dead Indian boy, wrapped in his buffalo robe, on top of a hill near where he had fallen. William F. Cody—Buffalo Bill—who was then post guide at Fort McPherson, brought in the boy's moccasins and some trinkets taken from the body, at which the newcomers from New Haven stared in wonder.

Professor Marsh had arranged that we should go first from Fort McPherson to the Loup Fork River to the north, where, it was understood, there were late Tertiary fossil beds of considerable interest. A troop of cavalry was to accompany us as escort, with six army wagons to carry the provisions and supplies, including tents, blankets, and ammunition.

The young men from the East, some of whom had never mounted a horse, were taken out to the corral near the post stables and there were introduced to a lot of Indian ponies captured from the Cheyennes the previous autumn at the Battle of Summit Springs. Major Frank North with two of his Pawnee Indian scouts had taken part in that fight and they chose for us the gentlest mounts.

We crossed the Platte River and, led by Major North and his Pawnees, started north through the desolate sand hills toward the hoped-for river. No one in the outfit, excepting the Pawnee Indians, had ever before been through the country, but by keeping north we could not fail to strike the Loup River. The sand hills were not high but they were very steep, and the sand was deep, making the pulling hard for the teams. Major North, riding ahead, selected the easiest way for the wagons, while still ahead of him the Indian scouts went forward and from the tops of the highest hills peered through the grass to see whether enemies could be discerned.

The country to be passed over was dangerous, for at any time one might meet parties of Sioux Indians, who would certainly attack us if they felt that they could safely do so. We were blissfully ignorant of all this and supposed that because we saw no Indians, there were none about and that there was no danger.

Perhaps none of the eastern members of the party had ever before been very far out of sight of a house, and none could understand the possible danger of the situation, because all the surroundings were something entirely outside of their experience. The first day's march was long, monotonous, and hot, and there was no water to drink. Some of the young men imagined that they were perishing from thirst and that they must have a drink of cold water.

At the end of the long day's march one of the soldiers, hot, thirsty, and utterly weary, was heard to exclaim, "What did God Almighty make such a country for?" To which one of his companions made the reply that "God Almighty made the country good enough, but it's this infernal geology that the professor talks about that has spoiled it all!"

Just before dark, water was found and we camped for our first night out of doors. That night at the camp fire Professor Marsh talked to us and to an audience of soldiers about the geological changes that had taken place here in past ages and about the discoveries of unknown animals that he hoped to make. Buffalo Bill, who had ridden out with us for the first day's march, was an interested auditor and was disposed to think that the professor was trying to see how much he could make his hearers believe of the stories he told them.

The hot, waterless marches continued, and two or three days satisfied the young men that they had seen quite enough of Nebraska. However, as the journey went on, they became more accustomed to the situation—to the heat, to the lack of shade, and to the absence of water—and began to take an interest in the country. Every day Major North took ahead with him one of the young men, whom he permitted to shoot at the antelope. No member of the party killed anything, which is not surprising in view of the fact that none of us knew anything of hunting or rifle shooting, or of the arms we were using.

At last we reached the Loup Fork, not without some alarms of Indians, for from time to time columns of smoke were seen,—signals indicating that the Sioux were communicating with one another. It was even said that an Indian had been seen watching the outfit from a distant hill.

The Loup River flows through a valley far below the general level of the prairie, and into this valley open many cañons, narrow and wide, in the sides of which were seen the strata of an ancient lake bottom through which the water had cut. There were many exposures of the so-called *mauvaises terres*, and in these bare clay surfaces fossil bones were found. The escort made short marches up the river, and the easterners, with a small guard of soldiers to act as lookouts, devoted themselves to bone hunting. After a little while the soldiers became as interested in collecting fossils as the members of the party, and brought in many specimens. As they gained experience, some of them became quite skillful collectors.

The region then examined was of late Tertiary age and gave us many Pliocene mammals—horses, camels, and other vertebrates—which tended to throw light on various problems more fully elucidated by recent investigations.

The country was full of game, antelope being by all odds the most abundant. This was long prior to any settlement on the plains and the antelope were still nearly in their primitive numbers. On the Loup Fork River elk were found and killed and fresh meat for the party was never lacking. More than once we came upon Indian burial places, the wrapped-up bodies resting on platforms, each supported by four poles standing in the ground. With the bodies had been placed the usual accompaniments of arms and implements, and beneath each platform were the bones of two or three horses, killed to provide the owner with mounts in his future life. The dried skulls of the Indians on these platforms were added to the party's collections.

One night a prairie fire, which, it was thought, had been kindled by the Sioux, crept down toward our camp from both sides of the river, but as we were in a bend, it was not difficult by back-firing to protect ourselves from the flames. The advance of the fire along the hills on either side of the river was interesting and—when our anxiety with regard to the camp had subsided—very beautiful. For the next day or two, however, the question of grass for the animals was one of difficulty.

We worked up the river quite a long way, but I have never known

7

which of the branches we followed. At last, turning southward, we set out again for the railroad, and once more entered an area where water was hard to get. What little we did find, was bitterly alkaline. This was a region of dry lakes, and water could be had only by digging. Some years later, when as a humble cow-puncher I worked cattle through this country, I often had excellent deer-hunting among these dry lakes.

Journeying south through this country we followed down the Birdwood River and one evening crossed the Platte, and at North Platte City had a real meal, sitting in chairs at a table and eating from china plates. There we learned of the Franco-German War, declared in our absence, and that night on our return to camp, Lieutenant Reilly ordered his men to fall in and with something of a flourish of oratory announced to them that war had been declared between France and Germany. The men, who were more or less surprised at the unusual order to get in the ranks while they were in camp, manifested slight interest, and when they were dismissed, I heard one of the soldiers declare with forcible profanity how little he cared about the news.

From Fort McPherson we proceeded west by rail to Cheyenne, and a few days later left Fort D. A. Russell, Wyoming Territory, to explore a region lying between the north and south forks of the Platte River. Before long we came upon some bad lands not previously known, the southwestern boundary of a Tertiary lake basin, in the margin of which were entombed and waiting to be excavated turtles, rhinoceroses, *Oreodon*, and the huge *Titanotherium*. These beds we followed for a long distance westward. At Antelope Station on the railroad, a locality from which Professor Marsh had secured some fossils the year before, we found several species of horse, one of them a little fellow only two feet high and having three toes.

Crossing the North Platte River we came upon and followed the old California and Oregon trail, along whose ruts so many searchers for wealth had traveled less than twenty years before. The grass was growing all along the road and where the wagons had passed was a continuous bed of sunflowers. Shortly before we reached Scotts Bluff we came upon another outcrop of fossil bones.

From the Platte we went to Horse Creek searching for other fossil grounds, and here two of the young men left our party, after being informed by the commanding officer that camp would be made about twenty miles farther along the creek, and followed up the stream to ,shoot the ducks that then were migrating in great numbers. The commanding officer did not know, nor did anyone else, that near here the creek made a great bend and that to follow it around to the place where the camp was to be pitched meant a journey of fifty or sixty miles.

The duck shooters killed some ducks, but as the sun drew toward the west, they began to be doubtful about reaching camp. They started back, intending to cut across country and strike the trail of the command, but before they had gone far, they were threatened by a prairie fire. One man dismounted and began to back-fire, but with the fire came a tremendous wind which swept on the flames at an inconceivably rapid rate. Finally he who was watching on his horse shouted to his companion to mount. He did so just as the flames swept toward them singeing the hair of men and horses; but two or three jumps took them to a burned space and the fire passed by on either side. The young men believed that the fire had obliterated the trail and rode back to the stream, feeling that this was a guide that would not fail them. They only now realized that to be far away from camp unarmed, except with shotguns, on the border of the Cheyenne Reservation was not a pleasant situation. They rode down the stream, stopped just as the sun set, built a fire, and made preparations for spending the night there. As soon as it grew dark, however, they remounted, rode into the stream, followed that down for a mile, so that no trail should be left, and then riding out on the bank spent the night there without fire.

Meantime Professor Marsh and all at the camp were much concerned about the absentees. Searching parties were sent out next day but found no trail they could follow. They came upon a couple of crippled horses abandoned by Indians, and this lowered the spirits of the searchers, who supposed that their companions had been killed, their horses taken, and these cripples left in their place. Meanwhile the lost ones, following the stream down to the camp of the day before, took the wagon trail there and that night appeared in camp.

After some weeks in this general region the party traveled west by rail to old Fort Bridger in Wyoming, a trading post established long before by the famous Jim Bridger. At and near Fort Bridger a long stay was made. South of the fort were great washed deposits of greenish sand and clay of Eocene age, and here we found great numbers of the extraordinary six-horned beasts later described by Marsh as Dinocerata. It was from this locality too that came *Eohippus*, the earliest horselike animal of which we know.

South of this great bone field, which was explored during early September, was Henry's Fork of Green River, on which was camped a little company of old-time trappers living with their Indian families in buffalo skin lodges. They still trapped the beaver and several times during our stay in this neighborhood I spent the night in their camp and in the morning went out with them to look at their catch. It was a glimpse of the old-time trapper's life in the Rocky Mountains of thirty years before, and a most interesting one. All the members of this little group wore buckskin clothing, and the men hunted and trapped, drawing their support from the country. One or two of them had come out to the Rocky Mountains in the year 1834. Another survivor of early days seen at Fort Bridger was "Uncle" Jack Robinson, who was of the famous band of trappers who had found the Arapaho Indian baby later known as Friday.

Professor Marsh wished to go still farther south to reach the junction of the Green and the White rivers in Utah. The way was unknown to anyone, but finally a Mexican, who knew a part of the route, went along as supposed guide. He did not know the mountains, however, and we were obliged to follow down the Green River, passing through Brown's Hole, finally to reach White River not very far above its junction with the Green. There were no roads and travel with wagons was impossible. With some difficulty the journey was made by pack train. On the way we saw many wonderful things which now can hardly be told of. Here is a paragraph written by one of the men which suggests a view seen from the eastern ends of the Uinta Mountains.

"After crossing an extensive table land a grand scene burst upon us. Fifteen hundred feet below us lay the bed of another great Tertiary lake. We stood at the brink of a vast basin, so desolate, wild and broken, so lifeless and silent that it seemed like the ruins of a world. A few solitary peaks rose to our level and showed that ages ago the plain behind us had extended unbroken to where a line of silver showed the Green River twenty miles away. The intermediate space was ragged with ridges and bluffs of every conceivable form, and rivulets that flowed from yawning cañons in the mountain sides stretched threads of green across the waste between their falling battlements. Yet, through the confusion could be seen an order that was eternal, for as age after age the ancient lake was filled and choked with layers of mud and sand, so on each crumbling bluff recurred strata of chocolate and greenish clays in unvaried succession, and a bright red ridge that stretched across the foreground, could be traced far off with beds of gray and yellow heaped above it."

At White River, not far from where it joins the Green, many Pliocene fossils were found, and before long, with pack animals heavily loaded, we crossed the Green River near the ancient trading post known as Fort Roubidoux and made our way to Fort Uinta, the agency of a section of the Ute Indians. From here a Shoshoni Indian guide led us through the Uinta Mountains, over a beautiful forested country with frequent open parks through which flowed clear sparkling trout streams. The region, known only to the Indians, had much game, and the journey in early autumn was full of joy. Going down one of the rough narrow mountain trails toward the valley of Henry's Fork we lost the pack mule which carried our mess outfit, and at the foot of the cliff were able to recover from its load only a few battered tin plates and broken knives and forks; even the saddle that the animal wore was smashed to matchwood.

It was here that a curious free Cretaceous crinoid *Uintacrinus* was discovered. This was described much later.

At Salt Lake City some of us met Brigham Young. From there we went on to California, visiting the Yosemite, the Mariposa Grove of "big trees" and the geysers. Returning eastward we stopped at some of the famous old-time placer mining districts in California, and thence went on to a point not far from Green River, Wyoming, where in an early Tertiary deposit many petrified fish and some fossil insects were found.

The plains of Kansas were the next collecting ground and here great numbers of Cretaceous reptiles were unearthed, among them giant mosasaurs and many fishes. From these beds came, a little later, the extraordinary birds with teeth—*Hesperornis* and *Ichthyornis*—and later still many pterodactyls. These bone fields are in a region that is now a great wheat- and corn-growing district. In Kansas some members of the party killed buffalo, which were abundant there.

The expedition now began to break up. Some of its members returned in late November, and before Christmas time the last of them had reached New York and New Haven.

In subsequent years Professor Marsh conducted other expeditions to the western country and all of them yielded rich results. Later his collections were made by hired collectors. The sum total of the material brought together is now preserved in the Washington and New Haven museums, and not all of it has yet been worked up.

A SUMMER HUNT

NOTES ON THE PAWNEES

IT WAS in the month of July, 1872. The Pawnees were preparing to start on their semi-annual buffalo hunt, and only the last religious rites remained to be performed before the nation should leave the village for the buffalo range.

"*Eh, idadi, whoop,*" came from without the lodge; and as I replied, "*Ehya, whoop,*" the sturdy figure of *Le-ta-kats-ta'-ka* appeared in the doorway.

"*Lau, idad, tŭt-tū-ta-rik ti-rah-rēk*—Come, brother, they are going to dance," he said, and then he turned and went out.

I rose from the pile of robes on which I had been dozing, and, after rolling them up, strolled out after him. The village seemed deserted, but off toward the medicine lodge, which stood upon its outskirts, I could see a throng of Indians; and a low murmur of voices and of footsteps, the hum which always accompanies any large assemblage, was borne to my ears on the evening breeze. The ceremonies, which comprised the consecration of the buffalo staves and the buffalo dance, were about to begin. The great dirt lodge was crowded. I pushed my way through the throng of women and boys, who made up the outer circle of spectators, and soon found myself among the men, who made way for me, until I reached a position from which I could see all that was going on within the circle about which they stood.

For several days the priests and the doctors had been preparing for this solemn religious ceremonial. They had fasted long; earnest prayers had been made to *Ti-ra'-wa*, and sacrifices had been offered. Now the twelve buffalo skulls had been arranged on the ground in a half-circle, and near them stood the chiefs and doctors, reverently holding in their hands the buffalo staves and sacred bows and arrows, and other implements of the chase. For a little while they stood silent, with bowed heads, but presently one and then another began to murmur their petitions to *A-ti-us Ti-ra'-wa*, the Spirit Father. At first their voices were low and mumbling, but gradually they became more earnest and lifted their eyes toward heaven. It was impossible to distinguish what each one said, but now and then disjointed sentences reached me. "Father, you are the Ruler—We are poor—Take pity on us—Send us plenty of buffalo, plenty of fat cows—Father, we are your children—help the people—send us plenty of meat so that we may be strong, and our bodies may increase and our flesh grow hard —Father, you see us, listen." As they prayed they moved their hands backward and forward over the implements which they held, and at length reverently deposited them on the ground within the line of buffalo skulls, and then stepped back, still continuing their prayers.

It was a touching sight to witness these men calling upon their God for help. All of them had passed middle life, and some were gray-haired, blind and tottering; but they prayed with a fervor and earnestness that compelled respect. They threw their souls into their prayers, and as a son might entreat his earthly father for some great gift, so they plead with *Ti-ra'-wa*. Their bodies quivered with emotion, and great drops of sweat stood upon their brows. They were thoroughly sincere.

After the last of the articles had been placed upon the ground, their voices grew lower and at length died away. A moment later a drum sounded, and a dozen or twenty young warriors sprang into the circle and began the buffalo dance. This was kept up without intermission for three days, and as soon as it was over, the tribe moved out of the village on the hunt.

From the village on the Loup, we traveled southward; for in those days the region between the Platte and the Smoky rivers swarmed with buffalo. With the Pawnees were a few Poncas, Omahas and Otoes, so that there were about four thousand Indians in the camp. It was the summer hunt of the tribe. Twice each year the agent permitted them to visit the buffalo range. The meat which they killed and dried on these hunts, the corn and squashes which they grew on their farms, and the small annuities received from the Government, were all they had to subsist on from season to season. Thus the occasion was one of importance to the Indians. Perhaps only the older heads among them fully appreciated its economic interest; but for all it was a holiday time; a temporary escape from confinement. Life on the reservation was monotonous. There was nothing to do except to sit in the sun and smoke, and tell stories of the former glories of the nation; of successful fights with the Sioux and Cheyennes, and of horse stealing expeditions, from which the heroes had returned with great herds of ponies and much glory. Now, for a little while, they returned to the old free life of earlier years, when the land had been all their own, and they had wandered at will over the broad expanse of the rolling prairie. Now, for a time, it was as it had been before the cornfields of the white man had begun to dot their river bottoms, before the sound of his rifle had made wild their game, before the locomotive's whistle had shrieked through the still, hot summer air. Half a year's provision was now to be secured. The comfort—almost the existence—of the tribe for the next six months depended on the accumulation of an abundant supply of dried buffalo meat, and no precaution was omitted to make the hunt successful. It would not do to permit each individual to hunt independently. Indiscriminate buffalo running by six or eight hundred men scattered over the prairie, each one working for himself alone, would result in the killing of some few buffalo, but would terrify and drive away all the others in the neighborhood. This matter was too important to be trusted to chance. The hunting was systematized.

The Pawnees

The government of the hunt was intrusted to the Pawnee soldiers. These were twenty-four warriors of mature age, not so old as to be unfitted for active work, yet with the fires of early youth somewhat tempered by years of experience; men whose judgment and discretion could at all times be relied on. These soldiers acted under the chiefs, but the practical guidance of the hunt was wholly in their hands. They determined the direction and length of each day's march, and the spot for camping. They selected the young men who should act as scouts, and arranged all the details of the approach and the charge when a herd of buffalo was discovered large enough to call for a general surround. All the men were under their control, and amenable to their discipline. They did not hesitate to exercise their authority, nor to severely punish any one who committed an act by which the success of the hunt might be imperilled.

The scouts sent out by the soldiers were chosen from among the younger men. They acted merely as spies, their office was to find the buffalo. They moved rapidly along, far in advance of the marching column, and from the tops of the highest hills carefully scanned the country before them in search of buffalo. If a herd was discerned, they were not to show themselves, nor in any way to alarm it. Having found the game, their duty was to observe its movement, learn where it was likely to be for the next few hours, and then to report as quickly as possible to the camp. The soldiers then determined what action should be taken. If the news was received late in the day, and the buffalo were at some distance, the camp would probably be moved as near as practicable to where the herd was feeding, and the chase would take place in the early morning. If, on the other hand, the scouts found the herd in the morning, the men would start off at once for the surround, leaving the women to follow, and make camp as near as possible to where the dead buffalo lay.

Day after day we traveled southward, crossing the Platte River, and then the Republican about due south of the present flourishing town of Kearney. South of the Platte a few scattering buffalo were found, but no large herds had been met with—nothing that called for a surround. At length we camped one night on the Beaver, a small affluent of the Republican, emptying into it from the south. With the gray dawn of morning, the camp, as usual, is astir. By the time our little party have turned out of our blankets, some of the Indians have already finished eating, and are catching up their horses and preparing to ride off over the bluffs, leaving the squaws to take down the lodges, pack the ponies, and pursue the designated line of march. Before we are ready to "pull out," most of the ponies have been packed, and a long, irregular line of Indians is creeping across the level valley, and beginning to wind up the face of the bluffs. The procession moves slowly, proceeding at a walk. Most of those who remain with the column are on foot, the squaws leading the ponies, and many of the men, wrapped in their blankets, and with only their bows and arrows on their backs, walking briskly over the prairie, a little to one side. These last are the poorer Indians —those who have but few horses. They travel on foot, letting their horses run without burdens, so that they may be fresh and strong, whenever they shall be needed for running the buffalo.

Side by side, at the head of the column, walk eight men who carry the buffalo staves. These are slender spruce poles, like a short lodge-pole, wrapped with blue and red cloth, and elaborately ornamented with bead work, and with the feathers of hawks, and of the war eagle. These sticks are carried by men selected by the chiefs and doctors in private council, and are religiously guarded. Upon the care of these emblems, and the respect paid to them, depends, in a great measure, the success of the hunt. While borne before the moving column, no one is permitted to cross the line of march in front of them.

Close behind the staff bearers follow a number of the principal men of the tribe; the head chief, old *Pi'ta Le-shar*, and a dozen or fifteen sub-chiefs or head men, all mounted on superb horses. Behind them comes the camp at large, a fantastically mingled multitude, marching without any appearance of order. Here most of the individuals are women, young girls and children, for the men who accompany the camp usually march singly, or by twos and threes, a little apart from the mob. Most of those rich enough in horses to be able to ride at all times, are scattered over the prairie for miles in every direction, picking up the small bands of buffalo, which have been passed by the scouts as not large enough to call for a general surround. The hunters are careful, however, not to follow too close upon the advance line, whose movements they can readily observe upon the bare bluffs far ahead of them.

At the time of which I am writing, the Pawnees had no wagons, all their possessions being transported on pack horses. The Indian pack pony is apt to be old and sedate, requiring no special guidance nor control. A strip of rawhide, knotted about the lower jaw, serves as a bridle, and is either tied up to the saddle or held in the rider's hand. In packing the animals a bundle of lodge-poles is tied on either side of the saddle, one end projecting forward toward the horse's head, the other dragging on the ground behind. This is the *travois*. Cross poles are often tied between these two dragging bundles, and on these are carried packages of meat and robes. Often, too, on a robe stretched between them, a sick or wounded Indian, unable to ride, is transported. The lodge-poles having been fastened to the saddle, the lodge is folded up and placed on it between them, and blankets, robes, and other articles are piled on top of this, until the horse has on its back what appears to be about as much as it can carry. The pack is then lashed firmly in position, and pots, buckets and other utensils are tied about it wherever there is room.

On top of the load so arranged one or two women, or three or four children, clamber and settle themselves comfortably there, and the old horse is turned loose. Each rider carries in her hand a whip, with which she strikes the horse at every step, not cruelly at all, but just from force of habit. If the pack is low, so that her feet reach down to the animal's sides, she keeps up also a constant drumming on his ribs with her heels. The old horse pays not the slightest attention to any of these demonstrations of impatience, but plods steadily along at a quiet walk, his eyes half closed and his ears nodding at each step. If the riders are women, each one holds a child or two in her arms, or on her back, or perhaps the baby board is hung over the end of a lodge-pole, and swings free. If the living load consists of children, they have in their arms a lot of puppies; for puppies occupy with relation to the small Indian girls the place which dolls hold among the white children. Many of the pack animals are mares with young colts, and these last, instead of following quietly at their mothers' heels, range here and there, sometimes before and sometimes behind their dams. They are thus constantly getting lost in the crowd, and then they charge backward and forward in wild affright, neighing shrilly, until they have again found their proper place in the line of march. Many of the yearling colts have very small and light packs tied on their backs, while the two-year-olds are often ridden by the tiniest of Indian boys, who are now giving them their first lesson in weight-carrying. Loose horses of all ages roam about at will, and their continual cries mingle with the barking of dogs, the calls of women and the yells of boys, and make an unceasing noise.

The boys are boiling over with animal spirits, and, like their civilized brothers of the same age, are continually running about, chasing each other, wrestling, shooting arrows and playing games, of which the familiar stick game seems the favorite.

Whenever the column draws near any cover, which may shelter game, such as a few bushes in a ravine, or the fringe of low willows along some little watercourse, the younger men and boys scatter out and surround it. They beat it in the most thorough manner, and any game which it contains is driven out on the prairie, surrounded and killed. The appearance even of a jackass rabbit throws the boys into a fever of excitement, and causes them to shriek and yell as if in a frenzy.

All the morning I rode with the Indians, either at the head of the column, chatting as best I could with *Pi'ta Le-shar* and other chiefs, or falling back and riding among the women and children, whom I never tired of watching. Frequently during the day I saw at a distance, on the prairie, small bunches of buffalo in full flight, hotly pursued by dark-skinned riders, and occasionally two or three men would ride up to the marching columns with heavy loads of freshly-killed meat. The quick-heaving, wet flanks of the ponies told a story of sharp, rapid chases, and their tossing heads and eager, excited looks showed how much interest they took in the hunt.

The report of firearms was seldom heard. Most of the Indians hunted with the primitive weapon of their forefathers—the bow and arrow. For buffalo running an arrow is nearly as effective as lead. The power of the bow in expert hands is tremendous. Riding within half a dozen yards of the victim's side, the practiced bowman will drive the dart so far through the body of the buffalo that its shaft may project a foot or more from the opposite side—sometimes indeed may pass quite through. Besides, the bow can be used very rapidly and accurately. I have seen an Indian take a sheaf of six arrows in his hand, and discharge them at a mark more rapidly and with more certainty of hitting his target than I could fire the six barrels of a revolver.

It was nearly noon, and I was riding along at the head of the column. I had but one horse, and did not care to wear him out by chasing around over the prairie, preferring to save him for some great effort. We were traveling along a smooth divide between two sets of ravines, which ran off, one to the east and the other to the west. *Pi'ta Le-shar* had just informed me by signs that we should make camp about two miles further on, by a stream whose course we could trace from where we then were. Suddenly, without the slightest warning, the huge dark bodies of half a dozen buffalo sprang into view, rising out of a ravine on our left not a hundred yards distant. When they saw the multitude before them, they stopped and stared at us.

They were too close for me to resist the temptation to pursue. As I lifted the reins from my pony's neck and bent forward, the little animal sprang into a sharp gallop toward the game, and as he did so I saw half a dozen Indians shoot out from the column and follow me. The buffalo wheeled, and in an instant were out of sight, but when I reached the edge of the bank down which they had plunged, I could see through the cloud of dust, which they left behind them, their uncouth forms dashing down the ravine. My nimble pony, as eager for the race as his rider, hurled himself down the steep pitch, and sped along the narrow broken bed of the gully. I could feel that sometimes he would lengthen his stride to leap wide ditches, where the water from some side ravine had cut away the ground, but I never knew of these until they were passed. My eyes were fixed on the fleeing herd; my ears were intent on the pursuing horsemen. Close behind me I could hear the quick pounding of many hoofs, and could feel that one of the horses, nearer than the rest, was steadily drawing up to me—but I was gaining on the buffalo. Already the confused rumble of their hoof-beats almost drowned those of the horses behind me, and the air was full of the dust and small pebbles thrown up by their hurrying feet. But they were still ahead of me, and the gulch was so narrow that I could not shoot. The leading horseman drew nearer and nearer, and was now almost at my side. I could see the lean head and long, slim neck of his pony under my right arm, and could hear the rider speak to his horse and urge him forward in the race. My horse did his best, but the other had the most speed. He shot by me, and a moment later was alongside the last buffalo.

As he passed me the young Indian made a laughing gesture of triumph, slipped an arrow on his bowstring, and drew it to its head; but just as he was about to let it fly, his horse, which was but a colt, took fright at the huge animal which it had overtaken, and shied violently to the right, almost unseating its rider. At the same moment the buffalo swerved a little to the left, and thus lost a few feet. Truly, the race is not always to the swift. As I passed the Indian, I could not restrain a little whoop of satisfaction, and then swinging my rifle around, I fired. The buffalo fell in its stride, tossing up a mightly cloud of the soft yellow earth, and my pony ran by him fifty yards before he could be checked. Then I turned and rode back to look at the game. The other Indians had passed me like a whirlwind, and, close at the heels of the herd, had swept around a point of bluff and out of sight. Only my rival remained, and he was excitedly arguing with his horse. The logic of a whip-handle, applied with vigor about the creature's ears, convinced it that it must approach the dead buffalo; and then the rider dismounting, and passing his lariat about the animal's horns, drew the pony's head to within a few feet of the terrifying mass, and fastened the rope. When he had accomplished this, he grinned pleasantly at me, and I responded in kind, and in dumb show transferred to him all my right and title in the dead buffalo. At this he smiled still more cheerfully, and set to work "butchering."

The animal was a superb specimen, just entering his prime, and was fat, round and sleek. His horns were symmetrically curved and beautifully polished. Not a scratch marred their shining surfaces, nor a splinter was frayed from their sharp points. The sweeping black beard was long and full, and the thick curls upon his hump and massive shoulders were soft and deep, while the short hair of his sides and hips was smooth as the coat of a horse. His size was

enormous. It seemed that he would have turned the scale at quite
two thousand pounds. Certainly his weight exceeded that of both
the fifteen-hand ponies that stood beside him.

A few moments later, I was again in the saddle, and riding on
along the course taken by the remaining buffalo, for I was anxious
to see what had become of them. On rounding the point of the
bluff, where I had last seen them, my curiosity was satisfied. The
valley here widened out until it was perhaps sixty yards across, and
on either side rose vertical bluffs of yellow chalk to a height of
forty feet. Scattered about over the little plain, lay half a dozen
buffalo, over each of which bent one or two Indians busily plying
the knife. At the foot of the bluff at one side of the valley stood four
or five others, looking at a cow, perched on a narrow shelf ten
feet below the top. I shall never understand how that animal reached
the position it occupied. There was evidently no way of getting to
it except by jumping up from below, which was obviously impossible
—or down from above, which seemed out of the question. The shelf
was so short that the animal could move neither backward nor forward, and was just wide enough for it to stand on. As I rode up and
joined the little group below it, the head and shoulders of a middle-
aged Indian appeared over the top of the bluff, above the cow. He
lay down flat on his breast, and holding in both hands an old-fashioned
muzzle-loading pistol, attempted to shoot the cow from above, but
his old arm would not go off. He snapped it half a dozen times,
and then, discouraged, called out something to us below. One of the
boys turned to me, and said very slowly and distinctly, "He say, you
shoot." I therefore dismounted, and fired at the cow, which responded
by shaking her head angrily, and whisking her short tail. Another
call came from the old fellow on top of the bluff, and the young man
said to me, "He say, you hit her; right spot." A moment later, the
cow bent forward and fell on her knees, and the Indian above dropped
down on her back.

Turning my horse's head in the direction from which I had come,
I rode up through a side ravine on to the high prairie. A mile away
I could see the column of marching Indians, plodding along at their
old slow pace. Here and there, over the rolling hills, dark forms were
visible, some of them in rapid motion, others apparently stationary.

Pawnee, Blackfoot and Cheyenne

Often it was impossible to determine whether these figures were horsemen or buffalo, but sometimes, far away, I could see a mimic chase in which pursuer and pursued appeared no larger than ants. As I came up with the Indians, they were just descending into the stream bottom, where camp was to be made. The small boys had, as usual, dispersed themselves over the valley and among the underbrush. Many of the squaws, leaving the ponies and packs to their sister-wives or children, were hurrying up or down the stream to gather wood. Already the leading ponies were being relieved of their loads. Suddenly, from the mouth of a little ravine coming down into the stream bottom, rose a chorus of shrill yelps and shrieks from childish throats, and a gang of wild turkeys were seen, running rapidly through the high grass toward the hills. A moment later, with a loud *quit-quit* of alarm, they took wing, but not before several of their number had fallen before the missiles of the boys. Most of them went up or down the creek, but one inexperienced bird took its course directly over our heads.

Those who have seen the Indian only on dress parade, talk of his stolidity, impassiveness, and his marvelous control over his countenance and his emotions. This demeanor he can and does assume, and when he is with white men, or among strangers, he is usually all that he has been pictured; but take him by himself, and he expresses his feelings with as little restraint as a child. So it was now. No grave chief, nor battle-scarred warrior, nor mighty worker of *ti-war'-uks-ti* (magic) was too dignified to express his interest at the appearance of this great bird sailing laboriously along, thirty or forty feet above him. It was as if the turkey had flown over a great company of schoolboys, and the utter abandonment of the excited multitude, the entire absence of restraint, the perfect naturalness of the expression of feeling, had in them something very delightful and infectious. Every Indian, who held in his hand anything that was light enough to throw, hurled it at the bird, and a cloud of whips, sticks, hatchets, fleshers, and arrows, rose to meet it as it passed along. One missile knocked from its tail a few long feathers, which drifted slowly down on the heads of the people. It kept on, but before it had passed beyond the long line of Indians extending back over the

22

plain, its strength became exhausted, it came to the ground, and was at once dispatched by those nearest to it.

Almost before the turkey's fate had been decided, many of the lodges had been pitched, and now the slender gray columns from a hundred camp-fires began to climb up through the still air toward the blue above. The women were hard at work cooking, or spreading out freshly killed robes, or putting up drying scaffolds, while the men lounged in the shade and smoked or chatted. Our wagon was halted at one side of the camp, and the tired horses and mules were stripped of saddles and harness, and picketed near at hand. The Indian pack ponies were collected and driven off on the upland in charge of several boys.

We had invitations to eat meat at several lodges that day. Usually we did not accept these freely proffered hospitalities, because we had no means of returning them, but one of these invitations came from a particular friend, and to-day we broke through our rule. We feasted on roast ribs, *ka'wis*, and dried meat, and really had a delightful time. It was about three o'clock when we finished the meal, and we were lounging about the lodge, smoking and chatting, in lazy after-dinner fashion, when we were startled by a series of yells and shouts, among which I distinguished the words "*Cha'-ra-rat wa-ta'* —The Sioux are coming." Our Indian companions snatched up their arms, and rushed out of the lodge, and we were not slow in following. "*Sūks-e-kitta-wit wis-kūts*—Get on your horses quick," shouted our host. The camp was in a state of wild excitement. Naked men were running to their horses, and jerking their lariats from the picket pins, sprang on their backs and rode hard for the hills; while women and boys rushed about, catching horses, and bringing them in among the lodges, where they were securely fastened. Less than a mile away, we saw the horse herd dashing along at top speed, and a little to one side of it a horseman riding in circles, and waving his blanket before him. It was evident that the Sioux were trying to run off the herd. We ran as hard as we could to the wagon, caught up rifles and cartridge belts, and buckling on the latter as we ran, kept on to the horses. There was no time to saddle up. We looped the ropes around their jaws, sprang on their naked backs, and were off. As we rode up on the prairie, the herd of ponies thundered by, and swept down the bluffs to the camp. The rolling expanse before us was dotted with Indians, each one urging forward his horse to its utmost speed. Many of them were already a long way in advance, and were passing over the furthest high bluff, which seemed to rise up and meet the sky. Hard as we might push our ponies, there was little hope that we would be in time to have any hand in the en-counter—if one took place—between the Pawnees and their hereditary foes.

We kept on until we reached the crest of the high bluff. From here we could see far off over the plain, dozens of black dots strung out after one another. Nearer at hand, other Indians, whose steeds, like ours, had proved too slow for the swift pursuit, were riding back toward us, showing in their faces the disappointment which they felt at being left behind. With these we turned about, and rode toward the camp. Among them was one of the herd boys, for the moment a hero, who had to repeat his story again and again. He had been sitting on top of a hill, not far from the horses, when he dis-covered several Sioux stealing toward them through a ravine. Signal-ing his comrades, they succeeded in getting the herd in motion before the robbers had approached very close to them. Eight of the slowest horses had dropped behind during the flight, and had no doubt fallen into the hands of the enemy.

One by one, the Indians came straggling back to camp during the afternoon and evening, but it was not until late that night that the main body of the pursuers came in. They had ten extra horses, two of which they had taken in turn from the Sioux. They had no scalps, however, for they had been unable to overtake the enemy.

Long we sat that night by the fire in *Pi'ta Le-shar's* lodge, talking over the exciting event of the afternoon; and as we rose to go to our wagons, and said good night, the old man, who had been silently gazing into the coals for some time, looked up at me and smiled, say-ing, "*Wa-ti-hes ti-kōt-it ti-ra-hah*—To-morrow we will kill buffalo."

When we turned out of our blankets the next morning, a heavy mist hung over the prairie. This was unfortunate, for so long as the fog lasted it would be impossible for the scouts to see far enough to discover the buffalo. The first few hours of the march were uneventful. Once or twice the huge bodies of a small band of buffalo loomed up through the white mist about us, their size and shape greatly exaggerated and distorted by its deceptive effect. As the sun climbed toward the zenith, the air grew brighter, and by mid-day the fog had risen from the ground, and though still clinging in white cottony wreaths about the tops of the higher bluffs near us, we now could see for quite a long distance over the prairie. A little later the sun burst forth, and the sky became clear. Soon after noon we went into camp.

We had but just begun our dinner, when a runner was seen coming at full gallop down the bluffs. It was one of the scouts. He dashed through the village, and did not check his pony's speed until he had reached old *Pi'ta Le-shar's* lodge. Here he stopped, and bending from his horse spoke a few words very earnestly, gesticulating and pointing back over the prairie in the direction whence he had come. As he rode on and past us, he called out, "*Te-co'di tŭt-tu-ta-rik ti-ra-hah*—I saw many buffalo," and we shouted back to him, "*Tū-ra-heh*—It is good."

At once the women began to take down the lodges and pack the ponies. Buffalo had been discovered about fifteen miles to the southwest, and orders had been issued to move the village to the creek on which they were feeding, while the men should go on at once and make the surround. Our teamster, to whom the Indians had already, from his occupation, given the name "Jackass Chief," was directed to move with the camp; and leaving everything save guns and ammunition belts in the wagon, we joined the crowd of men who were riding out of the village.

The scene that we now beheld was such as might have been witnessed here a hundred years ago. It is one that can never be seen again. Here were eight hundred warriors, stark naked, and mounted on naked animals. A strip of rawhide, or a lariat, knotted about the lower jaw, was all their horses' furniture. Among all these men there was not a gun nor a pistol, nor any indication that they had ever met with the white men. For the moment they had put aside whatever they had learned of civilization. Their bows and arrows they held in their hands. Armed with these ancestral weapons, they had become once more the simple children of the plains, about to slay the wild cattle that *Ti-ra'-wa* had given them for food. Here was barbarism pure and simple. Here was nature.

A brief halt was made on the upper prairie, until all the riders had come up, and then, at a moderate gallop, we set off. A few yards in advance rode the twenty-four soldiers, at first curbing in their spirited little steeds, till the horses' chins almost touched their chests, and occasionally, by a simple motion of the hand, waving back some impetuous boy, who pressed too close upon them. Many of the Indians led a spare horse, still riding the one that had carried them through the day. Often two men would be seen mounted on the same animal, the one behind having the lariats of two led horses wound about his arm. Here and there a man, with his arm over the horse's neck, would run along on foot by the side of the animal which was to serve him in the charge.

As we proceeded, the pace became gradually a little more rapid. The horses went along easily and without effort. Each naked Indian seemed a part of his steed, and rose and fell with it in the rhythmic swing of its stride. The plain was peopled with Centaurs. Out over each horse's croup floated the long black hair of his rider, spread out on the wings of the breeze. Gradually the slow gallop became a fast one. The flanks of the horses showed here and there patches of wet, which glistened in the slanting rays of the westering sun. Eight, ten, a dozen miles had been left behind us, and we were approaching the top of a high bluff, when the signal was given to halt. In a moment every man was off his horse, but not a pony of them all showed any sign of distress, nor gave any evidence of the work he had done, except by his wet flanks and his slightly accelerated breathing. Two or three of the soldiers rode up nearly to the top of the hill, dismounted and then peered over, and a moment later, at another signal, all mounted and the swift gallop began again. Over the ridge we passed, down the smooth slope, and across a wide level plain, where the prairie dogs and the owls and the rattlesnakes had their home. Through the dog town we hurried on thundering hoofs, no doubt amazing the dogs, and perhaps even arousing some slight interest in the sluggish, stupid snakes. Bad places these to ride through at such a pace, for a little carelessness on your horse's part might cost him a broken leg and you an ugly tumble. But no one took much thought of dog town or horse or possible accident, for the minds of all were upon the next high ridge, behind which we felt sure that the buffalo would be found.

And so it proved. Just before reaching it we were again halted. Two of the soldiers reconnoitered, and then signaled that the buffalo were in sight. The tired horses were now turned loose and the extra ones mounted. As we rode slowly up over the ridge, we saw spread out before us a wide valley black with buffalo. Two miles away, on the other side, rose steep ragged bluffs, up which the clumsy buffalo would make but slow progress, while the ponies could run there nearly as fast as on level ground. It was the very place that would have been chosen for a surround.

At least a thousand buffalo were lying down in the midst of this amphitheater. Here and there, away from the main herd on the lower hills, were old bulls, singly and by twos and threes, some of them quietly chewing the cud, others sullenly pawing up the dust or grinding their battered horns into the yellow dirt of the hillsides. Not the slightest notice was taken of us as we rode down the slope at a pace that was almost a run, but still held in check by the soldiers. The order for the charge had not yet been given. Our line was now much more extended than it had been; each man pressing as far forward as he dared, and those on either flank being so far ahead of the center that they were almost on a line with the soldiers. We had covered perhaps half the distance between the hilltop and the buffalo, when some of the outlying bulls seemed to observe us, and after looking for a moment or two, these started in rapid flight. This attracted the attention of the herd, and when we were yet half a mile from them, they took the alarm. At once all were on their feet. For a moment they gazed bewildered at the dark line that was sweeping toward them, and then, down went every huge head and up flew every little tail, and the herd was off in a headlong stampede for the opposite hills. As they sprang to their feet, the oldest man of the soldiers, who was riding in the center of the line, turned back toward us, and uttered a shrill *Loo'-ah!* It was the word we had waited for.

Like an arrow from a bow each horse darted forward. Now all restraint was removed, and each man might do his best. What had been only a wild gallop became a mad race. Each rider hoped to be the first to reach the top of the opposite ridge, and to turn the buffalo back into the valley, so that the surround might be completely successful. How swift those little ponies were, and how admirably the Indians managed to get out of them all their speed! I had not gone much more than half-way across the valley when I saw the leading Indians pass the head of the herd, and begin to turn the buffalo. This was the first object of the chase, for in a stampede, the cows and young are always in the lead, the bulls bringing up the rear. This position is not taken from chivalric motives on the part of the males, but simply because they cannot run so fast as their wives and children. Bulls are never killed when cows and heifers can be had.

Back came the herd, and I soon found myself in the midst of a throng of buffalo, horses and Indians. There was no yelling nor shouting on the part of the men, but their stern set faces, and the fierce gleam of their eyes, told of the fires of excitement that were burning within them. Three or four times my rifle spoke out, and to some purpose; and one shot, placed too far back, drew on me a quick savage charge from a vicious young cow. My pony, while a good cattle horse, was new at buffalo running, and his deliberation in the matter of dodging caused me an anxious second or two, as I saw the cow's head sweep close to his flank. It was far more interesting to watch the scene than to take part in it, and I soon rode to a little knoll from which I could overlook the whole plain. Many brown bodies lay stretched upon the ground, and many more were dashing here and there, closely attended by relentless pursuers. It was sad to see so much death, but the people must have food, and none of this meat would be wasted.

Before I turned my horse's head toward the camp, the broad disk of the setting sun had rested on the tops of the western bluffs, and tipped their crests with fire. His horizontal beams lit up with a picturesque redness the dusky forms which moved about over the valley. Up the ravines and over the hills were stringing long lines of squaws, leading patient ponies, whose backs were piled high with dark dripping meat, and with soft shaggy skins. Late into the night the work continued and the loads kept coming into the camp. About the flickering fires in and before the lodges there was feasting and merriment. Marrow bones were tossed among the red embers, calf's head was baked in the hot earth, fat ribs were roasted, *ka'-wis* boiled, and *boudins* eaten raw.

With laughter and singing and story telling and dance the night wore away.

Over the plain where the buffalo had fallen, the gray wolf was prowling, and, with the coyote, the fox and the badger, tore at the bones of the slain. When day came, the golden eagle and the buzzard perched upon the naked red skeletons, and took their toll. And far away to the southward, a few frightened buffalo, some of which had arrows sticking in their sore sides, were cropping the short grass of the prairie.

FRANK NORTH AND HIS SCOUTS

PANI LE-SHAR AND HIS SCOUTS

No ACCOUNT of the Pawnees' warfare would give any just impression of their prowess if it omitted to mention *Pa'-ni Le-shar* and the forces which he commanded. The Pawnee Scouts, under the gallant and able leadership of Frank North, did splendid service against hostile Indians. They saved hundreds of lives and millions of dollars' worth of property, and in their campaign wiped out in blood the memory of many an injury done to their race by the Sioux, the Cheyennes, the Arapahoes and the Kiowas.

Frank North was born in Ohio, March 10, 1840. When about fifteen years of age he accompanied his family westward to Council Bluffs, and a little later across the Missouri River into Nebraska. At about this time, his father, who was a surveyor, was lost in a snowstorm, and the responsibility of caring for his family fell in large measure on the boy. Soon after this he obtained employment as clerk in the trader's store at the Pawnee agency, and thus made the acquaintance of the tribe. His strong character early brought him to the notice of their principal men, and almost before attaining manhood he had become a person of influence in the councils of the Pawnee Nation.

Pawnee, Blackfoot and Cheyenne

In the year 1864 Frank North was authorized to enlist a company of Pawnee scouts to be employed against the bands of hostile Indians, whose depredations were at that time becoming very troublesome. The command was organized that autumn, and did some service along the old emigrant trail. It was not until the summer of 1865, however, that it saw any serious fighting. In that year General Connor of California commanded a large expedition to the Powder River country, and the Pawnee scouts accompanied him and rendered brilliant service.

Later, during the building of the Union Pacific Railway, the depredations of the hostile Sioux, Cheyennes and Arapahoes became so serious along the line of the road that the Government authorized Mr. North to enlist a battalion of scouts from the Pawnee Nation, and offered him the command with the rank of major. Several companies of these scouts were so enlisted, and for years the battalion did good service on the plains and in the mountains in Nebraska, Kansas and Wyoming, serving under Generals Auger, Emory, Carr, Royal, Mackenzie and Crook, some of the most successful Indian fighters in that Department. The Pawnee scouts were everywhere, and at all times brave men, good soldiers and victorious warriors. The amount of property saved to the Government, the settlers and the railroad through the efforts of Major North's command can scarcely be computed. In all his service of almost constant fighting, extending over a period of more than ten years, he never lost a man on the battle field, and this caused him to be regarded by the Pawnees as divinely favored.

It is impossible within the limits of a few pages to give even a sketch of the services performed by Frank North and his scouts. Two or three isolated episodes in his career will show something of the constant danger and hardship of the life he led, and of the courage, coolness and determination of the leader and his men.

Such an episode, memorable alike for its danger, the completeness of the victory gained, and the fact that it won for him the title by which he was ever after known among the Pawnees, marked his first campaign. It was in the Powder River country, and Captain North had started with a detachment of his scouts in pursuit of a party of Indians, whose trail he had found. For some weeks his men had been hard worked; and at this time their horses were so jaded that although they had come within sight of the Cheyennes, they were unable to overtake them and force them to a fight. Captain North, who was mounted on a fresh horse, rode far ahead of his men, who were constantly falling further and further behind. At length, realizing the futility of continuing the pursuit, North dismounted, fired a parting shot at the Indians, and was about to ride back toward camp, when the fleeing Cheyennes, about twenty-five in number, turned and charged him. He then discovered that he had outridden all his men. Not one of them was in sight. Hastily dismounting, he prepared to receive the enemy, and firing as they advanced, killed one. The rest sheered off, and rode out of rifle shot, and then formed again for another charge. Feeling for a cartridge to reload his rifle, North made the startling discovery that he had but three left, all the others having been lost during his rapid ride. He found, too, that his horse had been wounded by a ball from the Cheyennes, and was in no condition for running; indeed, it could not be ridden. His situation seemed well nigh hopeless, but he prepared to make the best of it, by retreating on foot, leading his wounded horse as a shelter, from behind which to fight. When the Cheyennes charged him he would face about, raise his gun to his shoulder, as if about to fire, and the Indians, who had already tasted the quality of his lead, would drop down behind their horses, and sheer off, never coming so close to him as to make it necessary for him to use one of his precious cartridges. After a long weary walk of twelve or fifteen miles, during which his moccasin-shod feet were cruelly lacerated by the thorns of the cactus, over which he walked, his pursuers left him, and he reached his command in safety. No sooner had he arrived at the camp than, taking a fresh horse and ordering out a well-mounted detachment of his men, he set out in pursuit of the enemy. All that afternoon they rode hard, and when night fell, dismounting a couple of Pawnees to follow the trail on foot, the pursuit was still kept up. Just after daylight, as they rode out into a little park in the mountains, a tiny column of blue smoke rising from a clump of cottonwood trees showed where the hostiles were camped. The Pawnees rode steadily forward in double file in military fashion; and the Cheyennes, supposing that they were white soldiers, jumped on their horses and rode out onto the open hillside where they formed a line of battle to meet the enemy. The Pawnees rode quietly onward until they were quite near the Cheyennes, and then loud and clear their ringing war whoop broke out upon the morning air. When the Cheyennes heard this war-cry, which told them that the attacking party were Pawnees, their hearts became like water, and they turned and fled. Already, however, seven of their number had fallen before the Pawnee bullets, and the fresher horses of the Pawnees easily overtook the tired ones ridden by the pursued. Of that party of Cheyennes not one escaped, and with twenty-seven scalps, and all the plunder, the victorious Pawnees returned that afternoon to their command.

Among the captured property were thirty-five horses and mules, some of which had been taken from a party of fifteen soldiers, killed to a man by these Cheyennes but a few days before; there were also the scalps of these soldiers, and wearing apparel belonging to white women and children, which justified the belief that they had recently massacred a party of emigrants.

It was on the occasion of the scalp dance which followed this victory, and when the Scouts were changing their names, as was the custom after a successful encounter with the enemy, that the Pawnees gave to Major North the title *Pa'-ni Le-shar* (Chief of the Pawnees), a name which has been borne by only one other white man, General John C. Fremont, the Pathfinder.

The story of the killing of Tall Bull, and the fight with Turkey Leg's band of Sioux, illustrate the readiness and the daring of Major North in battle. Tall Bull was a chief who commanded a large village of renegade Sioux and Cheyennes, who had given great trouble by their depredations. Major North, with his Pawnees and some white United States troops, had been looking for this village for some time, and at length succeeded in surprising it near Summit Springs. The village was captured in the charge and many of the hostiles killed. Others fled or concealed themselves in the ravines and washouts, which seamed the prairie, and made a desperate fight. The Pawnees were scattered about in little parties, killing the Indians thus concealed, when Major North and his brother came riding rapidly along, side by side, over the open prairie. They had approached within fifty or sixty yards of a narrow steep-walled ravine, of the existence of which they were ignorant, when an Indian raised his head above its side and fired. The ball whistled between the heads of the two riders; Major North threw up his hands and reeled in the saddle as if about to fall, and the

Indian's head disappeared from sight. Springing from his horse, the Major handed his bridle rein to his brother and directed him to ride away at a gallop. The tramp of the two horses sounded more and more faintly on the hard ground, and the Indian, thinking that the whites were riding off, raised his head to note the effect of his shot. North's rifle was already leveled at the spot where the head had disappeared, and as the black hair came into view the finger pressed the trigger more and more closely, and as the eyes appeared above the ground, a ball pierced the brain of Tall Bull. A hundred yards up the ravine was found his war pony, stabbed to the heart, and by it sat his squaw, awaiting with Indian patience whatever fate might come to her.

During one of the summer hunts, on which Major North accompanied the Pawnees, they were one day scattered out over the prairie running buffalo, when all at once North heard the whistle of rifle balls and saw the dirt thrown up about his horse by the bullets. He called to a Pawnee near him to tell those boys to be more careful about shooting. The Pawnee looked in the direction from which the balls were coming, and after an instant called back, "They are Sioux, you had better run." It was a large party of Sioux under the Chief Turkey Leg.

North and the Pawnee rode for the bluffs near at hand, and before reaching them were joined by C. D. Morse, his brother-in-law, and half a dozen Pawnees. The little party was surrounded by the Sioux and took refuge in a shallow washout at the head of a ravine, where they were somewhat sheltered from the enemy's fire by the sunflower stalks and the low edges of the bank. Their horses were at once killed, and the Sioux, who were numerous, became very bold, charging up to the edge of the washout, and shooting down into it.

They were led by an Indian, apparently of some importance, who was conspicuous by a large American flag which he carried. This man was constantly exhorting his men, and would lead them part way on the charge, turning off, however, before coming within range of the washout, where North and his brother-in-law, with the seven Pawnees, were lying concealed. After each charge he would ride to the top of a hill near at hand, and make a speech to his warriors. It occurred to Major North that if he could kill the man who carried the flag the other Sioux might lose some of their courage. As they were retiring from a charge, therefore, he crept cautiously down the ravine, concealed by the long grass which grew in its bed, until he had come within rifle range of the hill from which the leader was making his speech, and by a careful shot killed him and regained the shelter of the washout without injury.

Disheartened by the fall of their leader, the Sioux made no further attempt to kill the besieged company, but after a little desultory long-range firing drew off, so that North and his little party regained the main village in safety.

The Pawnee Scouts were last called out in 1876, when General Mackenzie fought the hostile Cheyennes in the Powder River country; and, led by Major North and his brother, they made that famous charge on the village which inflicted on the hostiles the crushing blow from which they never recovered. How *Pa'-ni Le-shar* held his men under fire that day, when the bullets were raining on them from the hillsides, was told in a letter written to me by a participant in the fight. "For cool bravery," it ran, "he beats anything that you ever saw. Why, at one time we were under such hot fire that even our scouts wanted to run, and to tell you the truth, I felt sort of that way myself; but Frank just straightened himself up on the old black horse and said, very quietly, 'The first one of *my* men that runs I will kill.' They didn't run."

If the full story of Major North's life were written it would constitute a history of the Indian wars in Nebraska and Wyoming from 1860 to 1876—a history so complete that there would be little left to add to it. Wherever the hostile Indians were worst there Frank North was to be found at the head of his Pawnee Scouts, doing the hardest of the fighting, and accomplishing work that could have been done by no other body of men.

From his long service in the army Major North was known to all officers who have ever been stationed in the field where his operations were conducted, and by all of them he was admired and respected. He was closely connected with the growth of the State of Nebraska. Several times he represented Platte county in the Legislature, and the strength and uprightness of his character won the confidence of all who knew him. He died at his home in Columbus, Nebraska, March 14, 1885, aged forty-five years.

His was a singularly lovable nature. If the stronger manly points of his character inspired respect and admiration, not less did his gentleness and consideration for others win the deepest affection. He was modest almost to diffidence, and it was with difficulty that he could be induced to speak of his own heroic achievements. And yet his face told the story of the power within the man.

The secret of Major North's success in commanding the Pawnees, who loved him as much as they respected him, lay in the unvarying firmness, justice, patience and kindness with which he treated them. He never demanded anything unreasonable of them, but when he gave an order, even though obedience involved great peril, or appeared to mean certain death, it was a command that must be carried out. He was their commander, but at the same time their brother and friend. Above all, he was their leader. In going into battle he never said to them, "Go," but always "Come on." It is little wonder, then, that the devotion felt for him by all the Pawnee Nation, and especially by the men who had served under him in battle, was as steadfast as it was touching.

THE PAWNEES AND THEIR STORIES

ONCE the Pawnees were a great people. They were very numerous. They were undisputed masters of a vast territory. They had everything that heart could wish. Their corn and their buffalo gave them food, clothing and shelter; they had weapons for war and for the chase. They roamed over the country without let or hindrance. In peace they were light-hearted and contented; in war cunning, fierce and successful. Their name was a terror to their enemies. This was in the past. Now they are few in number, poor, a prey to disease, a vanishing race.

My acquaintance with the tribe began in 1870. From that time to the present I have had frequent intercourse with them; have lived in their villages; and been with them on their buffalo hunts. During the weeks and months spent in camp and village, I have listened to many stories of Pawnee heroes and to folk-tales of the miraculous doings of the olden time. In my intercourse with the tribe, extending over a period of nearly twenty years, I have been deeply impressed by the high qualities of the Pawnee character; and the more familiar I have become with this people, the more strongly have I felt that a permanent record should be made of the tales which reflect that character. Unless thus collected now, much of this lore must inevitably be forgotten.

For the Pawnees are passing away. When I first joined them on their buffalo hunts from their old home on the Loup Fork in Nebraska, the tribe numbered three thousand; last March in the Indian Territory I found but eight hundred. And more rapidly than the dwindling of the people are their traditions lapsing from memory under the changed conditions of the tribe's life. The lore, which sprang up as an indigenous growth of the wide-stretching prairie and the wilderness where the wild Pawnee warrior hunted free, finds scanty nurture in the uncongenial soil of fields tilled by Pawnee followers of the plow. With the new modes of living come new views of life, new motives, new sympathies—in a word, civilization. To earn a living by toil, to wrest subsistence from the earth, this is the problem confronting the Pawnees to-day, the task which is engaging the sinew and purpose of the tribe. In the transition stage, the memory of the old days, of old manners and rites and ceremonies and of old heroes, is with the elders of the race, those ancient braves whose lives bridge the past and the present. When I visited the Agency last March, it was to write down from the lips of these old men such material as I could collect. When they shall die much of the unwritten lore will perish too, for with them will cease that sympathetic and perfect credence, which alone gives to folk-lore vitality and lastingness. What is written in this volume then belongs distinctly to the wild Indian.

The task that I have set for myself is that of a recorder. No attempt has been made to give a literary color to the hero stories and folk-tales here written out. I have scrupulously avoided putting into them anything of my own. The stories are told to the reader as they were told to me. They are not elaborated. I have tried to show how Indians think and speak, rather than to make their stories more entertaining by dressing them up to suit the civilized taste. My object in giving these narratives in their present shape is to make a book which shall be true to life, and shall faithfully reflect the Pawnee character, as the story tellers have themselves painted it. In a very few cases I have added some words explaining matters so well understood by those familiar with the Indians as to need no explanation. If these tales have any ethnological value, it will be enhanced by their being given in the precise form in which they were told by those to whom they have been handed down from generation to generation; but quite apart from this is another point which is entitled to consideration.

The entire ignorance concerning Indians, which prevails among the general public, can be dispelled only by letting that public understand something of the ways of life of the wild Indian, something of the subjects about which he thinks and talks, as well as of how he looks at these subjects, and what he has to say about them.

The late Mrs. Jackson's charming story, "Ramona," did much to bring the more intelligent class of readers in touch with the Indians, and to awaken sympathy for them by pointing out the unnumbered wrongs perpetrated on this race by the Government. Mrs. Jackson's book was a story, a novel; wonderfully well told and full of truth and feeling; but while it may have been a relation of facts, it did not profess to treat of actual persons. It is looked upon by many readers as a mere romance. It is a book about which I was once asked, skeptically, "Did you ever see any Indians like those?" In the Pawnee stories here set down there is no romance nor coloring. The Indians themselves are talking, and whatever the faults and weak points of these tales—and some of them are sufficiently obvious—they at least give the reader a true conception of Indians as they have actually lived. They are stories of Indians by Indians. There is about them nothing of the white man; and the intelligent person, who is sufficiently interested in the subject to read this book through, will gain from it a new insight into Indian character.

The Indian of Cooper—with his bravery, his endurance, his acuteness, his high qualities of honesty, generosity, courtesy and hospitality —has been laughed at for half a century. Yet every man who has mingled much with the Indians in their homes has known individuals who might have sat for the portraits which Cooper drew of some of his aboriginal heroes. There are good men among Indians, just as among the whites. The prevalent notion of the Indian has been formed from the worst class of this people, the lazy, filthy beggars who haunt the settlements of the West, who to their own vices have added new ones picked up from their surroundings, and who are hopelessly degraded. These are not typical Indians, and it is unjust to judge a whole race from such degenerate specimens. There is still another notion of the Indian fondly cherished by many worthy people, whose sympathies have been wrought upon by the cruelty and injustice with which we have treated this race. These good people look upon all Indians as simple children of nature, who would do no wrong if they had not been contaminated by contact with vicious whites. It is unnecessary to say that this notion of the Indian is also incorrect.

The Indian is neither a fiend nor a saint. There are good ones and bad ones. As a rule, perhaps they try to act up to their ideas of what is right, but the standard of a race of barbarians cannot be the same as that of a civilized people, and in judging of their character we must make allowances for this difference. The standard of right and wrong among civilized people is a growth, the product of the experience of thousands of years. The Indian races have not been through a like experience. They have regarded as virtues some things which seem to us the worst of crimes. The Indian differs from the white man in education and manner of life, and so, of course, in his modes of thought. He has not been taught the lesson of self-control, which his surroundings oblige each civilized man to begin to learn as a child. He has known until recent times no law save that of strength. He has been taught that war is the noblest of pursuits—the only one worthy of man. And that war has consisted in making forays upon his enemies, taking their possessions, and, if possible, their lives and their scalps. His warfare consisted in surprises rather than open combat. A scalp taken was a trophy of victory; and the scalp of a woman was almost as eagerly sought as that of a brave or of a chief. It was an evidence of injury inflicted on the enemy. To steal horses from the enemy was an achievement creditable and also profitable.

We commonly speak of the raids of war parties as horse stealing expeditions, but this is wholly misleading, because to the civilized understanding the phrase horse stealing carries with it an idea of dishonesty. No such meaning attaches to the Indian equivalent of this phrase. They take horses by stratagem or secretly, by the usual, and to them legitimate, methods of warfare. To speak of their stealing horses, using that verb in the sense which we commonly give it, would be like saying that an army stole the cannon which it captured in an engagement with the enemy. Captured horses were the legitimate spoils of war. The wealth of the Indians was in their horses. They had no fortified places, no ships of war, no cannon, no works of art. Their only valuable possessions were their horses. These were the only property that could be carried off. Therefore, when an expedition was made against a hostile tribe, scalps and horses were naturally its object. Horses, being their only valuable possessions, constituted their medium of exchange, so far as they had any. Did a man wish to purchase an ornament, or an article of dress which took his fancy, he gave a horse for it. If he bought a wife he paid for her in horses. The most valuable present that could be made was a good horse; and horses were often given by the well-to-do to their friends and relations who had been sick or unfortunate. On the other hand, when, as was sometimes the case, a conquered tribe was condemned to pay a war indemnity, they paid it in horses. It is related that when the Skidi broke their treaty with the other bands, and were afterward conquered by them, they were obligated to pay such a fine.

This view of Indian warfare being understood, the motive of the hero stories here given, and of many of the folk-tales, becomes plain.

The Pawnees are essentially a religious people. They worship *Ti-ra'-wa*, who is in and of everything. Unlike many of the Indian tribes of the West, they do not adore any material thing. They regard certain places as sacred, but these are so only because blessed by the Divine presence. The Pawnee Deity is not personified. He is intangible, quite as much so as the God of the Christians. The sacred character of *Ti-ra'-wa* extends to animal nature. The fishes which swim in the rivers, the birds of the air and the beasts which roam over the prairie, have sometimes intelligence, knowledge and power far beyond those of man. But they are not gods. Their miraculous attributes are given them by the Ruler, whose servants they are, and who often makes them the medium of his communications to man. They are his messengers—his angels—and their powers are always used for good.

Prayers are made to them; sometimes for direct help in time of need, but more often for intercession. Often in the folk-tales it will be seen that when the blessing asked for is some small thing, a prayer is made to the animals (*Na-hu'rac*), but if the petitioners are asking for some great thing, something which is very difficult to grant, then the prayer is made to "One Above," to "The Ruler," that is, to the Supreme Being.

Nothing of importance was ever undertaken without a prayer for help, for success. All the serious undertakings of the year, whose success would affect the general welfare, were preceded by religious ceremonies, when all the tribe took part, and prayers were made and sacrifices offered to *Ti-ra'-wa;* and in all lesser enterprises, the individuals who were interested humbled themselves and implored the Divine assistance. A party starting off on the warpath prayed for success and made a burnt offering. Prayer and sacrifice always marked the beginning of the feast, and often its end. Success in their undertakings was acknowledged by grateful offerings to the Ruler. The victorious warrior sometimes sacrificed the scalp torn from the head of his enemy, and this was burned with elaborate ceremonies by the High Priest. He who brought back from a foray many horses, gave one to the priest as a thank-offering to the Ruler. One of the well-known Seven Brothers said to me, "It is our aim, after we have been helped, to give thanks."

The feeling of these Indians toward their God is one of humility and reverence. They do not love him, but they look to him for help at all times. The young are exhorted to humble themselves before him, to pray to him, to look to One Above, to ask help from the Ruler. In the stories which are included in this book the allusions constantly made to *Ti-ra'-wa*—the Supreme Power—the prayers offered and the humility and self-abnegation so often expressed, show faith, profound religious feelings, and great elevation of thought.

Among tribal names of North American Indians, none is more familiar to us than Pawnee; yet of no tribe is less known. Frequent allusions to them occur in the writings of early travelers in the West; but only one satisfactory attempt has been made to write a connected history of this family. In the *Magazine of American History* for

1880–81 Mr. John B. Dunbar published a most interesting account of this tribe, but his sketch is mainly historical, and does not profess to treat exhaustively of the lives and modes of thought of this people. It is, however, a history of very great importance and value, and in preparing the historical matter which is included in this volume, I have not hesitated to draw on Mr. Dunbar's papers, which must form the basis of any subsequent account of the Pawnees, and which should be read by all who are interested in this people.

I owe much of my interest in and knowledge of the Pawnees to my long intimacy with the late Major Frank North, who from his extended intercourse and close connection with this people—a connection which lasted more than thirty years—was unquestionably better informed about them than any other white man has ever been; and with Capt. L. H. North, his brother, who was for many years associated with Major North in command of the Pawnee Scouts.

In gathering the material here presented I have been assisted also by James R. Murie, a nephew of Comanche Chief; by Ralph J. Weeks, a half-brother of Lone Chief; by Harry Kuhns, by Eagle Chief and Bear Chief, Skidis; by Good Chief and Curly Chief, Kit-ke-hahk-is; by Secret Pipe Chief and Frank White, Chau-is, and by many others of my Pawnee friends, to all of whom my acknowledgments are due.

In the pronunciation of the few Pawnee words used in these stories, the vowel sounds, as nearly as I can give them, are as follows: *a* as in father, *e* as the *a* in ale, *i* as *e* in cede, *ū* long as *oo* in pool, *ŭ* short as in us, *au* as *ou* in house. These sounds depend somewhat on the letters which follow the vowels, and the spelling does not always conform to the rule laid down. The last two syllables in the word Pita-hau-erat, for example, are pronounced *irăt* or *idot*. The sounds of *d, l, n* and *r* are difficult to express by English letters; *r* sometimes has its own sound quite distinctly, at others more the sound of *d; n* often has a *d* sound, and *l* a sound of *n*. It will be noted that throughout I have used the familiar English word Pawnee instead of the evidently more correct *Pa'-ni*.

Finally I have refrained from commenting on the stories, though there is abundant opportunity for comment.

HERO STORIES

COMANCHE CHIEF, THE PEACE-MAKER

I

MANY years ago there lived in the Ski'-di village a young man, about sixteen years old. His name was *Kut-a'wi-kutz* (the hawk). At this time the Pawnees wore their hair in the ancient fashion, cut as the Osages wear theirs; the whole head was shaved except a roach running back from the forehead beyond the scalp lock.

A war party went off to the south and he joined them as a servant. They went a long way and a long way, traveling far, but they got no horses and came back. Afterward another party started off on the warpath, and he went with it. They traveled many days, going to the southwest, and at length they came to a camp, and hid themselves to wait until it was dark. It was a camp of the Comanches.

When night had come they all went into the camp to steal horses. This young man went to a lodge near which stood three horses, two spotted horses and one gray. They were tied near the door of the lodge, and from this he thought they must be fast, for the Indians usually tie up their best horses close to the lodge door, where they will be under their eyes as much as possible. He went to the lodge to cut the ropes, and just as he was about to do so he thought he heard some one inside. He stepped up close to the lodge, and looked in through a little opening between the door and the lodge, and saw a small fire burning, and on the other side of the fire was sitting a young girl, combing her long hair. The young man looked around the lodge to see who else was there, and saw only an old man and an old woman, and the firemaker. He cut the ropes of the two spotted horses standing outside, led the horses out of the camp, and met his companion. To him he said, "Now, brother, you take these horses and go to the hill

42

where we were hiding to-day, and wait for me there. I have seen another fine spotted horse that I want to get; I will go back for it and will meet you before morning at that place."

He went back, as if to get the spotted horse, but returned to the lodge where the girl was. He went all around it, and looked at it carefully. He saw that there were feathers on the lodge, and rows of animals hoofs hanging down the sides, which rattled in the wind, and to one of the lodge-poles was tied a buffalo tail, which hung down. Then he went back to the door and looked in at the girl again. She had braided her hair and was sitting there by the fire. He stayed there a long time that night looking at her. Toward morning he went to look for his companion. When he met him he told him that some one had taken the spotted horse before he got to it; he could not find it. When the party all met next morning, they found that they had taken a lot of horses, and they started north to go home. They reached the Pawnee village, and every one was glad of their success.

After this, whenever this young man saw anything that was nice or pretty, such as medals, ear-rings, finger rings for women, beadwork leggings, bracelets, necklaces, wampum, beads—things that the Comanches did not have—he would give a pony for it. For one year he went on like this, gathering together these pretty things. When the year had gone by he had no horses left; he had given them all away to get these presents. He packed all these things up in a bundle, and then spoke one night to his friend, saying, "I intend to go off on the warpath again, and I would like to have you go with me; we two will go alone." His friend agreed to go.

II

Before the time came to start, other young men heard of it, and several joined them. There were eight of them in all. *Kut-a'wi-kutz* was the leader. He told his young men that they were going to a certain place where he knew there were lots of spotted horses to steal. They started out on foot. After traveling many days, they came to the place where the camp had been at the time he saw the girl. There was now no camp there.

They went on further, and at length came to a camp and hid themselves. When night came the leader told his men to remain where they were hiding, and he would go into the camp and see if there were any horses to take. He went through all the camp looking for the lodge in which he had seen the girl, but he did not find it. Then he went back to where the young men were hiding, and told them that this was not the camp they were looking for; that they did not have here the spotted horses that they wanted. In the camp of the year before there had been many spotted horses.

The young men did not understand this, and some of them did not like to leave this camp without taking any horses, but he was the leader and they did as he said. They left that camp and went on further.

After traveling some days they came to another camp, and hid themselves near it. When night came on *Kut-a'wi-kutz* said to his young men, "You stay here where you are hiding, and I will go into this camp and see if it is the one we are looking for." He went through the camp but did not find the lodge he sought. He returned to the hiding place, and told the party there that this was not the camp they were looking for, that the spotted horses were not there. They left the camp and went on.

When they had come close to the mountains they saw another camp. *Kut-a'wi-kutz* went into this camp alone, and when he had been through it, he went back to his party and told them that this was the camp they had been looking for. Then he sent the young men into the camp to steal horses, and he put on his fine leggings and moccasins that he had in his bundle, and painted himself and went with them. He took a horse and his friend took one. They met outside the village. He told his friend to get on his own horse and lead the other, and with the rest of the party to go off east from the camp to a certain place, and there to wait for him. "I have seen," he said, "another fine horse that I like, and I wish to go back and get it."

His friend looked sorrowfully at him and said, "Why are you all dressed up like this, and why is your face painted? What are you doing or what is in your mind? Perhaps you intend to do some great thing to-night that you do not want me, your friend, to know about. I have seen for a long time that you are hiding something from me."

Kut-a'wi-kutz caught his friend in his arms and hugged him and kissed him and said, "You are my friend; who is so near to me as you are? Go on as I have said, and if it turns out well I will tell you all. I will catch up with you before very long."

His friend said, "No, I will stay with you. I will not go on. I love you as a brother, and I will stay with you, and if you are going to do some great thing I will die with you."

When *Kut-a'wi-kutz* found that his friend was resolved to remain with him, he yielded and told him his secret. He said to him, "My brother, when we were on the warpath a year ago, and I took those two spotted horses, I heard a little noise in the lodge by which they were tied. I looked in and I saw there a girl sitting by the fire combing her hair. She was very pretty. When I took the spotted horses away, I could not put that girl out of my mind. I remembered her. Brother, when we went back home that girl was constantly in my mind. I could not forget her. I came this time on purpose to get her, even if it shall cost me my life. She is in this camp, and I have found the lodge where she lives."

His friend said, "My brother, whatever you say shall be done. I stay with you. You go into the camp. I will take the horses and go to that high rocky hill east of the camp, and will hide the horses there. When you are in the village I will be up in one of the trees on the top of the hill, looking down on the camp. If I hear shooting and see lots of people running to the lodge I will know that you are killed, and I will kill myself. I will not go home alone. If I do not see you by noon, I will kill myself."

Kut-a'wi-kutz said, "It is good. If I am successful I will go up there after you, and take you down into the camp."

They parted. The friend hid the horses and went up on the hill. *Kut-a'wi-kutz* went into the camp.

III

It was now the middle of the night. When he came to the lodge, he saw there was a fire in it. He did not go in at once; he wanted the fire to go out. He stayed around the lodge, and gradually the fire died down. It was dark. He went into the lodge. He was painted and finely dressed, and had his bundle with him. He took his moccasins off and his leggings, and hung them up over the girl's bed; then strings of beads, then five or six medals, bracelets, ear-bobs, beaded leggings, everything he had—his shirt. He took his blanket, and spread it over the bed where the girl was lying, stepped over the bed, and crept under his own blanket, and lay down by her side.

When he lay down she woke up, and found that there was some one lying by her, and she spoke to him, but he did not answer. He could not understand her, for he did not know Comanche. She talked for a long time, but he did not speak. Then she began to feel of him, and when she put her hands on his head—*Pi-ta'-da*—Pawnee—an enemy! Then she raised herself up, took a handful of grass from under the bed, spread the fire and put the grass on it. The fire blazed up and she saw him. Then she sprang up and took the top blanket, which was his, off the bed, and put it about her, and sat by the fire. She called her father and said, "Father get up; there is a man here."

The old man got up, and got his pipe and began smoking. This old man was the Head Chief of the Comanches. He called the servant, and told him to make a fire. The girl got up and went over to where her mother was lying and called her. The mother got up; and they all sat by the fire.

The old man smoked for a long time. Every now and then he would look at the bed to see who it could be that was lying there, and then he would look at all the things hanging up over the bed—at the medals and other things. He did not know what they were for, and he wondered. At length the old man told the servant to go and call the chiefs of the tribe, and tell them to come to his lodge.

Presently the chiefs came in one by one and sat down. When they had come there was still one brave who ought to have come that was not there. His name was Skin Shirt; the father wanted him. He sent for him three times. He sent word back to the chief to go on with the council, and that he would agree to whatever they decided. The fourth time he was sent for he came, and took a seat by the chief, the girl's father. This brave spoke to *Kut-a'wi-kutz*, and told him to get up, and take a seat among them. He did so. The girl was sitting on the other side of the fire. When he got up, he had to take the blanket that was left, which was the girl's. He put it around him, and sat down among them.

The Pawnees

When the chiefs came in, there was among them a Pawnee who had been captured long ago and adopted by the Comanches, and was now himself a chief; he talked with *Kut-a'wi-kutz* and interpreted for him, telling him everything that was said as each one spoke.

After the young man had seated himself, the chief filled his pipe, and gave the pipe to his brave to decide what should be done with this enemy. The brave took the pipe, but he did not wish to decide, so he did not light it, but passed it on to another chief to decide. He passed it on to another, and he to another, and so it went until the pipe came back to the Head Chief. When he got it again, he asked *Kut-a'wi-kutz,* "Why have you come here this night and lain down in my lodge, you who are an enemy to my people? And why have you hung up in the lodge all these strange things which we see here? I do not understand it, and I wish to know your reasons."

The boy said to him, "A long time ago I came south on the warpath to steal horses. I traveled until I came to your camp. I saw three horses tied outside a lodge, two spotted horses and a gray. While I was cutting one of the ropes, I heard a little noise inside the lodge, and pushing aside the door I looked in, and saw that girl combing her hair. I stole the two spotted horses, and took them out of the camp, and gave them to a friend of mine, and came back to your lodge, and kept looking at the girl. I stayed there until she went to bed. For a long year I have been buying presents; beads and many other things, for I had made up my mind that I would go after this girl. I came down here to find her. I have been to where you were camped last year, and to two other camps that I discovered. She was not in these and I left them, and came on until I found the right camp. This is the fourth place. Now I am here. I made up my mind to do this thing, and if her relations do not like it they can do as they please. I would be happy to die on her account."

When he had spoken the old chief laughed. He said: "Those two spotted horses that you stole I did not care much about. The gray horse was the best one of the three, and you left him. I was glad that you did not take him. He was the best of all." Then for a little while there was silence in the lodge.

Then the chief, the girl's father, began to talk again; he said, "If I wanted to decide what should be done with this man, I would decide right now, but here is my brave, Skin Shirt, I want him to decide. If I were to decide, it would be against this man, but he has my daughter's blanket on, and she has his, and I do not want to decide. I pass the pipe to my brave, and want him to light it."

The brave said, "I want this chief next to me to decide," and he passed him the pipe, and so it went on around the circle until it came to the Head Chief again. He was just about to take it and decide the question, when they heard outside the lodge the noise made by some one coming, shouting and laughing; then the door was pushed aside and an old man came in, and as he passed the door he stumbled and fell on his knees. It was the girl's grandfather. He had been outside the lodge, listening.

The pipe was passed to the chief, and he gave it again to his brave to decide. While the brave was sitting there, holding the pipe, the old grandfather said, "Give me the pipe; if you men cannot decide, let me do it. In my time we did not do things this way. I never passed the pipe; I could always decide for myself."

Then Skin Shirt passed him the pipe, and he lit it and smoked. Then he said, "I do not wish to condemn to death a man who is wearing my granddaughter's blanket." The interpreter began to tell *Kut-a'wi-kutz* that the old man was going to decide in his favor, and that when he got through speaking he must get up and pass his hands over him, and thank him for taking pity on him, and so to all the others. The old man continued, "Now, chiefs, do not think hardly of what I am going to say, nor be dissatisfied with my decision. I am old. I have heard in my time that there is a tribe up north that is raising from the ground something that is long and white, and something that is round; and that these things are good to eat. Now, chiefs, before I die, I want to eat of these things, and I want my granddaughter to go and take her seat by this man, and for them to be man and wife. Since I was young we have been enemies, but now I want the two tribes to come together, join hands and be friends." And so it was decided.

The young man got up and passed his hands over the old man, and over the brave, and passed around the circle and blessed them all. The Pawnee, who was interpreter, now told him to get up, and get a medal and put it on the brave, and then another and put it on the chief, and so on until all the presents were gone. And he did so, and put on them the medals, and ear-rings, and strings of beads, and breast-plates of wampum, until each had something. And these things were new to them, and they felt proud to be wearing them, and thought how nice they looked.

IV

By this time it was daylight, and it had got noised abroad through the camp that there was a Pawnee at the Head Chief's lodge, and all the people gathered there. They called out, "Bring him out; we want him out here." They crowded about the lodge, all the people, the old men and the women and the young men, so many that at last they pushed the lodge down. They shouted: "Let us have the Pawnee. Last night they stole many horses from us." The chiefs and braves got around the Pawnee, and kept the Comanches off from him, and protected him from the people. The Cheyennes were camped close by, near the hill southeast of the Comanches, and they, too, had heard that the Comanches had a Pawnee in the camp. They came over, and rode about in the crowd to try and get the Pawnee, and they rode over a Comanche or two, and knocked them down. So Skin Shirt got his bow and arrows, and jumped on his horse, and rode out and drove the Cheyennes away back to their camp again.

The Cheyennes saw that the Comanches did not want the Pawnee killed, so they sent a message inviting him over to a feast with them, intending to kill him, but Skin Shirt told them that he was married into the tribe. While the Cheyennes were parading round the Comanche camp, they were shooting off their guns in the air, just to make a noise. Now, the young Pawnee on the hill, who was watching the camp to see what would happen to his friend, saw the crowd and heard the shooting, and made up his mind that *Kut-a'wi-kutz* had been killed. So he took his knife, and put the handle against a tree and the point against his breast, and put his arms around the tree and hugged it, and the knife blade passed through his heart and he fell down and died.

In the afternoon when all the excitement had quieted down, the Cheyennes came over again to the Comanche camp, and invited the Pawnee and his wife to go to their village, and visit with them. Then

Skin Shirt said, "All right, we will go." Three chiefs of the Comanches went ahead, the Pawnee followed with his wife, and Skin Shirt went behind. They went to the Cheyenne camp. The Cheyennes received them and made a great feast for them, and gave the Pawnee many horses. Then they went back to the Comanche camp. *Kut-a'wi-kutz* never went up to the hill until the next morning. Then he went, singing the song he had told his friend he would sing. He called to him, but there was no reply. He called again. It was all silent. He looked for his friend, and at last he found him there dead at the foot of the tree.

V

Kut-a'wi-kutz then stayed with the Comanches. The Cheyennes came north and east, and the Comanches went on west, nearer to the mountains. While the Pawnee was with the Comanches, they had several wars with the Utes, Lipans and Tonkaways. *Kut-a'wi-kutz* proved himself a brave man, and, as the son-in-law of the chief, he soon gained great influence, and was himself made a chief.

After some years the old man, his wife's grandfather, told the Pawnee that he thought it was time that he should eat some of those things that he had long wanted to eat that grew up north; that he was getting pretty old now. *Kut-a'wi-kutz* said, "It is time. We will go." So he had his horses packed, and with his immediate family and the old man, started north toward the Pawnee country. At this time he was called *Kut-a'wi-kutz-u si-ti'-da-rit*, which means "See! The Hawk." When going into battle he would ride straight out to strike his enemy, and the Comanches who were looking at him would say, "See! The Hawk." So that became his name.

They traveled a long time until they came to the Pawnee ground. As they were traveling along, they came to a field where were growing corn, beans and squashes. The Pawnee said to the old man, "Grandfather, look at that field. There are the things that you have desired to eat." He got off his horse and went into the field, and pulled some corn, some beans and some squashes, and took them to the old man, and gave them to him. The old man supposed they were to be eaten just as they were, and he tried to bite the squashes. This made the Pawnee laugh. When they came to the village, the Pawnees were very glad to see him who had been lost long ago. He told the people that he had brought these Indians to eat of the corn and other things; that they were his kinsfolk. He told them, too, about the young man who had killed himself. His relations went out into the fields, and gathered corn and beans and squashes, and cooked them for the Comanches.

They stayed there a long time at the Pawnee village. When they were getting ready to return, the Pawnees dried their corn, and gave a great deal of it to the Comanches, packing many horses with it for the Indians at home. Then the Comanches started south again, and some of the Pawnee young men, relations of *Kut-a'wi-kutz*, joined him, and went back with them. After they had returned to the Comanche camp, the old grandfather died, happy because he had eaten the things he wanted to eat.

Soon after this, *Kut-a'wi-kutz* started back to the Pawnee village, and some young men of the Comanches joined him. Some time after reaching the village he went south again, accompanied by some young Pawnees, but leaving most of the Comanches behind. He had arranged with the chiefs of the Pawnees that they should journey south, meet the Comanches on the plains and make peace. When he reached the Comanches, the whole village started north to visit the Pawnees, and met them on their way south. When they met, the two tribes made friends, smoked together, ate together, became friends.

After they had camped together for some time, some Comanches stayed in the Pawnee camp, and some Pawnees in the Comanche camp. *Kut-a'wi-kutz* was called by the Pawnees Comanche Chief. He would have remained with the Comanches, but when he went back with them his wife fell sick. The Comanche doctors could not help her, and he wanted to take her north to see the Pawnee doctors, but the Comanches would not let him. They kept him there, and his wife died. Then he was angry, for he thought if he had taken her north her life might have been saved.

So he left the Comanches, and went and lived with the Pawnees, and was known among them always as Comanche Chief, the Peace-Maker, because he made peace between the Pawnees and Comanches. He was chief of the Ski'-di band, and a progressive man of modern times. He sent his children East to school at Carlisle, Pa.

Comanche Chief died September 9th, 1888.

THE PRISONERS
OF COURT HOUSE ROCK

COURT HOUSE ROCK is a high, square-shaped bluff, or butte, on the North Platte River. It is composed of a hard, yellowish clay, which is but slowly eroded by the weather, though soft enough to be cut readily with a knife. On all sides except one, this rock or butte is nearly or quite vertical, and its sides, smoothed and polished by the wind and the rain, offer no projecting points, to serve as foot or hand holds for one who might wish to climb up or down. On one side there is a way by which an active man may reach the summit, where he finds a flat tableland of moderate extent.

A number of years ago a war party of Skidi, who were camped near Court House Rock, were surprised by a party of Sioux. There were many of them, and they drove the Skidi back, and at length these were obliged to climb the steep side of Court House Rock. The Sioux dared not follow them up on to the rock, but guarded the only place where it was possible to come down, and camped all around the rock below to starve the Skidi out. The Skidi had nothing to eat nor to drink, and suffered terribly from hunger and still more from thirst. The leader of the party suffered most of any, for he thought that he would surely lose all his men. He felt that this was the worst of all. He must not only die, but must also be disgraced, because under his leadership the young men of his party had been lost. He used to go off at night, apart from the others, and pray to *Ti-ra'-wa* for help; for some way to save his party.

One night while he was praying, something spoke to him, and said, "Look hard for a place where you may get down from this rock, and so save both your men and yourself." He kept on praying that night, and when day came, he looked all along the edge of the rock for a place where it might be possible to get down. At last he found near the edge of the cliff a point of the soft clay rock sticking up above the level of the rest. The side of the rock below it was straight up and down, and smooth. At night he took his knife, and began to cut about the base of this point of rock, and night after night he kept at this until he had cut away the base of the point, so that it was no larger around than a man's body. Then he secretly took all the lariats that the party had, and tied them together, and let them down, and found that his rope was long enough to reach the ground. He put the rope around the point, and made a loop in it for his feet, and slowly let himself down to the ground. He got there safely, and then climbed back again. The next night he called his men about him, and told them how it was, and that they might all be saved. Then he ordered the youngest and least important man of the party to let himself down, and after him the next youngest, and so on, up to the more important men, and last of all the leader's turn came. He let himself down, and they all crept through the Sioux camp and escaped.

They never knew how long the Sioux stayed there watching the rock. Probably until they thought that the Skidi had all starved to death.

FOLK TALES

THE DUN HORSE

I

MANY years ago, there lived in the Pawnee tribe an old woman and her grandson, a boy about sixteen years old. These people had no relations and were very poor. They were so poor that they were despised by the rest of the tribe. They had nothing of their own; and always, after the village started to move the camp from one place to another, these two would stay behind the rest, to look over the old camp, and pick up anything that the other Indians had thrown away, as worn out or useless. In this way they would sometimes get pieces of robes, worn out moccasins with holes in them, and bits of meat.

Now, it happened one day, after the tribe had moved away from the camp, that this old woman and her boy were following along the trail behind the rest, when they came to a miserable old worn out dun horse, which they supposed had been abandoned by some Indians. He was thin and exhausted, was blind of one eye, had a bad sore back, and one of his forelegs was very much swollen. In fact, he was so worthless that none of the Pawnees had been willing to take the trouble to try to drive him along with them. But when the old woman and her boy came along, the boy said, "Come now, we will take this old horse, for we can make him carry our pack." So the old woman put her pack on the horse, and drove him along, but he limped and could only go very slowly.

II

The tribe moved up on the North Platte, until they came to Court House Rock. The two poor Indians followed them, and camped with the others. One day while they were here, the young men who had been sent out to look for buffalo, came hurrying into camp and told the chiefs that a large herd of buffalo were near, and that among them was a spotted calf.

The Head Chief of the Pawnees had a very beautiful daughter, and when he heard about the spotted calf, he ordered his old crier to go about through the village, and call out that the man who killed the spotted calf should have his daughter for his wife. For a spotted robe is *ti-war'-uks-ti*—big medicine.

The buffalo were feeding about four miles from the village, and the chiefs decided that the charge should be made from there. In this way, the man who had the fastest horse would be the most likely to kill the calf. Then all the warriors and the young men picked out their best and fastest horses, and made ready to start. Among those who prepared for the charge was the poor boy on the old dun horse. But when they saw him, all the rich young braves on their fast horses pointed at him, and said, "Oh, see; there is the horse that is going to catch the spotted calf"; and they laughed at him, so that the poor boy was ashamed, and rode off to one side of the crowd, where he could not hear their jokes and laughter.

When he had ridden off some little way, the horse stopped, and turned his head round, and spoke to the boy. He said, "Take me down to the creek, and plaster me all over with mud. Cover my head and neck and body and legs." When the boy heard the horse speak, he was afraid; but he did as he was told. Then the horse said, "Now mount, but do not ride back to the warriors, who laugh at you because you have such a poor horse. Stay right here, until the word is given to charge." So the boy stayed there.

And presently all the fine horses were drawn up in line and pranced about, and were so eager to go that their riders could hardly hold them in; and at last the old crier gave the word, "*Loo-ah*"—Go! Then the Pawnees all leaned forward on their horses and yelled, and away they went. Suddenly, away off to the right, was seen the old dun horse. He did not seem to run. He seemed to sail along like a bird. He passed all the fastest horses, and in a moment he was among the buffalo. First he picked out the spotted calf, and charging up alongside of it, *U-ra-rish!* straight flew the arrow. The calf fell. The boy drew another arrow, and killed a fat cow that was running by. Then he dismounted and began to skin the calf, before any of the other warriors had come up. But when the rider got off the old dun horse, how changed he was! He pranced about and would hardly stand still near the dead buffalo. His back was all right again; his legs were well and fine; and both his eyes were clear and bright.

The boy skinned the calf and the cow that he had killed, and then he packed all the meat on the horse, and put the spotted robe on top of the load, and started back to the camp on foot, leading the dun horse. But even with this heavy load the horse pranced all the time, and was scared at everything he saw. On the way to camp, one of the rich young chiefs of the tribe rode up by the boy, and offered him twelve good horses for the spotted robe, so that he could marry the Head Chief's beautiful daughter; but the boy laughed at him and would not sell the robe.

Now, while the boy walked to the camp leading the dun horse, most of the warriors rode back, and one of those that came first to the village, went to the old woman, and said to her, "Your grandson has killed the spotted calf." And the old woman said, "Why do you come to tell me this? You ought to be ashamed to make fun of my boy, because he is poor." The warrior said, "What I have told you is true," and then he rode away. After a little while another brave rode up to the old woman, and said to her, "Your grandson has killed the spotted calf." Then the old woman began to cry, she felt so badly because every one made fun of her boy, because he was poor.

Pretty soon the boy came along, leading the horse up to the lodge where he and his grandmother lived. It was a little lodge, just big enough for two, and was made of old pieces of skin that the old woman had picked up, and was tied together with strings of rawhide and sinew. It was the meanest and worst lodge in the village. When the old woman saw her boy leading the dun horse with the load of meat and the robes on it, she was very much surprised. The boy said to her, "Here, I have brought you plenty of meat to eat, and here is a robe, that you may have for yourself. Take the meat off the horse." Then the old woman laughed, for her heart was glad. But when she went to take the meat from the horse's back, he snorted and jumped about, and acted like a wild horse. The old woman looked at him in wonder, and could hardly believe that it was the same horse. So the boy had to take off the meat, for the horse would not let the old woman come near him.

III

That night the horse spoke again to the boy and said, "*Wa-ti-hes Chah'-ra-rat wa-ta.* To-morrow the Sioux are coming—a large war party. They will attack the village, and you will have a great battle. Now, when the Sioux are drawn up in line of battle, and are all ready to fight, you jump on to me, and ride as hard as you can, right into the middle of the Sioux, and up to their Head Chief, their greatest warrior, and count *coup* [1] on him, and kill him, and then ride back. Do this four times, and count *coup* on four of the bravest Sioux, and

[1] An explanation of this term is found on p. 111.

kill them, but don't go again. If you go the fifth time, may be you will be killed, or else you will lose me. *La-ku'-ta-chix*—remember." So the boy promised.

The next day it happened as the horse had said, and the Sioux came down and formed in line of battle. Then the boy took his bow and arrows, and jumped on the dun horse, and charged into the midst of them. And when the Sioux saw that he was going to strike their Head Chief, they all shot their arrows at him, and the arrows flew so thickly across each other that they darkened the sky, but none of them hit the boy. And he counted *coup* on the Chief, and killed him, and then rode back. After that he charged again among the Sioux, where they were gathered thickest, and counted *coup* on their bravest warrior, and killed him. And then twice more, until he had gone four times as the horse had told him.

But the Sioux and the Pawnees kept on fighting, and the boy stood around and watched the battle. And at last he said to himself, "I have been four times and have killed four Sioux, and I am all right, I am not hurt anywhere; why may I not go again?" So he jumped on the dun horse, and charged again. But when he got among the Sioux, one Sioux warrior drew an arrow and shot. The arrow struck the dun horse behind the forelegs and pierced him through. And the horse fell down dead. But the boy jumped off, and fought his way through the Sioux, and ran away as fast as he could to the Pawnees. Now, as soon as the horse was killed, the Sioux said to each other, "This horse was like a man. He was brave. He was not like a horse." And they took their knives and hatchets, and hacked the dun horse and gashed his flesh, and cut him into small pieces.

The Pawnees and Sioux fought all day long, but toward night the Sioux broke and fled.

IV

The boy felt very badly that he had lost his horse; and, after the fight was over, he went out from the village to where it had taken place, to mourn for his horse. He went to the spot where the horse lay, and gathered up all the pieces of flesh, which the Sioux had cut off, and the legs and the hoofs, and put them all together in a pile. Then he went off to the top of a hill near by, and sat down and drew his robe over his head, and began to mourn for his horse.

As he sat there, he heard a great wind storm coming up, and it passed over him with a loud rushing sound, and after the wind came a rain. The boy looked down from where he sat to the pile of flesh and bones, which was all that was left of his horse, and he could just see it through the rain. And the rain passed by, and his heart was very heavy, and he kept on mourning.

And pretty soon came another rushing wind, and after it a rain; and as he looked through the driving rain toward the spot where the pieces lay, he thought that they seemed to come together and take shape, and that the pile looked like a horse lying down, but he could not see well for the thick rain.

After this, came a third storm like the others; and now when he looked toward the horse he thought he saw its tail move from side to side two or three times, and that it lifted its head from the ground. The boy was afraid, and wanted to run away, but he stayed.

And as he waited, there came another storm. And while the rain fell, looking through the rain, the boy saw the horse raise himself up on his forelegs and look about. Then the dun horse stood up.

V

The boy left the place where he had been sitting on the hilltop, and went down to him. When the boy had come near to him, the horse spoke and said, "You have seen how it has been this day; and from this you may know how it will be after this. But *Ti-ra'-wa* has been good, and has let me come back to you. After this, do what I tell you; not any more, not any less." Then the horse said, "Now lead me off, far away from the camp, behind that big hill, and leave me there to-night, and in the morning come for me;" and the boy did as he was told.

And when he went for the horse in the morning, he found with him a beautiful white gelding, much more handsome than any horse in the tribe. That night the dun horse told the boy to take him again to the place behind the big hill, and to come for him the next morning; and when the boy went for him again, he found with him a beautiful black gelding. And so for ten nights, he left the horse among the hills, and each morning he found a different colored horse, a bay, a roan, a gray, a blue, a spotted horse, and all of them finer than any horses that the Pawnees had ever had in their tribe before.

Now the boy was rich, and he married the beautiful daughter of the Head Chief, and when he became older, he was made Head Chief himself. He had many children by his beautiful wife, and one day when his oldest boy died, he wrapped him in the spotted calf robe and buried him in it. He always took good care of his old grandmother, and kept her in his own lodge until she died. The dun horse was never ridden except at feasts, and when they were going to have a doctors' dance, but he was always led about with the Chief, wherever he went. The horse lived in the village for many years, until he became very old. And at last he died.

THE BEAR MAN

There was once a young boy, who, when he was playing with his fellows, used often to imitate the ways of a bear, and to pretend that he was one. The boys did not know much about bears. They only knew that there were such animals.

Now, it had happened that before this boy was born his mother had been left alone at home, for his father had gone on the warpath toward the enemy, and this was about five or six months before the babe would be born. As the man was going on the warpath, he came upon a little bear cub, very small, whose mother had gone away; and he caught it. He did not want to kill it because it was so young and helpless. It seemed to him like a little child. It looked up to him, and cried after him, because it knew no better; and he hated to kill it or to leave it there. After he had thought about this for a while, he put a string around its neck and tied some medicine smoking stuff, Indian tobacco, to it, and said, "*Pi-rau'*—child you are a *Nahu'rac;*

Ti-ra'-wa made you, and takes care of you. He will look after you, but I put these things about your neck to show that I have good feelings toward you. I hope that when my child is born, the *Nahu'rac* will take care of him, and see that he grows up a good man, and I hope that *Ti-ra'-wa* will take care of you and of mine." He looked at the little bear for quite a long time, and talked to it, and then he went on his way.

When he returned to the village from his warpath, he told his wife about the little bear, and how he had looked at it and talked to it.

When his child was born it had all the ways of a bear. So it is among the Pawnees. A woman, before her child is born, must not look hard at any animal, for the child may be like it. There was a woman in the Kit-ke-hahk'-i band, who caught a rabbit, and, because it was gentle and soft, she took it up in her hands and held it before her face and petted it, and when her child was born it had a split nose, like a rabbit. This man is still alive.

This boy, who was like a bear, as he grew up, had still more the ways of a bear. Often he would go off by himself, and try to pray to the bear, because he felt like a bear. He used to say, in a joking way, to the other young men, that he could make himself a bear.

After he had come to be a man, he started out once on the warpath with a party of about thirty-five others. He was the leader of the party. They went away up on the Running Water, and before they had come to any village, they were discovered by Sioux. The enemy pursued them, and surrounded them, and fought with them. The Pawnees were overpowered, their enemies were so many, and all were killed.

The country where this took place is rocky, and much cedar grows there. Many bears lived there. The battle was fought in the morning; and the Pawnees were all killed in a hollow. Right after the fight, in the afternoon, two bears came traveling along by this place. When they came to the spot where the Pawnees had been killed, they found one of the bodies, and the she bear recognized it as that of the boy who was like a bear. She called to the he bear, and said, "Here is the man that was very good to us. He often sacrificed smokes to us, and every time he ate he used always to take a piece of food and give it to us, saying, 'Here is something for you to eat. Eat this.'

Here is the one that always imitated us, and sung about us, and talked about us. Can you do anything for him?" The he bear said, "I fear I cannot do it. I have not the power, but I will try. I can do anything if the sun is shining. I seem to have more power when the sun is shining on me." That day it was cloudy and cold and snowing. Every now and then the clouds would pass, and the sun come out for a little while, and then the clouds would cover it up again.

The man was all cut up, pretty nearly hacked in small pieces, for he was the bravest of all. The two bears gathered up the pieces of the man, and put them together, and then the he bear lay down and took the man on his breast, and the she bear lay on top of it to warm the body. They worked over it with their medicine, and every now and then the he bear would cry out, and say, "*A-ti'-us*—Father, help me. I wish the sun was shining." After a while the dead body grew warm, and then began to breathe a little. It was still all cut up, but it began to have life. Pretty soon the man began to move, and to come to life, and then he became conscious and had life.

When he came to himself and opened his eyes he was in the presence of two bears. The he bear spoke to him, and said, "It is not through me that you are living. It was the she bear who asked for help for you, and had you brought back to life. Now, you are not yet whole and well. You must come away with us, and live with us for a time, until your wounds are healed." The bears took him away with them. But the man was very weak, and every now and then, as they were going along, he would faint and fall down; but still they would help him up and support him; and they took him along with them, until they came to a cave in the rocks among the cedars, which was their home. When he entered the cave, he found there their young ones that they had left behind when they started out.

The man was all cut up and gashed. He had also been scalped, and had no hair on his head. He lived with the bears until he was quite healed of his wounds, and also had come to understand all their ways. The two old bears taught him everything that they knew. The he bear said to him, "None of all the beings and animals that roam over the country are as great and as wise as the bears. No animal is equal to us. When we get hungry, we go out and kill something and eat it. I did not make the wisdom that I have. I am an animal, and

61

I look to one above. He made me, and he made me to be great. I am made to live here and to be great, but still there will be an end to my days, just as with all of us that *Ti-ra'-wa* has created upon this earth. I am going to make you a great man; but you must not deceive yourself. You must not think that I am great, or can do great things of myself. You must always look up above for the giver of all power. You shall be great in war and great in wealth.

"Now you are well, and I shall take you back to your home, and after this I want you to imitate us. This shall be a part of your greatness. I shall look after you. I shall give to you a part of myself. If I am killed, you shall be killed. If I grow old, you shall be old.

"I want you to look at one of the trees that *Ti-ra'-wa* made in this earth, and place your dependence on it. *Ti-ra'-wa* made this tree (pointing to a cedar). It never gets old. It is always green and young. Take notice of this tree, and always have it with you; and when you are in the lodge and it thunders and lightens, throw some of it on the fire and let the smoke rise. Hold that fast."

The he bear took the skin of a bear, and made a cap for him, to hide his naked skull. His wounds were now all healed, and he was well and strong. The man's people had nearly forgotten him, it had been so long ago, and they had supposed that the whole party had been killed.

Soon after this the he bear said, "Now we will take that journey." They started, and went to the village, and waited near it till it was night. Then the bear said to him, "Go into the village, and tell your father that you are here. Then get for me a piece of buffalo meat, and a blue bead, and some Indian tobacco, and some sweet smelling clay."

The man went into the village, and his father was very much surprised, and very glad to see him again. He got the presents, and brought them to the bear, and gave them to him, and the bear talked to him.

When they were about to part, the bear came up to him, and put his arms about him, and hugged him, and put his mouth against the man's mouth, and said, "As the fur that I am in has touched you it will make you great, and this will be a blessing to you." His paws were around the man's shoulders, and he drew them down his arms, until they came to his hands, and he held them, and said, "As my hands, have touched your hands, they are made great, not to fear anything. I have rubbed my hands down over you, so that you shall be as tough as I am. Because my mouth has touched your mouth you shall be made wise." Then he left him, and went away.

So this man was the greatest of all warriors, and was brave. He was like a bear. He originated the bear dance which still exists among the tribe of Pawnees. He came to be an old man, and at last died of old age. I suspect the old bear died at the same time.

THE BOY WHO WAS SACRIFICED

THERE was a time, far back, when some people thought that it was good to sacrifice to *Ti-ra'-wa* whatever they had that was most precious to them. The sacrifice of the animal, the burnt offering, has always been made by all the Pawnees; that is one of the things handed down from the ruler. It is very old. The Skidi have always performed the sacrifice of the captive. Each one of these is sacred and solemn, but it is not like giving up something that belongs to you, and that you love. It is a sacrifice, but it does not cost much.

Many years ago, in the Skidi village on the Loup, there lived a man, who believed that if he sacrificed his son to *Ti-ra'-wa*, it would be a blessing to him. He thought that if he did this thing, perhaps *Ti-ra'-wa* would speak to him face to face, and that he could talk to him just as two people would talk to one another, and that in this way would learn many things that other people did not understand. His child was a nice boy about ten years old, strong, growing up well, and the man loved him. It made him feel badly to think of killing him. He meditated long about this, but the more he thought about it, the more he believed that this sacrifice would please *Ti-ra'-wa*. There were many things that he wanted to understand, and to do; and he thought if he gave up his son, these good things would come to him. So he resolved to make the sacrifice.

One morning he started out from the village, and took the boy with him. They went over to the Platte. When they got to the river,

63

as they were walking along, the man took his knife from its sheath, and caught the boy by the shoulder, and stabbed him quickly, and cut him open. When the boy was dead, he threw the body into the river, and then went back to the village. When he got there, he went into his lodge and sat down. After a time he said to his wife, "Where is the boy?" The woman said, "He went out with you, when you went over to see the horses." The man answered, "No; I went out to where the horses are feeding, and looked at them, but he did not go with me."

The man went out, and looked for the boy all through the village, but he could not find him. At night when the boy did not come home, they began to get frightened, and for two days they hunted for the boy, and at last they got the old crier to call out for him from the top of the lodge, and ask if any one had seen him, but none of the people knew what had become of the boy. Now the mother was mourning, and the father pretended to feel very badly. They could not find the boy; and soon after this the tribe started on the summer hunt, and the father and mother went with them. The village made a good hunt, killing plenty of buffalo, and made much dried meat.

After the boy had been thrown into the river, he floated down with the current, sometimes turning over and over in the swift water, and sometimes grounding for a little while on a sand bar, and then being floated off again, and being carried further down. At length he came near to the place where the whirlpool is, under the bluff at *Pa-hŭk'*, where is the lodge of the *Nahu'rac*. There were two buzzards sitting on the bluff, just above this place, and as they sat there, one of them stretched out his neck and looked up the river, and after he had looked, he said to the other, "I see a body." Then both the buzzards flew down to where the boy was floating in the water, and got down under him, and raised him on their backs, and lifted him up out of the water, and flew up to the bluff, carrying the boy on their backs, and placed him on the ground on top of the bluff over the big cave, which is the home of the *Nahu'rac*. In this lodge were all kinds of animals, and all kinds of birds. There were bears, and mountain lions, and buffalo, and elk, and beaver, and otter, and deer; all kinds of animals, great and small, and all kinds of birds.

There is a little bird, smaller than a pigeon. Its back is blue, and its breast white, and its head is spotted. It flies swiftly over the water, and when it sees a fish, it dives down into the water to catch it. This bird is a servant or a messenger for the *Nahu'rac*. Such a bird came flying by just as the buzzards put the body on the ground, and he stopped and looked at it. When he saw how it was—for he knew all that had happened—he flew down into the lodge and told the *Nahu'rac* about the boy. The bird said, "There is a boy up here on the hill. He is dead, and he is poor, and I want to have him brought to life again." Then he told the *Nahu'rac* all the things that had happened. When the messenger bird had done speaking, the *Nahu'rac* earnestly counselled together for a long time to decide what should be done, and each one made a speech, giving his opinion about the matter, but they could not make up their minds what ought to be done.

The little bird was coaxing the *Nahu'rac*, and saying, "Come, now, we want to save his life." But the *Nahu'rac* could not decide. At last the chief of the *Nahu'rac* said, "No, messenger, we cannot decide this here. You will have to go to the other council lodges, and see what they say about it." The bird said, "I am going," and flew swiftly out of the lodge and up the river, till he came to the *Nahu'rac* lodge near the Lone Tree. When he got there, he told them all about the boy, and said that the council at *Pa-hŭk'* could not decide what should be done. The *Nahu'rac* here talked, and at last they said, "We cannot decide. The council at *Pa-hŭk'* must decide." Then the bird went to the lodge on the Loup, and the *Nahu'rac* there said that they could not decide. Then he went to *Kitz-a-witz-ŭk*, and to *Pa-hŭr'*; and at each place the *Nahu'rac* considered and talked about it, and then said, "We cannot decide what shall be done. The council at *Pa-hŭk'* must decide for themselves."

At last, after he had visited all the council lodges of the *Nahu'rac*, the bird flew swiftly back to the lodge at *Pa-hŭk'*, and told them there what the animals at the other lodges had said. In the council of the *Nahu'rac* at *Pa-hŭk'*, there were four chiefs, who sat there as judges to determine such matters as this, after they had all been talked over, and to decide what should be done. When the messenger bird came back, and told the *Nahu'rac* what the other councils had said, these judges considered for a time, and then spoke together, and at length the chief of the judges said to the bird, "Now, messenger, we have concluded that we will not decide this question ourselves. You decide it, and say what shall be done."

The messenger was not long in deciding. He did not hesitate. He said, "I want this boy brought back to life." Then all the *Nahu'rac* stood up, and went to where the boy lay, and stood around him and prayed, and at last the boy breathed once, and then after a little while he breathed again, and at last he came to life and sat up. He looked about and saw all these animals standing around him, and he wondered. He said to himself, "Why, my father stabbed me, and killed me, and now here I am among this great crowd of animals. What does this mean?" He was surprised.

The *Nahu'rac* all went back into the lodge, and took the boy with them. When all were seated in the lodge, the four judges talked to each other, and the chief one stood up, and said, "Now, my people, we have brought this boy back to life, but he is poor, and we must do something for him. Let us teach him all we know, and make him one of us." Then the *Nahu'rac* all made a noise. They were glad. Then they began to sing and they danced. They taught the boy all their secrets, and all their ways. They taught him how to cut a man open and cure him again, and how to shoot an arrow through a man and then cure him, and how to cut a man's tongue out and then to put it back, and how to make well a broken leg, and many other things. After they had done all these things, they said to the boy, "Now we have brought you back to life, and have taught you all these things, so that you are one of us. Now you must stop with us one season. Your people have gone off on the summer hunt. You must stay with us until the autumn. Then you can go back to your people." So the boy stayed with the *Nahu'rac* in their lodge.

At length the Skidi had returned from the hunt with plenty of dried meat. Soon after this, the *Nahu'rac* said one day to the boy, "Your people have got back from the hunt. Now you can go back to the village. Go back and get a lot of nice dried meat, and bring it back to us here, and we will have a feast."

The boy went home to the village. He got there in the night, and went to his father's lodge, and went in. There was a little fire burning in the lodge. It was nearly out, and gave only a little light, but he knew the place where his mother slept. He went up to her, and put out his hand and touched her, and pushed her a little. She awoke, and sat up and looked at him, and he said, "I've come back." When she saw him, and heard him speak, she was very much surprised, and her heart was glad to see her boy again. She called to his father, and he woke up. When he saw the boy he was afraid, for he thought it was a ghost. The boy told them nothing of what had happened, or where he had been. He just said, "I have come back again."

In the morning all the people were surprised to hear that he had come back, and to see him, and they stood around looking at him, and asking him questions, but he said nothing. The next day the people still questioned him, and at last the boy said, "I have been all summer with friends, with people who have been good to me. I should like to take them a present of some nice dried meat, so that we can have a feast." The people said that this was good. They picked out four strong horses, and loaded them with dried meat, the nicest pieces. The boy's father gave some of it, and all the other people brought pieces and put them on the horses, until they had big loads. They sent two young men with the boy, to help him load and drive the horses, and they started to go to the *Nahu'rac* lodge at *Pa-huk'*.

When they had come pretty near the place, the boy sent the young men back to the village, and he went on alone, driving the pack-horses before him. When he reached the home of the *Nahu'rac*, he unloaded the horses, and turned them loose, and then went into the lodge. When he went in, and when the *Nahu'rac* saw him, they all made a hissing noise. They were glad to see him. The boy brought into the lodge all the dried meat, and they had a great feast. After the feast they had a doctors' dance, and the boy was made a doctor, and again was taught all that the *Nahu'rac* knew. After that he could do many wonderful things. He could sometimes go to a man that had been dead for a day, and then bring him back to life.

No one ever knew what the father had done, for the boy never told any one. He knew that he could never have learned all these wonderful things unless his father had sacrificed him.

THE SNAKE BROTHER

ONE time, long ago, a big party of Pawnees went on the warpath down to the south. They could find no enemies anywhere, and they went a long way south. In this party were two brothers, poor boys, and one day as they were traveling along, apart from the others, in a piece of woods where it was very thick, they got lost. When they found that they were lost, they tried to go back to the camp, but they could not find the others, and at last gave up looking for them and started to go back north to their home. They had no food with them, and were looking about for something to kill, so that they might eat. As they were going along, they came upon a dead buffalo that had been killed some time, and there was nothing of it left but the bones, so they took some of the marrow bones, and carried them along with them, until they made a camp.

Not far beyond here they stopped to rest. There was a tree growing near where they stopped, and as they looked up into it, they saw a squirrel run up the tree. One of the brothers caught up his bow and arrows, and the other said, "Oh, kill him, kill him, quick." The boy shot and killed it, and they skinned it, and roasted it over the fire. While they were cooking it the elder brother said, "I wonder if it is good to eat the marrow and the squirrel together." The younger said, "No, it is not good to do so. This is not real meat." The elder thought the two kinds of food would be good together, and they disputed about this for some time. The elder brother kept coaxing the younger to eat the squirrel and the marrow together, but the younger said, "Oh, brother, I do not like to do this. To me it does not seem good. But if you wish to do it, why don't you?" The elder said, "I think I will do so"; and he did so, taking a bite of squirrel, and then a bite of marrow. He said, "It is nice, you had better take some." But the younger brother would not. He ate only the marrow. After they had eaten they did not go on further, but slept there.

The Pawnees

About the middle of the night, the elder brother felt a noise in his feet, and he sat up and felt of his legs and feet, and he found that his feet were stuck together, and were beginning to get round, like a snake, and had a rattle on the end of them, and that his legs were round and like the tail of a great big rattlesnake. He reached over, and put his hands on his brother, and shook him, and said to him, "Get up. There is something the matter with me." The younger brother woke up, and felt of his brother, and found how it was; as if he was changing into a snake, beginning at his feet. When he saw this he felt very badly. Then the older brother began to talk to the younger, and to give him good advice, for he felt very sad.

He said, "Now I am going to die, and leave my young brother here alone on this prairie. He is so young, he will not be able to find his way home, and he must die, too. Surely this has happened because I ate the marrow and the squirrel together." While he was talking, the change had moved up to his waist.

After a little while he got more hopeful, and he said, "Now, brother, I know that you will get home safely. I will protect you. I know that I am going to be a snake, and I shall stay right here. You see that hole," and he pointed to a hole in the bank. "When I have changed into a snake, take me in your arms, and carry me over to that hole. I am going to stay there forever. That will be my home, for that is the house of the snakes. When you go back home, you must tell our father and mother how it was, and whenever you want to go on the warpath, take a big party and come down this way, and come right here, to this very place, and you will see me, for I shall be here. Now, brother, when you go back home, some time after you have reached home, I want you to come back all alone; come right here. You know what I told you; do not be afraid of me. I believe this was to happen to me, and I could not help it. After you have once come all alone, then the second time you may bring some others with you, but the first time come alone." So he talked to his brother, and as he spoke the change kept going on. While it was moving up his body, until it got to his head, he was still like a man in his mind, but all his body was like a great big snake. Then he spoke to his brother, and said, "Now, brother, cover up my head with the robe, and after a little while take it off again." The younger brother did as he was told, and when, after a while, he took the robe off, there he saw an immense snake's head as broad as his two hands. The elder brother had completely changed into a snake.

The young man took the snake in his arms, and carried him over to the hole, and put him on the ground by it. He felt very sad to go away and leave his brother here. Before he started, he spoke good words to the snake, and said, "Now, brother, I am going home, and I ask you to take pity on me, and to protect me. I do not know the country I am going through, and you must take care of me. Do not forget the promises you have made me." After he had spoken he did not wait to see the snake go into the hole, but started on his journey, and went off toward his home.

When he reached the village, he told all these things to his father and his mother. He said to all his relations, "Do not mourn for him. He is alive and he is well. The only trouble is, that he is in the shape of a snake." After he had been home ten days, he told his mother to make for him five pairs of moccasins, that he was going on the warpath for himself. His mother did so, and he stuffed them full of parched corn, and took a little sack of pounded buffalo meat on his back, and started back to see his brother.

It took him seven days' fast traveling to get to where he left the snake. When he had come near the place, he saw there the hole where he had left his brother. He went up close to the hole and began to speak. He said, "Brother, I am here. I have come on the warpath, and I am here to see you. You told me to come, and to come alone. I have done what you bade me, and am here. Now, brother, remember to keep your promises. I want to see you this afternoon."

He stood there a little while, and then there began in the hole a rattling and a rustling and scraping noise, and presently dust began to roll out, and then out of the hole came this great big snake, which was his brother. First came out this great snake, and after him many other large ones came out, and crept all about, but the great snake, his brother, lay just outside the hole. The boy went up to the big snake and took it in his arms, and hugged it, and spoke to it, and the snake put out its tongue, as if it were kissing him. Then the boy put it down on the ground, and all the other snakes came back, and went in the hole, and after them all, last, the big snake went in the hole.

Then the boy left this place, and went on a little further, and about sunset he came to a little creek, and here he lay down and slept. In the night he dreamed of his brother, who spoke to him and said, "Now, brother, I am glad that you have come down to see me, as I told you to. And now I say to you, be brave. Have courage. To-morrow morning when you awake, dress yourself up as if you were going to fight. Paint your face, put feathers in your head, make yourself ready to fight."

The next morning the boy woke up, and as the snake had told him in the dream, so he did. He painted his face and tied feathers in his head, and dressed himself up for the fight. Then he started on. Pretty soon he came to a little hill, and as he looked over it, he saw people coming toward him; people and many horses. He thought they were Sioux, and when he saw them, he went back a little, to find a place where he could hide. He went back to the little creek where he had slept, and there he sat down in the brush. When he had hidden himself in the brush, he waited; and the people came straight toward where he had hidden himself, and camped just below where he was. After a little while he raised himself up and looked at them, and saw only two persons, and presently he saw that one of them was a woman. He watched for a long time, looking about to see if there were any more, but he could see only these two. Then he considered what he should do. While he was thinking, it came to him what the snake brother had said to him in the night, and then he knew what to do.

He crept slowly along through the brush toward their camp, and when he got close to them, about twenty yards distant, he raised up his head and looked. He saw the woman cooking, and there were hanging on a little tree the man's bow and arrows and shield and spear, but the man he could not see. He was lying down asleep somewhere near by. The boy waited and watched. He was excited, and his heart was pounding against his ribs. After a little while, the woman left the fire and walked away toward the horses. Perhaps her husband had said to her, "The horses are going off, you had better go and turn them back." When she went toward the horses, the boy was going to run up to the man and kill him, but before doing so he changed his mind; for he thought, "If I kill him, perhaps the woman will get on a horse, and ride away, driving the other horses with her." So he waited until the woman had come back. When she had returned to the fire, he ran up toward her, and she heard him coming, and ran to wake her husband; but just as she got to him, the boy was by her side. He shot two arrows into the man and killed him and counted *coup* on him, and captured the woman. He took the whole scalp of his enemy's head.

Then he took the woman and went down to where the horses were, and they got on two of them, and rode back to where his brother, the snake, lived, driving the horses before them. Just before they got to the hole, the boy took his lariat and caught a nice spotted horse and a mule, and tied them up to the tree, and called up the woman, and tied her up against the tree as tight as he could tie her. When he had done this, he went up to the hole and began to talk. He said, "Oh, my brother, I see now that what you have promised me comes true. I did what you told me. Now here are these two animals and the woman; I give them to you for being good to me. They are yours. I am glad for what you have done for me this day." When he had finished saying this he spoke again, saying, "Now, brother, I want to see you once more. I am going off, and I want to see you before I go." After a little while he heard again the rattling sound in the hole, and saw the dust coming out of it, and then his brother came out of the hole, and then afterward the smaller snakes; and these all went down to the tree and climbed up into it. The tree was thick with them. Then the boy did as he had done before. He went close to the hole, and took his brother up in his arms and hugged him, and the great snake thrust out his tongue, as if kissing him. Then the boy spoke again and said, "Now, brother, I am going away, and I give you these two animals and this woman to keep. They are yours." Then he started for his home, and after a long time he arrived at the village.

After a time, he determined to start off again on the warpath, and this time he took a party with him. He had told the whole tribe what had happened, and how his brother had protected and helped him; and he said to those warriors who were going with him, "Let each one of you take a present with you for my brother; some beads or eagle feathers or some tobacco as an offering, so that he may help you." They started south to go to the place where his brother lived. When they got there the young man said to the others, "Now you must, each one of you, give something to my brother. Call him by his kin name, and ask him to help you, and to make you successful; and leave the things before the hole." They did as he said, and when they had made their presents, they went by. They saw nothing, for the brother did not call out the great snake.

Two or three days after they had passed the place, they found a camp of Sioux and took a lot of horses and killed some of the enemy. Then they went back, and when they came to the snake's home, they took a horse and led it up near the hole and killed it, and gave it to him, and left the scalps at the mouth of the hole as presents to him. When they reached the village, there was great joy and a good time. They had all kinds of dances, for they were glad that the war party had killed some Sioux.

After that another war party started out, and the brother said to them, "Go straight to my brother, and make him a present, and ask him to give you good luck, and you will be successful." And it happened as he had said.

The brother was always fortunate in war. He became a chief and was very rich, having many horses. Ever after that time, when he took the lead of a war party, all the poor men would come and say, "I want to go with you." They knew that his brother was a snake, and would give him good luck.

O'RE-KA-RAHR

A LONG time ago, as the tribe were on their summer hunt, a man and his wife got to quarreling. They had a child, a boy about ten months old. It was while they were traveling along, going from one camp to another, that they began to quarrel. At length the wife became very angry, and threw the baby to the man saying, "You take that baby. It belongs to you, for it is a man child. I am not going to nurse it for you any longer." Then she went away.

The man took the child and carried it along with him. He felt very badly, both on his own account and on account of his child. He was so unhappy that he almost wanted to kill himself. He was so poor-minded because it was a disgrace that he, being a man, should be obliged to take care of his child until it was grown up, and he had no female relatives to whom he could turn it over to be reared. So he was very unhappy, and determined to leave the tribe and wander off alone, far from his people.

He did so. He carried the child on his back, as a woman does. When it cried for its mother's milk, he had none to give it. He could only cry with it. He hated to kill the child, or to leave it behind to die on the prairie. He wandered off to the south. He traveled on for a time, until he came near to where the buffalo were. By this time, the child had changed from a very fat baby to a very thin one, because it had not been nursed. When he got to the buffalo, he killed a cow, and took its udder, and while it was fresh he let the child suck it, until it became sour. Then he killed another cow, and did the same thing. In every way he did the best he could to nourish the child. Sometimes he would get a slice of meat, and half cook it, and let the child suck the juice. The child began to improve, and to get a little stronger. In this way he supported it for quite a long time, and it did pretty well, and at last it got used to this food, and became strong and well. By this time he had gone a long way.

At length he found that the child could sit up alone. Then he began to give it all sorts of playthings, so that it could amuse itself. First he made for it a little bow and some arrows, and taught it how to use them. He made other things for the child to play with, and at last it got to be contented playing alone. Then the father would leave the child for a few minutes, and go off a little way, perhaps to the top of a hill near by, to look off over the country, but he would look back at the child every few steps to see that it was all right. When he would come back he would find the child safe, playing, well contented. After a while he got so that he would leave it for about an hour, and when he came back, find it safe and contented, playing. By this time the child had begun to walk. Finally the father went off once for half a day, and when he came back, he found the child playing about safe. It did not seem to mind much about the father being absent. About this time he killed a buffalo cow, and made some dried meat, and put it in a certain place, and told the child when it was hungry to go there and get a piece.

He now went off and was gone a whole day, and when he came back at night the child was safe. Finally he made his preparations and went off to stay over night, and be gone two days. He did so, and when he came back, the boy was asleep. A second time he went away and was absent for two days, going quite a long distance. When he came back he found that the child was painted with white clay. The father thought this was strange. He said to himself, "Something must have come and talked to my child, and is taking care of him while I am gone."

When he came back the third time after a two days' journey, he found that the child had about his neck a string of *pa'hut*. The fourth long journey he took lasted three days, and when he returned, he found his boy still wearing this same string of beads, and with a feather tied in his head. Now his father knew that something was looking after his child while he was away, and when he went off, he would pray for the child. He would say, "*No'-a*, whatever it is that is taking pity on my child, also take pity on me."

The child had now grown so large that it could talk with him, and one day it said, "Father, you go away, and you be gone for four days; I will be all right here. When you come back you will find me safe."

The man went. He started to go way down south, to be gone for four days. After he had been gone two days and two nights, he saw a signal smoke and went toward it. As he raised up his head and peeped over a hill before crossing it, he saw, far off, a lot of people and horses coming toward the river which lay between him and them. He lay on the hill a long time, watching to see where they would camp. When they had made camp, he went into a ravine, and crept down close to the camp, until he could see that it was just one lodge, and that about it were a whole herd of horses. He waited until evening, and then went over to the lodge. It was after dark when he went. The lodge was all surrounded by horses; everywhere nothing but horses, there were so many. He crept close to the lodge, and looked in through an opening by the door, and saw lying down opposite the door a great big man, and on either side a woman; only three persons in all. As he looked at these persons, he thought he recognized one of the women. He kept looking at her, and at last he remembered who she was, and that she had been captured long ago from the Pawnees. Her people were still living. The man was a Comanche.

While the Pawnee was watching, the man inside the lodge asked for something, and the captive woman stood up to go out of the lodge, and the Pawnee stepped to one side, out of sight. The woman came out into the darkness, and went out among the horses. The Pawnee stepped up behind her very softly, and put his hand on her shoulder, and said to her in Pawnee, "Friend, do you belong to my tribe?" The woman started to scream, but he put his hand on her mouth, and said to her, "Be quiet. Keep still. Do not call out." She answered him, "Yes, I belong to your tribe." Then she said in a very low voice that shook, for she was afraid, "Do you belong to my tribe?" The man said, "Yes." Then he asked her, "Who is that other woman that I see in the lodge?" She answered him, "She also belongs to our tribe, and is a prisoner." Then the man said, "You just wait and keep still. I am going to kill that man." The woman said, "That is good. That is good. This man is the biggest man of all the Comanches. He has come first to this place, and all the rest of the Comanches are coming here to meet him. I am glad that my people are living, and that I am going back to see them once more. Do not fail to kill him. I will tell the other woman to be ready, that our friend is here, and we will wait and watch."

When the woman went into the lodge, she whispered to the other woman, and said, "Be ready. A friend who belongs to our tribe is here. Take your hatchet, and be prepared to help to kill our husband."

The two women waited, and the Pawnee made ready to shoot the Comanche with his bow and arrow. The woman had said to him, "Push aside the door a little and be ready." He made a little bit of an opening by the door, just big enough to let an arrow pass through, and when the time came he let it go. *U'-ra-rĭsh!* the arrow flew straight, and pierced the Comanche through the heart. So he died, and the Pawnee counted *coup* on him and took his scalp.

The women felt so glad to meet a friend that they put their arms around the man and patted him. They were going back home to see their relations. They asked him, "How many of you are here?" He answered, "I am alone." They were surprised.

They took down the lodge, and packed everything on the horses, and drove off the herd, leaving the dead body of the enemy in the camp. All night they traveled, and all the next day; and as they were going, he told them how it came about that he was alone. They told him that there were about three hundred head of horses in the herd that they had with them. When they had come pretty close to where he had left the child, he told them about the boy being there all alone; and the women just ran their horses to get to the boy; whichever got there first, he should be hers. When they came to the boy, they took him in their arms and petted him, and took him as their own.

Now the father was no longer sad. He had recovered two captured women, had killed his enemy, and had taken a lot of horses.

They went on, and traveled far, and at length, one night, they came to the Pawnee tribe, and camped with them. The horses just surrounded the lodge, you could just see the top of it over their backs. The next morning all the people wondered who these strangers could be. They found out that the man and child, who were lost, had returned, and with them two women, captured long ago by the Comanches. So there was great joy in the tribe. Then the man gave his relations many horses. In those days the Pawnees had not many horses, and it seems that this man brought good luck in horses to the tribe. Ever since that time they have had many horses. The mother of the child came to see it, she was so glad it was alive, but she was whipped out of the lodge.

The child grew to be a man, and was wealthy. After he had grown up, he told his father that ever since he could remember anything, a buck deer had talked to him, and taken care of him; that it had saved them, and brought them good fortune. In order that the *O're-ka-rahr* might be remembered, he established a dance, called the deer dance, which has been kept up to this day.

Many wonderful things happened to this same young man. Once he went on a war party against the Cheyennes, and stole some horses from them. The Cheyennes followed and overtook them, and they had a great fight. The first man killed was this young man. He was very brave, and the Cheyennes cut him up into small pieces, but that night it lightened and thundered and rained, and soon after the storm was over, the young man came walking into camp alive. He was all scarred over, where he had been cut up, but he had come to life because the deer had looked after him. He lived long to show the scars of the battles he had been through.

THE GHOST BRIDE

In a place where we used to have a village, a young woman died just before the tribe started on the hunt. When she died they dressed her up in her finest clothes, and buried her, and soon after this the tribe started on the hunt.

A party of young men had gone off to visit another tribe, and they did not get back until after this girl had died and the tribe had left the village. Most of this party did not go back to the village, but met the tribe and went with them on the hunt. Among the young men who had been away was one who had loved this girl who had died. He went back alone to the village. It was empty and silent, but before he reached it, he could see, far off, some one sitting on top of a lodge. When he came near, he saw that it was the girl he loved. He did not know that she had died, and he wondered to see her there alone, for the time was coming when he would be her husband and she his wife. When she saw him coming, she came down from the top of the lodge and went inside. When he came close to her, he spoke and said, "Why are you here alone in the village?" She answered him, "They have gone off on the hunt. I was sulky with my relations, and they went off and left me behind." The man wanted her now to be his wife, but the girl said to him, "No, not yet, but later we will be married." She said to him, "You must not be afraid. To-night there will be dances here; the ghosts will dance." This is an old custom of the Pawnees. When they danced they used to go from one lodge to another, singing, dancing and hallooing. So now, when the tribe had gone and the village was deserted, the ghosts did this. He could hear them coming along the empty streets, and going from one lodge to another. They came into the lodge where he was, and danced about, and whooped and sang, and sometimes they almost touched him, and he came pretty near being scared.

The next day, the young man persuaded the girl to go on with him, and follow the tribe, to join it on the hunt. They started to travel together, and she promised him that she would surely be his wife, but not until the time came. They overtook the tribe; but before they got to the camp, the girl stopped. She said, "Now we have arrived, but you must go first to the village, and prepare a place for me. Where I sleep, let it be behind a curtain. For four days and four nights I must remain behind this curtain. Do not speak of me. Do not mention my name to any one."

The young man left her there and went into the camp. When he got to his lodge, he told a woman, one of his relations, to go out to a certain place and bring in a woman, who was waiting there for him. His relative asked him, "Who is the woman?" And to avoid speaking her name, he told who were her father and mother. His relation, in surprise, said, "It cannot be that girl, for she died some days before we started on the hunt."

When the woman went to look for the girl she could not find her. The girl had disappeared. The young man had disobeyed her, and had told who she was. She had told him that she must stay behind a curtain for four days, and that no one must know who she was. Instead of doing what she had said, he told who she was, and the girl disappeared because she was a ghost. If he had obeyed the girl, she would have lived a second time upon earth. That same night this young man died in sleep.

Then the people were convinced that there must be a life after this one.

HOW THE DEER LOST HIS GALL

A LONG time ago, the deer and the antelope met upon the prairie. At that time both of them had dew-claws, and both had galls. After they had talked for a little while, each one of them began to boast about how fast he could run. Each one, the deer and the antelope, claimed that he could run faster than any other animal, and at length they became very angry in their dispute, and determined that they would have a race.

They staked their galls on the race, and it was run on the prairie. The antelope ran the faster, and won, and took the deer's gall. The deer felt very badly that he had lost it, and he seemed so miserable that the antelope felt sorry for him, and to cheer him up, he took off his dew-claws and gave them to him.

Since that time the deer has had no gall, and the antelope no dew-claws.

NOTE.—A story somewhat similar to this is current among the Blackfeet tribes of the northern country. In this tale the antelope won the deer's gall, as in the Pawnee story. Then the deer said, "You have won, but that race was not a fair one, for it was over the prairie alone. We ought to run another race in the timber to decide which is really the faster." They agreed to run this second race, and on it they bet their dew-claws. The deer ran the faster through the thick timber and over the logs, and beat the antelope, and took his dew-claws. Since then the antelope has had no dew-claws, and the deer no gall.

THE BLACKFEET

GRINNELL AND THE BLACKFEET

WE WERE sitting about the fire in the lodge on Two Medicine. Double Runner, Small Leggings, Mad Wolf, and the Little Blackfoot were smoking and talking, and I was writing in my note-book. As I put aside the book, and reached out my hand for the pipe, Double Runner bent over and picked up a scrap of printed paper, which had fallen to the ground. He looked at it for a moment without speaking, and then, holding it up and calling me by name, said:—

"*Pi-nut-ú-ye is-tsím-okan*, this is education. Here is the difference between you and me, between the Indians and the white people. You know what this means. I do not. If I did know, I would be as smart as you. If all my people knew, the white people would not always get the best of us."

"*Nísah* (elder brother), your words are true. Therefore you ought to see that your children go to school, so that they may get the white man's knowledge. When they are men, they will have to trade with the white people; and if they know nothing, they can never get rich. The times have changed. It will never again be as it was when you and I were young."

"You say well, *Pi-nut-ú-ye is-tsím-okan*, I have seen the days; and I know it is so. The old things are passing away, and the children of my children will be like white people. None of them will know how it used to be in their father's days unless they read the things which we have told you, and which you are all the time writing down in your books."

"They are all written down, *Nísah*, the story of the three tribes, Sík-si-kau, Kaínah, and Pikúni."

STORY OF THE THREE TRIBES

THE PAST AND THE PRESENT

FIFTY years ago the name Blackfoot was one of terrible meaning to the white traveller who passed across that desolate buffalo-trodden waste which lay to the north of the Yellowstone River and east of the Rocky Mountains. This was the Blackfoot land, the undisputed home of a people which is said to have numbered in one of its tribes— the Pi-kŭn'-i—8000 lodges, or 40,000 persons. Besides these, there were the Blackfeet and the Bloods, three tribes of one nation, speaking the same language, having the same customs, and holding the same religious faith.

But this land had not always been the home of the Blackfeet. Long ago, before the coming of the white men, they had lived in another country far to the north and east, about Lesser Slave Lake, ranging between Peace River and the Saskatchewan, and having for their neighbors on the north the Beaver Indians. Then the Blackfeet were a timber people. It is said that about two hundred years ago the Chippeweyans from the east invaded this country and drove them south and west. Whether or no this is true, it is quite certain that not many generations back the Blackfeet lived on the North Saskatchewan River and to the north of that stream. Gradually working their way westward, they at length reached the Rocky Mountains, and, finding game abundant, remained there until they obtained horses, in the very earliest years of the present century. When they secured horses and guns, they took courage and began to venture out on to the plains and to go to war. From this time on, the Blackfeet made constant war on their neighbors to the south, and in a few years controlled the whole country between the Saskatchewan on the north and the Yellowstone on the south.

It was, indeed, a glorious country which the Blackfeet had wrested from their southern enemies. Here nature has reared great mountains and spread out broad prairies. Along the western border of this region, the Rocky Mountains lift their snow-clad peaks above the clouds. Here and there, from north to south, and from east to west, lie minor ranges, black with pine forests if seen near at hand, or in the distance mere gray silhouettes against a sky of blue. Between these mountain ranges lies everywhere the great prairie; a monotonous waste to the stranger's eye, but not without its charm. It is brown and bare; for, except during a few short weeks in spring, the sparse bunch-grass is sear and yellow, and the silver gray of the wormwood lends an added dreariness to the landscape. Yet this seemingly desert waste has a beauty of its own. At intervals it is marked with green winding river valleys, and everywhere it is gashed with deep ravines, their sides painted in strange colors of red and gray and brown, and their perpendicular walls crowned with fantastic columns and figures of stone or clay, carved out by the winds and the rains of ages. Here and there, rising out of the plain, are curious sharp ridges, or square-topped buttes with vertical sides, sometimes bare, and sometimes dotted with pines—short, sturdy trees, whose gnarled trunks and thick, knotted branches have been twisted and wrung into curious forms by the winds which blow unceasingly, hour after hour, day after day, and month after month, over mountain range and prairie, through gorge and coulée.

These prairies now seem bare of life, but it was not always so. Not very long ago, they were trodden by multitudinous herds of buffalo and antelope; then, along the wooded river valleys and on the pine-clad slopes of the mountains, elk, deer, and wild sheep fed in great numbers. They are all gone now. The winter's wind still whistles over Montana prairies, but nature's shaggy-headed wild cattle no longer feel its biting blasts. Where once the scorching breath of summer stirred only the short stems of the buffalo-grass, it now billows the fields of the white man's grain. Half-hidden by the scanty herbage, a few bleached skeletons alone remain to tell us of the buffalo; and the broad, deep trails, over which the dark herds passed by thousands, are now grass-grown and fast disappearing under the effacing hand of time. The buffalo have disappeared, and the fate of the buffalo has almost overtaken the Blackfeet.

As known to the whites, the Blackfeet were true prairie Indians, seldom venturing into the mountains, except when they crossed them to war with the Kutenais, the Flatheads, or the Snakes. They subsisted almost wholly on the flesh of the buffalo. They were hardy, untiring, brave, ferocious. Swift to move, whether on foot or horseback, they made long journeys to war, and with telling force struck their enemies. They had conquered and driven out from the territory which they occupied the tribes who once inhabited it, and maintained a desultory and successful warfare against all invaders, fighting with the Crees on the north, the Assinaboines on the east, the Crows on the south, and the Snakes, Kalispels, and Kutenais on the southwest and west. In those days the Blackfeet were rich and powerful. The buffalo fed and clothed them, and they needed nothing beyond what nature supplied. This was their time of success and happiness.

Crowded into a little corner of the great territory which they once dominated, and holding this corner by an uncertain tenure, a few Blackfeet still exist, the pitiful remnant of a once mighty people. Huddled together about their agencies, they are facing the problem before them, striving, helplessly but bravely, to accommodate themselves to the new order of things; trying in the face of adverse surroundings to wrench themselves loose from their accustomed ways of life; to give up inherited habits and form new ones; to break away from all that is natural to them, from all that they have been taught—to reverse their whole mode of existence. They are striving to earn their living, as the white man earns his, by toil. The struggle is hard and slow, and in carrying it on they are wasting away and growing fewer in numbers. But though unused to labor, ignorant of agriculture, unacquainted with tools or seeds or soils, knowing nothing of the ways of life in permanent houses or of the laws of health, scantily fed, often utterly discouraged by failure, they are still making a noble fight for existence.

Only within a few years—since the buffalo disappeared—has this change been going on; so recently has it come that the old order and the new meet face to face. In the trees along the river valleys, still quietly resting on their aërial sepulchres, sleep the forms of the ancient hunter-warrior who conquered and held this broad land; while, not far away, Blackfoot farmers now rudely cultivate their little crops, and gather scanty harvests from narrow fields.

It is the meeting of the past and the present, of savagery and civilization. The issue cannot be doubtful. Old methods must pass away. The
Blackfeet will become civilized, but at a terrible cost. To me there is
an interest, profound and pathetic, in watching the progress of the
struggle.

DAILY LIFE AND CUSTOMS

INDIANS are usually represented as being a silent, sullen race, seldom
speaking, and never laughing nor joking. However true this may be in
regard to some tribes, it certainly was not the case with most of those
who lived upon the great Plains. These people were generally talkative,
merry, and light-hearted; they delighted in fun, and were a race of
jokers. It is true that, in the presence of strangers, they were grave,
silent, and reserved, but this is nothing more than the shyness and em-
barrassment felt by a child in the presence of strangers. As the Indian
becomes acquainted, this reserve wears off; he is at his ease again and
appears in his true colors, a light-hearted child. Certainly the Blackfeet
never were a taciturn and gloomy people. Before the disappearance of
the buffalo, they were happy and cheerful. Why should they not have
been? Food and clothing were to be had for the killing and tanning.
All fur animals were abundant, and thus the people were rich. Meat,
really the only food they cared for, was plenty and cost nothing.
Their robes and furs were exchanged with the traders for bright-
colored blankets and finery. So they wanted nothing.

It is but nine years since the buffalo disappeared from the land.
Only nine years have passed since these people gave up that wild, free
life which was natural to them, and ah! how dear! Let us go back in
memory to those happy days and see how they passed the time.

The sun is just rising. Thin columns of smoke are creeping from the
smoke holes of the lodges, and ascending in the still morning air.
Everywhere the women are busy, carrying water and wood, and preparing the simple meal. And now we see the men come out, and start

87

for the river. Some are followed by their children; some are even carrying those too small to walk. They have reached the water's edge. Off drop their blankets, and with a plunge and a shivering *ah-h-h* they dash into the icy waters. Winter and summer, storm or shine, this was their daily custom. They said it made them tough and healthy, and enabled them to endure the bitter cold while hunting on the bare bleak prairie. By the time they have returned to the lodges, the women have prepared the early meal. A dish of boiled meat—some three or four pounds—is set before each man; the children are served as much as they can eat, and the wives take the rest. The horses are now seen coming in, hundreds and thousands of them, driven by boys and young men who started out after them at daylight. If buffalo are close at hand, and it has been decided to make a run, each hunter catches his favorite buffalo horse, and they all start out together; they are followed by women, on the travois or pack horses, who will do most of the butchering, and transport the meat and hides to camp. If there is no band of buffalo near by, they go off, singly or by twos and threes, to still-hunt scattering buffalo, or deer, or elk, or such other game as may be found. The women remaining in camp are not idle. All day long they tan robes, dry meat, sew moccasins, and perform a thousand and one other tasks. The young men who have stayed at home carefully comb and braid their hair, paint their faces, and, if the weather is pleasant, ride or walk around the camp so that the young women may look at them and see how pretty they are.

Feasting began early in the morning, and will be carried on far into the night. A man who gives a feast has his wives cook the choicest food they have, and when all is ready, he goes outside the lodge and shouts the invitation, calling out each guest's name three times, saying that he is invited to eat, and concludes by announcing that a certain number of pipes—generally three—will be smoked. The guests having assembled, each one is served with a dish of food. Be the quantity large or small, it is all that he will get. If he does not eat it all, he may carry home what remains. The host does not eat with his guests. He cuts up some tobacco, and carefully mixes it with *l'herbe*, and when all have finished eating, he fills and lights a pipe, which is smoked and passed from one to another, beginning with the first man on his left. When the last person on the left of the host has smoked, the pipe is passed back around the circle to the one on the right of the door, and smoked to the left again. The guests do not all talk at once. When a person begins to speak, he expects every one to listen, and is never interrupted. During the day the topics for conversation are about the hunting, war, stories of strange adventures, besides a good deal of good-natured joking and chaffing. When the third and last pipeful of tobacco has been smoked, the host ostentatiously knocks out the ashes and says "*Kyi,*" whereupon all the guests rise and file out. Seldom a day passed but each lodge-owner in camp gave from one to three feasts. In fact almost all a man did, when in camp, was to go from one of these gatherings to another.

A favorite pastime in the day was gambling with a small wheel called *it-se'-wah*. This wheel was about four inches in diameter, and had five spokes, on which were strung different-colored beads, made of bone or horn. A level, smooth piece of ground was selected, at each end of which was placed a log. At each end of the course were two men, who gambled against each other. A crowd always surrounded them, betting on the sides. The wheel was rolled along the course, and each man at the end whence it started, darted an arrow at it. The cast was made just before the wheel reached the log at the opposite end of the track, and points were counted according as the arrow passed between the spokes, or when the wheel, stopped by the log, was in contact with the arrow, the position and nearness of the different beads to the arrow representing a certain number of points. The player who first scored ten points won. It was a very difficult game, and one had to be very skilful to win.

Another popular game was what with more southern tribes is called "hands"; it is like "Button, button, who's got the button?" Two small, oblong bones were used, one of which had a black ring around it. Those who participated in this game, numbering from two to a dozen, were divided into two equal parties, ranged on either side of the lodge. Wagers were made, each person betting with the one directly opposite him. Then a man took the bones, and, by skilfully moving his hands and changing the objects from one to the other, sought to make it impossible for the person opposite him to decide which hand held the marked one. Ten points were the game, counted by sticks, and the side which first got the number took the stakes. A song always accompanied this game, a weird, unearthly air,—if it can be so called,—but when heard at a little distance, very pleasant and soothing. At first a scarcely audible murmur, like the gentle soughing of an evening breeze, it gradually increased in volume and reached a very high pitch, sank quickly to a low bass sound, rose and fell, and gradually died away, to be again repeated. The person concealing the bones swayed his body, arms, and hands in time to the air, and went through all manner of graceful and intricate movements for the purpose of confusing the guesser. The stakes were sometimes very high, two or three horses or more, and men have been known to lose everything they possessed, even to their clothing.

The children, at least the boys, played about and did as they pleased. Not so with the girls. Their duties began at a very early age. They carried wood and water for their mothers, sewed moccasins, and as soon as they were strong enough, were taught to tan robes and furs, make lodges, travois, and do all other woman's—and so menial—work. The boys played at mimic warfare, hunted around in the brush with their bows and arrows, made mud images of animals, and in summer spent about half their time in the water. In winter, they spun tops on the ice, slid down hill on a contrivance made of buffalo ribs, and hunted rabbits.

Shortly after noon, the hunters began to return, bringing in deer, antelope, buffalo, elk, occasionally bear, and, sometimes, beaver which they had trapped. The camp began to be more lively. In all directions persons could be heard shouting out invitations to feasts. Here a man was lying back on his couch singing and drumming; there a group of young men were holding a war dance; everywhere the people were eating, singing, talking, and joking. As the light faded from the western sky and darkness spread over the camp, the noise and laughter increased. In many lodges, the people held social dances, the women, dressed in their best gowns, ranged on one side, the men on the other; all sung, and three or four drummers furnished an accompaniment; the music was lively if somewhat jerky. At intervals the people rose and danced, the "step" being a bending of the knees and swinging of the body, the women holding their arms and hands in various graceful positions.

With the night came the rehearsal of the wonderous doings of the gods. These tales may not be told in the daytime. Old Man would not like that, and would cause any one who narrated them while it was light to become blind. All Indians are natural orators, but some far exceed others in their powers of expression. Their attitudes, gestures, and signs are so suggestive that they alone would enable one to understand the stories they relate. I have seen these storytellers so much in earnest, so entirely carried away by the tale they were relating, that they fairly trembled with excitement. They held their little audiences spell-bound. The women dropped their half-sewn moccasin from their listless hands, and the men let the pipe go out. These stories for the most part were about the ancient gods and their miraculous doings. They were generally related by the old men, warriors who had seen their best days. Many of them are recorded in this book. They are the explanations of the phenomena of life, and contain many a moral for the instruction of youth.

The *I-kŭn-ŭh'-kah-tsi* contributed not a little to the entertainment of every-day life. Frequent dances were held by the different bands of the society, and the whole camp always turned out to see them. The animal-head masks, brightly painted bodies, and queer performances were dear to the Indian heart.

Such was the every-day life of the Blackfeet in the buffalo days. When the camp moved, the women packed up their possessions, tore down the lodges, and loaded everything on the backs of the ponies or on the travois. Meantime the chiefs had started on, and the soldiers— the Brave band of the *I-kŭn-ŭh'-kah-tsi*—followed after them. After these leaders had gone a short distance, a halt was made to allow the column to close up. The women, children, horses, and dogs of the camp marched in a disorderly, straggling fashion, often strung out in a line a mile or two long. Many of the men rode at a considerable distance ahead, and on each side of the marching column, hunting for any game that might be found, or looking over the country for signs of enemies.

Before the Blackfeet obtained horses in the very first years of the present century, and when their only beasts of burden were dogs, their possessions were transported by these animals or on men's backs. We may image that in those days the journeys made were short ones, the camp travelling but a few miles.

In moving the camp in ancient days, the heaviest and bulkiest things to be transported were the lodges. These were sometimes very large, often consisting of thirty cowskins, and, when set up, containing two or three fires like this ╱★★★╲ or in ground plan like this ⊙~★~⊙. The skins of these large lodges were sewn together in strips, of which there would be sometimes as many as four; and, when the lodge was set up, these strips were pinned together as the front of a common lodge is pinned to-day. The dogs carried the provisions, tools, and utensils, sometimes the lodge strips, if these were small enough, or anything that was heavy, and yet could be packed in small compass; for since dogs are small animals, and low standing, they cannot carry bulky burdens. Still, some of the dogs were large enough to carry a load of one hundred pounds. Dogs also hauled the travois, on which were bundles and sometimes babies. This was not always a safe means of transportation for infants, as is indicated by an incident related by John Monroe's mother as having occurred in her father's time. The camp, on foot of course, was crossing a strip of open prairie lying between two pieces of timber, when a herd of buffalo, stampeding, rushed through the marching column. The loaded dogs rushed after the buffalo, dragging the travois after them and scattering their loads over the prairie. Among the lost chattels were two babies, dropped off somewhere in the long grass, which were never found.

There were certain special customs and beliefs which were a part of the every-day life of the people.

In passing the pipe when smoking, it goes from the host, who takes the first smoke, to the left, passing from hand to hand to the door. It may not be passed across the door to the man on the other side, but must come back,—no one smoking,—pass the host, and go round to the man across the door from the last smoker. This man smokes and passes it to the one on his left, and so it goes on until it reaches the host again. A person entering a lodge where people are smoking must not pass in front of them, that is, between the smokers and the fire.

A solemn form of affirmation, the equivalent of the civilized oath, is connected with smoking, which, as is well known, is with many tribes of Indians a sacred ceremony. If a man sitting in a lodge tells his companions some very improbable story, something that they find it very hard to believe, and they want to test him, to see if he is really telling the truth, the pipe is given to a medicine man, who paints the stem red and prays over it, asking that if the man's story is true he may have long life, but if it is false his life may end in a short time. The pipe is then filled and lighted, and passed to the man, who has seen and overheard what has been done and said. The medicine man says to him: "Accept this pipe, but remember that, if you smoke, your story must be as sure as that there is a hole through this pipe, and as straight as the hole through this stem. So your life shall be long and you shall survive, but if you have spoken falsely your days are counted." The man may refuse the pipe, saying, "I have told you the truth; it is useless to smoke this pipe." If he declines to smoke, no one believes what he has said; he is looked upon as having lied. If, however, he takes the pipe and smokes, every one believes him. It is the most solemn form of oath. The Blackfoot pipes are usually made of black or green slate or sandstone.

The Blackfeet do not whip their children, but still they are not without some training. Children must be taught, or they will not know anything; if they do not know anything, they will have no sense; and if they have no sense they will not know how to act. They are instructed in manners, as well as in other more general and more important matters.

If a number of boys were in a lodge where older people were sitting, very likely the young people would be talking and laughing about their own concerns, and making so much noise that the elders could say nothing. If this continued too long, one of the older men would be likely to get up and go out and get a long stick and bring it in with him. When he had seated himself, he would hold it up, so that the children could see it and would repeat a cautionary formula, "I will give you gum!" This was a warning to them to make less noise, and was always heeded—for a time. After a little, however, the boys might forget and begin to chatter again, and presently the man, without further warning, would reach over and rap one of them on the head with the stick, when quiet would again be had for a time.

In the same way, in winter, when the lodge was full of old and young people, and through lack of attention the fire died down, some older person would call out, "Look out for the skunk!" which would be a warning to the boys to put some sticks on the fire. If this was not done at once, the man who had called out might throw a stick of wood across the lodge into the group of children, hitting and hurting one or more of them. It was taught also that, if, when young and old were in the lodge and the fire had burned low, an older person were to lay the unburned ends of the sticks upon the fire, all the children in the lodge would have the scab, or itch. So, at the call "Look out for the scab!" some child would always jump to the fire, and lay up the sticks.

There were various ways of teaching and training the children. Men would make long speeches to groups of boys, playing in the camps, telling them what they ought to do to be successful in life. They would point out to them that to accomplish anything they must be brave and untiring in war; that long life was not desirable; that the old people always had a hard time, were given the worst side of the lodge and generally neglected; that when the camp was moved they suffered from cold; that their sight was dim, so that they could not see far; that their teeth were gone, so that they could not chew their food. Only discomfort and misery await the old. Much better, while the body is strong and in its prime, while the sight is clear, the teeth sound, and the hair still black and long, to die in battle fighting bravely. The example of successful warriors would be held up to them, and the boys urged to emulate their brave deeds. To such advice some boys would listen, while others would not heed it.

The girls also were instructed. All Indians like to see women more or less sober and serious-minded, not giggling all the time, not silly. A Blackfoot man who had two or three girls would, as they grew large, often talk to them and give them good advice. After watching them, and taking the measure of their characters, he would one day get a buffalo's front foot and ornament it fantastically with feathers. When the time came, he would call one of his daughters to him and say to her: "Now I wish you to stand here in front of me and look me straight in the eye without laughing. No matter what I may do, do not laugh." Then he would sing a funny song, shaking the foot in the girl's face in time to the song, and looking her steadily in the eye. Very likely before he had finished, she would begin to giggle. If she did this, the father would stop singing and tell her to finish laughing; and when she was serious again, he would again warn her not to laugh, and then would repeat his song. This time perhaps she would not laugh while he was singing. He would go through with this same performance before all his daughters. To such as seemed to have the steadiest characters, he would give good advice. He would talk to each girl of the duties of a woman's life and warn her against the dangers which she might expect to meet.

At the time of the Medicine Lodge, he would take her to the lodge and point out to her the Medicine Lodge woman. He would say: "There is a good woman. She has built this Medicine Lodge, and is greatly honored and respected by all the people. Once she was a girl just like you; and you, if you are good and live a pure life, may some day be as great as she is now. Remember this, and try to live a worthy life."

At the time of the Medicine Lodge, the boys in the camp also gathered to see the young men count their *coups*. A man would get up, holding in one hand a bundle of small sticks, and, taking one stick from the bundle, he would recount some brave deed, throwing away a stick as he completed the narrative of each *coup*, until the sticks were all gone, when he sat down, and another man stood up to begin his recital. As the boys saw and heard all this, and saw how respected those men were who had done the most and bravest things, they said to themselves, "That man was once a boy like us, and we, if we have strong hearts, may do as much as he has done." So even the very small boys used often to steal off from the camp, and follow war parties. Often they went without the knowledge of their parents, and poorly provided, without food or extra moccasins. They would get to the enemy's camp, watch the ways of the young men, and so learn about going to war, how to act when on the war trail so as to be successful. Also they came to know the country.

The Blackfeet men often went off by themselves to fast and dream for power. By no means every one did this, and, of those who attempted it, only a few endured to the end,—that is, fasted the whole four days,—and obtained the help sought. The attempt was not usually made by young boys before they had gone on their first war journey. It was often undertaken by men who were quite mature. Those who underwent this suffering were obliged to abstain from food or drink for four days and four nights, resting for two nights on the right side, and for two nights on the left. It was deemed essential that the place to which a man resorted for this purpose should be unfrequented, where few or no persons had walked; and it must also be a place that tried the nerve, where there was some danger. Such situations were mountain peaks; or narrow ledges on cut cliffs, where a careless movement might cause a man to fall to his death on the rocks below; or islands in lakes, which could only be reached by means of a raft, and where there was danger that a person might be seized and carried off by the *Sū'-yē tŭp'-pi*, or Under Water People; or places where the dead had been buried, and where there was much danger from ghosts. Or a man might lie in a well-worn buffalo trail, where the animals were frequently passing, and so he might be trodden on by a travelling band of buffalo; or he might choose a locality where bears were abundant and dangerous. Wherever he went, the man built himself a little lodge of brush, moss, and leaves, to keep off the rain; and, after making his prayers to the sun and singing his sacred songs, he crept into the hut and began his fast. He was not allowed to take any covering with him, nor to roof over his shelter with skins. He always had with him a pipe, and this lay by him, filled, so that, when the spirit, or dream, came, it could smoke. They did not appeal to any special class of helpers, but prayed to all alike. Often by the end of the fourth day, a secret helper— usually, but by no means always, in the form of some animal—appeared to the man in a dream, and talked with him, advising him, marking out his course through life, and giving him its power. There were some, however, on whom the power would not work, and a much greater number who gave up the fast, discouraged, before the prescribed time had been completed, either not being able to endure the lack of food and water, or being frightened by the strangeness or loneliness of their surroundings, or by something that they thought they saw or heard. It was no disgrace to fail, nor was the failure necessarily known, for the seeker after power did not always, nor perhaps often, tell any one what he was going to do.

Three modes of burial were practised by the Blackfeet. They buried their dead on platforms placed in trees, on platforms in lodges, and on the ground in lodges. If a man dies in a lodge, it is never used again. The people would be afraid of the man's ghost. The lodge is often used to wrap the body in, or perhaps the man may be buried in it.

As soon as a person is dead, be it man, woman, or child, the body is immediately prepared for burial, by the nearest female relations. Until recently, the corpse was wrapped in a number of robes, then in a lodge covering, laced with rawhide ropes, and placed on a platform of lodge poles, arranged on the branches of some convenient tree. Some times the outer wrapping—the lodge covering—was omitted. If the deceased was a man, his weapons, and often his medicine, were buried with him. With women a few cooking utensils and implements for tanning robes were placed on the scaffolds. When a man was buried on a platform in a lodge, the platform was usually suspended from the lodge poles.

Sometimes, when a great chief or noted warrior died, his lodge would be moved some little distance from the camp, and set up in a patch of brush. It would be carefully pegged down all around, and stones piled on the edges to make it additionally firm. For still greater security, a rope fastened to the lodge poles, where they come together at the smoke hole, came down, and was securely tied to a peg in the ground in the centre of the lodge, where the fireplace would ordinarily be. Then the beds were made up all around the lodge, and on one of them was placed the corpse, lying as if asleep. The man's weapons, pipe, war clothing, and medicine were placed near him, and the door then closed. No one ever again entered such a lodge. Outside the lodge, a number of his horses, often twenty or more, were killed, so that he might have plenty to ride on his journey to the Sand Hills, and to use after arriving there. If a man had a favorite horse, he might order it to be killed at this grave, and his order was always carried out. In ancient times, it is said, dogs were killed at the grave.

Women mourn for deceased relations by cutting their hair short. For the loss of a husband or son (but not a daughter), they not only cut their hair, but often take off one or more joints of their fingers, and always scarify the calves of their legs. Besides this, for a month or so, they daily repair to some place near camp, generally a hill or little rise of ground, and there cry and lament, calling the name of the deceased over and over again. This may be called a chant or song, for there is a certain tune to it. It is in a minor key and very doleful. Any one hearing it for the first time, even though wholly unacquainted with Indian customs, would at once know that it was a mourning song, or at least was the utterance of one in deep distress. There is no fixed period for the length of time one must mourn. Some keep up this daily lament for a few weeks only, and others much longer. I once came across an old wrinkled woman, who was crouched in the sage brush, crying and lamenting for some one, as if her heart would break. On inquiring if any one had lately died, I was told she was mourning for a son she had lost more than twenty years before.

Men mourn by cutting a little of their hair, going without leggings, and for the loss of a son, sometimes scarify their legs. This last, however, is never done for the loss of a wife, daughter, or any relative except a son.

Many Blackfeet change their names every season. Whenever a Blackfoot counts a new *coup*, he is entitled to a new name. A Blackfoot will never tell his name if he can avoid it. He believes that if he should speak his name, he would be unfortunate in all his undertakings.

It was considered a gross breach of propriety for a man to meet his mother-in-law, and if by any mischance he did so, or what was worse, if he spoke to her, she demanded a very heavy payment, which he was obliged to make. The mother-in-law was equally anxious to avoid meeting or speaking to her son-in-law.

HOW THE BLACKFOOT LIVED

THE primitive clothing of the Blackfeet was made of the dressed skins of certain animals. Women seldom wore a head covering. Men, however, in winter generally used a cap made of the skin of some small animal, such as the antelope, wolf, badger, or coyote. As the skin from the head of these animals often formed part of the cap, the ears being left on, it made a very odd-looking head-dress. Sometimes a cap was made of the skin of some large bird, such as the sage-hen, duck, owl, or swan.

The ancient dress of the women was a shirt of cowskin, with long sleeves tied at the wrist, a skirt reaching half-way from knees to ankles, and leggings tied above the knees, with sometimes a supporting string running from the belt to the leggings. In more modern times, this was modified, and a woman's dress consisted of a gown or smock, reaching from the neck to below the knees. There were no sleeves, the armholes being provided with top coverings, a sort of cape or flap, which reached to the elbows. Leggings were of course still worn. They reached to the knee, and were generally made, as was the gown, of the tanned skins of elk, deer, sheep, or antelope. Moccasins for winter use were made of buffalo robe, and of tanned buffalo cowskin for summer wear. The latter were always made with parfleche soles, which greatly increased their durability, and were often ornamented over the instep or toes with a three-pronged figure, worked in porcupine quills or beads, the three prongs representing, it is said, the three divisions or tribes of the nation. The men wore a shirt, breech-clout, leggings which reached to the thighs, and moccasins. In winter both men and women wore a robe of tanned buffalo skin, and sometimes of beaver. In summer a lighter robe was worn, made of cowskin or buckskin, from which the hair had been removed. Both sexes wore belts, which supported and confined the clothing, and to which were attached knifesheaths and other useful articles.

Necklaces and ear-rings were worn by all, and were made of shells, bone, wood, and the teeth and claws of animals. Elk tushes were highly prized, and were used for ornamenting women's dresses. A gown profusely decorated with them was worth two good horses. Eagle feathers were used by the men to make head-dresses and to ornament shields and also weapons. Small bunches of owl or grouse feathers were sometimes tied to the scalp locks. It is doubtful if the women ever took particular care of their hair. The men, however, spent a great deal of time brushing, braiding, and ornamenting their scalp locks. Their hair was usually worn in two braids, one on each side of the head. Less frequently, four braids were made, one behind and in front of each ear. Sometimes, the hair of the forehead was cut off square, and brushed straight up; and not infrequently it was made into a huge topknot and wound with otter fur. Often a slender lock, wound with brass wire or braided, hung down from one side of the forehead over the face.

As a rule, the men are tall, straight, and well formed. Their features are regular, the eyes being large and well set, and the nose generally moderately large, straight, and thin. Their chests are splendidly developed. The women are quite tall for their sex, but, as a rule, not so good-looking as the men. Their hands are large, coarse, and knotted by hard labor; and they early become wrinkled and careworn. They generally have splendid constitutions. I have known them to resume work a day after childbirth; and once, when travelling, I knew a woman to halt, give birth to a child, and catch up with the camp inside of four hours.

As a rule, children are hardy and vigorous. They are allowed to do about as they please from the time they are able to walk. I have often seen them playing in winter in the snow, and spinning tops on the ice, barefooted and half-naked. Under such conditions, those which have feeble constitutions soon die. Only the hardiest reach maturity and old age.

It is said that very long ago the people made houses of mud, sticks, and stones. It is not known what was their size or shape, and no traces of them are known to have been found. For a very long time, the lodge seems to have been their only dwelling. In ancient times, before they had knives of metal, stones were used to hold down the edges of the lodge, to keep it from being blown away. These varied in size from six inches to a foot or more in diameter. Everywhere on the prairie, one may now see circles of these stones, and, within these circles, the smaller ones, which surrounded the fireplace. Some of them have lain so long that only the tops now project above the turf, and undoubtedly many of them are buried out of sight.

Lodges were always made of tanned cowskin, nicely cut and sewn together, so as to form an almost perfect cone. At the top were two large flaps, called ears, which were kept extended or closed, according to the direction and strength of the wind, to create a draft and keep the lodge free from smoke. The lodge covering was supported by light, straight pine or spruce poles, about eighteen of which were required. Twelve cowskins made a lodge about fourteen feet in diameter at the base, and ten feet high. I have heard of a modern one which contained forty skins. It was over thirty feet in diameter, and was so heavy that the skins were sewn in two pieces which buttoned together.

An average-sized dwelling of this kind contained eighteen skins and was about sixteen feet in diameter. The lower edge of the lodge proper was fastened, by wooden pegs, to within an inch or two of the ground. Inside, a lining, made of brightly painted cowskin, reached from the ground to a height of five or six feet. An air space of the thickness of the lodge poles—two or three inches—was thus left between the lining and the lodge covering, and the cold air, rushing up through it from the outside, made a draft, which aided the ears in freeing the lodge of smoke. The door was three or four feet high and was covered by a flap of skin, which hung down on the outside. Thus made, with plenty of buffalo robes for seats and bedding, and a good stock of firewood, a lodge was very comfortable, even in the coldest weather.

It was not uncommon to decorate the outside of the lodge with buffalo tails and brightly painted pictures of animals. Inside, the space around was partitioned off into couches, or seats, each about six feet in length. At the foot and head of every couch, a mat, made of straight, peeled willow twigs, fastened side by side, was suspended on a tripod at an angle of forty-five degrees, so that between the couches spaces were left like an inverted V, thus $\wedge$, making convenient places to store articles which were not in use. The owner of the lodge always occupied the seat or couch at the back of the lodge, directly opposite the door-way, the places on his right being occupied by his wives and daughters; though sometimes a Blackfoot had so many wives that they occupied the whole lodge. The places on his left were reserved for his sons and visitors. When a visitor entered a lodge, he was assigned a seat according to his rank,—the nearer to the host, the greater the honor.

Bows were generally made of ash wood, which grows east of the mountains toward the Sand Hills. When for any reason they could not obtain ash, they used the wood of the choke-cherry tree, but this had not strength nor spring enough to be of much service. I have been told also that sometimes they used hazel wood for bows.

Arrows were made of shoots of the sarvis berry wood, which was straight, very heavy, and not brittle. They were smoothed and straightened by a stone implement. The grooves were made by pushing the shafts through a rib or other flat bone in which had been made a hole, circular except for one or two projections on the inside. These projections worked out the groove. The object of these grooves is said to have been to allow the blood to flow freely. Each man marked his arrows by painting them, or by some special combination of colored feathers. The arrow heads were of two kinds,—barbed slender points for war, and barbless for hunting. Knives were originally made of stone, as were also war clubs, mauls, and some of the scrapers for fleshing and graining hides. Some of the flint knives were long, others short. A stick was fitted to them, forming a wooden handle. The handles of mauls and war clubs were usually made of green sticks fitted as closely as possible into a groove made in the stone, the whole being bound together by a covering of hide put on green, tightly fitted and strongly sewed. This, as it shrunk in drying, bound the different parts of the implement together in the strongest possible manner. Short, heavy spears were used, the points being of stone or bone, barbed.

I have heard no explanation among the Blackfeet of the origin of fire. In ancient times, it was obtained by means of fire sticks, as described elsewhere. The starting of the spark with these sticks is said to have been hard work. At almost their first meeting with the whites, they obtained flints and steels, and learned how to use them.

In ancient times,—in the days of fire sticks and even later, within the memory of men now living,—fire used to be carried from place to place in a "fire horn." This was a buffalo horn slung by a string over the shoulder like a powder horn. The horn was lined with moist, rotten wood, and the open end had a wooden stopper or plug fitted to it. On leaving camp in the morning, the man who carried the horn took from the fire a small live coal and put it in the horn, and on this coal placed a piece of punk, and then plugged up the horn with the stopper. The punk smouldered in this almost air-tight chamber, and, in the course of two or three hours, the man looked at it, and if it was nearly consumed, put another piece of punk in the horn. The first young men who reached the appointed camping ground would gather two or three large piles of wood in different places, and as soon as some one who carried a fire horn reached camp, he turned out his spark at one of these piles of wood, and a little blowing and nursing gave a blaze which started the fire. The other fires were kindled from this first one, and when the women reached camp and had put the lodges up, they went to these fires, and got coals with which to start those in their lodges. This custom of borrowing coals persisted up to the last days of the buffalo, and indeed may even be noticed still.

The punk here mentioned is a fungus, which grows on the birch tree. The Indians used to gather this in large quantities and dry it. It was very abundant at the Touchwood Hills (whence the name) on Beaver Creek, a tributary of the Saskatchewan from the south.

The Blackfeet made buckets, cups, basins, and dishes from the lining of the buffalo's paunch. This was torn off in large pieces, and was stretched over a flattened willow or cherry hoop at the bottom and top. These hoops were sometimes inside and sometimes outside the bucket or dish. In the latter case, the hoop at the bottom was often sewed to the paunch, which came down over it, double on the outside, the needle holes being pitched with gum or tallow. The hoop at the upper edge was also sewed to the paunch, and a rawhide bail passed under it, to carry it by.

These buckets were shaped somewhat like our wooden ones, and were of different sizes, some of them holding four or five gallons. They were more or less flexible, and when carried in a pack, they could be flattened down like a crush hat, and so took up but little room. If set on the ground when full, they would stand up for a while, but as they soon softened and fell down, they were usually hung up by the bail on a little tripod. Cups were made in the same way as buckets, but on a smaller scale and without the bail. Of course, nothing hot could be placed in these vessels.

It is doubtful if the Blackfeet ever made any pottery or basket ware. They, however, made bowls and kettles of stone. There is an ancient children's song which consists of a series of questions asked an elk, and its replies to the same. In one place, the questioner sings,

"Elk, what is your bowl (or dish)?" and the elk answers, "*Ok-wi-tok-so-ka*," stone bowl. On this point, Wolf Calf, a very old man, states that in early days the Blackfeet sometimes boiled their meat in a stone bowl made out of a hard clayey rock. Choosing a fragment of the right size and shape, they would pound it with another heavier rock, dealing light blows until a hollow had been made in the top. This hollow was made deeper by pounding and grinding; and when it was deep enough, they put water in it, and set it on the fire, and the water would boil. These pots were strong and would last a long time. I do not remember that any other tribe of Plains Indians made such stone bowls or mortars, though, of course, they were commonly made, and in singular perfection, by the Pacific Coast tribes; and I have known of rare cases in which basalt mortars and small soapstone ollas have been found on the central plateau of the continent in southern Wyoming. These articles, however, had no doubt been obtained by trade from Western tribes.

Serviceable ladles and spoons were made of wood and of buffalo and mountain sheep horn. Basins or flat dishes were sometimes made of mountain sheep horn, boiled, split, and flattened, and also of split buffalo horn, fitted and sewn together with sinew, making a flaring, saucer-shaped dish. These were used as plates or eating dishes. Of course, they leaked a little, for the joints were not tight. Wooden bowls and dishes were made from knots and protuberances of trees, dug out and smoothed by fire and the knife or by the latter alone.

It is not known that these people ever made spears, hooks, or other implements for capturing fish. They appear never to have used boats of any kind, not even "bull boats." Their highest idea of navigation was to lash together a few sticks or logs, on which to transport their possessions across a river.

Red, brown, yellow, and white paints were made by burning clays of these colors, which were then pulverized and mixed with a little grease. Black paint was made of charred wood.

Bags and sacks were made of parfleche, usually ornamented with buckskin fringe, and painted with various designs in bright colors. Figures having sharp angles are most common.

The diet of the Blackfeet was more varied than one would think. Large quantities of sarvis berries (*Amelanchier alnifolia*) were gathered whenever there was a crop (which occurs every other year), dried, and stored for future use. These were gathered by women, who collected the branches laden with ripe fruit, and beat them over a robe spread upon the ground. Choke-cherries were also gathered when ripe, and pounded up, stones and all. A bushel of the fruit, after being pounded up and dried, was reduced to a very small quantity. This food was sometimes eaten by itself, but more often was used to flavor soups and to mix with pemmican. Bull berries (*Shepherdia argentea*) were a favorite fruit, and were gathered in large quantities, as was also the white berry of the red willow. This last is an exceedingly bitter, acrid fruit, and to the taste of most white men wholly unpleasant and repugnant. The Blackfeet, however, are very fond of it; perhaps because it contains some property necessary to the nourishment of the body, which is lacking in their every-day food.

The camas root, which grows abundantly in certain localities on the east slope of the Rockies, was also dug, cooked, and dried. The bulbs were roasted in pits, as by the Indians on the west side of the Rocky Mountains, the Kalispels, and others. It is gathered while in the bloom—June 15 to July 15. A large pit is dug in which a hot fire is built, the bottom being first lined with flat stones. After keeping up this fire for several hours, until the stones and earth are thoroughly heated, the coals and ashes are removed. The pit is then lined with grass, and is filled almost to the top with camas bulbs. Over these, grass is laid, then twigs, and then earth to a depth of four inches. On this a fire is built, which is kept up for from one to three days, according to the quantity of the bulbs in the pit.

When the pit is opened, the small children gather about it to suck the syrup, which has collected on the twigs and grass, and which is very sweet. The fresh-roasted camas tastes something like a roasted chestnut, with a little of the flavor of the sweet potato. After being cooked, the roots are spread out in the sun to dry, and are then put in sacks to be stored away. Sometimes a few are pounded up with sarvis berries, and dried.

Bitter-root is gathered, dried, and boiled with a little sugar. It is a slender root, an inch or two long and as thick as a goose quill, white in color, and looking like short lengths of spaghetti. It is very starchy.

In the spring, a certain root called *mats* was eaten in great quantities. This plant was known to the early French employees of the Hudson's Bay and American Fur Companies as *pomme blanche* (*Psoralea esculenta*).

All parts of such animals as the buffalo, elk, deer, etc., were eaten, save only the lungs, gall, and one or two other organs. A favorite way of eating the paunch or stomach was in the raw state. Liver, too, was sometimes eaten raw. The unborn calf of a fresh-killed animal, especially buffalo, was considered a great delicacy. The meat of this, when boiled, is white, tasteless, and insipid. The small intestines of the buffalo were sometimes dried, but more often were stuffed with long, thin strips of meat. During the stuffing process, the entrail was turned inside out, thus confining with the meat the sweet white fat that covers the intestine. The next step was to roast it a little, after which the ends were tied to prevent the escape of the juices, and it was thoroughly boiled in water. This is a very great delicacy, and when properly prepared is equally appreciated by whites and Indians.

As a rule, there were but two ways of cooking meat,—boiling and roasting. If roasted, it was throughly cooked; but if boiled, it was only left in the water long enough to lose the red color, say five or ten minutes. Before they got kettles from the whites, the Blackfeet often boiled meat in a green hide. A hole was dug in the ground, and the skin, flesh side up, was laid in it, being supported about the edges of the hole by pegs. The meat and water having been placed in this hollow, red-hot stones were dropped in the water until it became hot and the meat was cooked.

In time of plenty, great quantities of dried meat were prepared for use when fresh meat could not be obtained. In making dried meat, the thicker parts of an animal were cut in large, thin sheets and hung in the sun to dry. If the weather was not fine, the meat was often hung up on lines or scaffolds in the upper part of the lodge. When properly cured and if of good quality, the sheets were about one-fourth of an inch thick and very brittle. The back fat of the buffalo was also dried, and eaten with the meat as we eat butter with bread. Pemmican was made of the flesh of the buffalo. The meat was dried in the usual way; and, for this use, only lean meat, such as the hams, loin, and shoulders, was chosen. When the time came for making the pemmican, two large fires were built of dry quaking aspen wood, and these were allowed to burn down to red coals. The old women brought the dried meat to these fires, and the sheets of meat were thrown on the coals of one of them, allowed to heat through, turned to keep them from burning, and then thrown on the flesh side of a dry hide, that lay on the ground near by. After a time, the roasting of this dried meat caused a smoke to rise from the fire in use, which gave the meat a bitter taste, if cooked in it. Then they turned to the other fire, and used that until the first one had burned clear again. After enough of the roasted meat had been thrown on the hide, it was flailed out with sticks, and being very brittle was easily broken up, and made small. It was constantly stirred and pounded until it was all fine. Meantime, the tallow of the buffalo had been melted in a large kettle, and the pemmican bags prepared. These were made of bull's hide, and were in two pieces, cut oblong, and with the corners rounded off. Two such pieces sewed together made a bag which would hold one hundred pounds. The pounded meat and tallow—the latter just beginning to cool—were put in a trough made of bull's hide, a wooden spade being used to stir the mixture. After it was thoroughly mixed, it was shovelled into one of the sacks, held open, and rammed down and packed tight with a big stick, every effort being made to expel all the air. When the bag was full and packed as tight as possible, it was sewn up. It was then put on the ground, and the women jumped on it to make it still more tight and solid. It was then laid away in the sun to cool and dry. It usually took the meat of two cows to make a bag of one hundred pounds; a very large bull might make a sack of from eighty to one hundred pounds.

A much finer grade of pemmican was made from the choicest parts of the buffalo with marrow fat. To this dried berries and pounded choke-cherries were added, making a delicious food, which was extremely nutritious. Pemmican was eaten either dry as it came from the sack, or stewed with water.

In the spring, the people had great feasts of the eggs of ducks and other water-fowl. A large quantity having been gathered, a hole was dug in the ground, and a little water put in it. At short intervals above the water, platforms of sticks were built, on which the eggs were laid. A smaller hole was dug at one side of the large hole, slanting into the bottom of it. When all was ready, the top of the larger hole was covered with mud, laid upon cross sticks, and red-hot stones were dropped into the slant, when they rolled down into the water, heating it, and so cooking the eggs by steam.

Fish were seldom eaten by these people in early days, but now they seem very fond of them. Turtles, frogs, and lizards are considered creatures of evil, and are never eaten. Dogs, considered a great delicacy by the Crees, Gros Ventres, Sioux, Assinaboines, and other surrounding tribes, were never eaten by the Blackfeet. No religious motive is assigned for this abstinence. I once heard a Piegan say that it was wrong to eat dogs. "They are our true friends," he said. "Men say they are our friends and then turn against us, but our dogs are always true. They mourn when we are absent, and are always glad when we return. They keep watch for us in the night when we sleep. So pity the poor dogs."

Snakes, grasshoppers, worms, and other insects were never eaten. Salt was an unknown condiment. Many are now very fond of it, but I know a number, especially old people, who never eat it.

THE BLACKFOOT IN WAR

The Blackfeet were a warlike people. How it may have been in the old days, before the coming of the white man, we do not know. Very likely, in early times, they were usually at peace with neighboring tribes, or, if quarrels took place, battles were fought, and men killed, this was only in angry dispute over what each party considered its rights. Their wars were probably not general, nor could they have been very bloody. When, however, horses came into the possession of the Indians, all this must have soon become changed. Hitherto there had really been no incentive to war. From time to time expeditions may have gone out to kill enemies,—for glory, or to take revenge for some injury,—but war had not yet been made desirable by the hope of plunder, for none of their neighbors—any more than themselves—had property which was worth capturing and taking away. Primitive arms, dogs, clothing, and dried meat were common to all the tribes, and were their only possessions, and usually each tribe had an abundance of all these. It was not worth any man's while to make long journeys and to run into danger merely to increase his store of such property, when his present possessions were more than sufficient to meet all his wants. Even if such things had seemed desirable plunder, the amount of it which could be carried away was limited, since—for a war party—the only means of transporting captured articles from place to place was on men's backs, nor could men burdened with loads either run or fight. But when horses became known, and the Indians began to realize what a change the possession of these animals was working in their mode of life, when they saw that, by enormously increasing the transporting power of each family, horses made far greater possessions practicable, that they insured the food supply, rendered the moving of the camp easier and more rapid, made possible long journeys with a minimum of effort, and that they had a value for trading, the Blackfoot mind received a new idea, the idea that it was desirable to accumulate property. The Blackfoot saw that, since horses could be exchanged for everything that was worth having, no one had as many horses as he needed. A pretty wife, a handsome war bonnet, a strong bow, a finely ornamented woman's dress,—any or all of these things a man might obtain, if he had horses to trade for them. The gambler at "hands," or at the ring game, could bet horses. The man who was devoted to his last married wife could give her a horse as an evidence of his affection.

We can readily understand what a change the advent of the horse must have worked in the minds of a people like the Blackfeet, and how this changed mental attitude would react on the Blackfoot way of living. At first, there were but few horses among them, but they knew that their neighbors to the west and south—across the mountains and on the great plains beyond the Missouri and the Yellowstone—had plenty of them; that the Kūtenais, the Kalispels, the Snakes, the Crows, and the Sioux were well provided. They soon learned that horses were easily driven off, and that, even if followed by those whose property they had taken, the pursued had a great advantage over the pursuers; and we may feel sure that it was not long before the idea of capturing horses from the enemy entered some Blackfoot head and was put into practice.

Now began a systematic sending forth of war parties against neighboring tribes for the purpose of capturing horses, which continued for about seventy-five or eighty years, and has only been abandoned within the last six or seven, and since the settlement of the country by the whites made it impossible for the Blackfeet longer to pass backward and forward through it on their raiding expeditions. Horse-taking at once became what might be called an established industry among the Blackfeet. Success brought wealth and fame, and there was a pleasing excitement about the war journey. Except during the bitterest weather of the winter, war parties of Blackfeet were constantly out, searching for camps of their enemies, from whom they might capture horses. Usually the only object of such an expedition was to secure plunder, but often enemies were killed, and sometimes the party set out with the distinct intention of taking both scalps and horses.

Until some time after they had obtained guns, the Blackfeet were on excellent terms with the northern Crees, but later the Chippeways from the east made war on the Blackfeet, and this brought about general hostilities against all Crees, which have continued up to within a few years. If I recollect aright, the last fight which occurred between the Pi-kun'-i and the Crees took place in 1886. In this skirmish, which followed an attempt by the Crees to capture some Piegan horses, my friend, Tail-feathers-coming-in-sight-over-the-Hill, killed and counted *coup* on a Cree whose scalp he afterward sent me, as an evidence of his prowess.

The Gros Ventres of the prairie, of Arapaho stock, known to the Blackfeet as *At-séna*, or Gut People, had been friends and allies of the Blackfeet from the time they first came into the country, early in this century, up to about the year 1862, when, according to Clark, peace was broken through a mistake. A war party of Snakes had gone to a Gros Ventres camp near the Bear Paw Mountains and there killed two Gros Ventres and taken a white pony, which they subsequently gave to a party of Piegans whom they met, and with whom they made peace. The Gros Ventres afterward saw this horse in the Piegan camp and supposed that the latter had killed their tribesmen, and this led to a long war. In the year 1867, the Piegans defeated the allied Crows and Gros Ventres in a great battle near the Cypress Mountains, in which about 450 of the enemy are said to have been killed.

An expression often used in these pages, and which is so familiar to one who has lived much with Indians as to need no explanation, is the phrase to count *coup*. Like many of the terms common in the Northwest, this one comes down to us from the old French trappers and traders, and a *coup* is, of course, a blow. As commonly used, the expression is almost a direct translation of the Indian phrase to strike the enemy, which is in ordinary use among all tribes. This striking is the literal inflicting a blow on an individual, and does not mean merely the attack on a body of enemies.

The most creditable act that an Indian can perform is to show that he is brave, to prove, by some daring deed, his physical courage, his lack of fear. In practice, this courage is shown by approaching near enough to an enemy to strike or touch him with something that is held in the hand—to come up within arm's length of him. To kill an enemy is praiseworthy, and the act of scalping him may be so under certain circumstances, but neither of these approaches in bravery the hitting or touching him with something held in the hand. This is counting *coup*.

The man who does this shows himself without fear and is respected accordingly. With certain tribes, as the Pawnees, Cheyennes, and others, it was not very uncommon for a warrior to dash up to an enemy and strike him before making any attempt to injure him, the effort to kill being secondary to the *coup*. The blow might be struck with anything held in the hand,—a whip, coupstick, club, lance, the muzzle of a gun, a bow, or what not. It did not necessarily follow that the person on whom the *coup* had been counted would be injured. The act was performed in the case of a woman, who might be captured, or even on a child, who was being made prisoner.

Often the dealing the *coup* showed a very high degree of courage. As already implied, it might be counted on a man who was defending himself most desperately, and was trying his best to kill the approaching enemy, or, even if the attempt was being made on a foe who had fallen, it was never certain that he was beyond the power of inflicting injury. He might be only wounded, and, just when the enemy had come close to him, and was about to strike, he might have strength enough left to raise himself up and shoot him dead. In their old wars, the Indians rarely took men captive. The warrior never expected quarter nor gave it, and usually men fought to the death, and died mute, defending themselves to the last—to the last, striving to inflict some injury on the enemy.

The striking the blow was an important event in a man's life, and he who performed this feat remembered it. He counted it. It was a proud day for the young warrior when he counted his first *coup*, and each subsequent one was remembered and numbered in the warrior's mind, just as an American of to-day remembers the number of times he has been elected to Congress. At certain dances and religious cere-monies, like that of the Medicine Lodge, the warriors counted—or rather re-counted—their *coups*.

While the *coup* was primarily, and usually, a blow with something held in the hand, other acts in warfare which involved great danger to him who performed them were also reckoned *coups* by some tribes. Thus, for a horseman to ride over and knock down an enemy, who was on foot, was regarded among the Blackfeet as a *coup*, for the horseman might be shot at close quarters, or might receive a lance thrust. It was the same to ride one's horse violently against a mounted foe. An old Pawnee told me of a *coup* that he had counted by running up to a fallen enemy and jumping on him with both feet. Sometimes the taking of horses counted a *coup*, but this was not always the case.

As suggested by what has been already stated, each tribe of the Plains Indians held its own view as to what constituted a *coup*. The Pawnees were very strict in their interpretation of the term, and with them an act of daring was not in itself deemed a *coup*. This was counted only when the person of an enemy was actually touched. One or two incidents which have occurred among the Pawnees will serve to illustrate their notions on this point.

In the year 1867, the Pawnee scouts had been sent up to Ogallalla, Nebraska, to guard the graders who were working on the Union Pacific railroad. While they were there, some Sioux came down from the hills and ran off a few mules, taking them across the North Platte.

Major North took twenty men and started after them. Crossing the river, and following it up on the north bank, he headed them off, and before long came in sight of them.

The six Sioux, when they found that they were pursued, left the mules that they had taken, and ran; and the Pawnees, after chasing them eight or ten miles, caught up with one of them, a brother of the well-known chief Spotted Tail. Baptiste Bahele, a half-breed Skidi, had a very fast horse, and was riding ahead of the other Pawnees, and shooting arrows at the Sioux, who was shooting back at him. At length Baptiste shot the enemy's horse in the hip, and the Indian dismounted and ran on foot toward a ravine. Baptiste shot at him again, and this time sent an arrow nearly through his body, so that the point projected in front. The Sioux caught the arrow by the point, pulled it through his body, and shot it back at his pursuer, and came very near hitting him. About that time, a ball from a carbine hit the Sioux and knocked him down.

Then there was a race between Baptiste and the Pawnee next behind him, to see which should count *coup* on the fallen man. Baptiste was nearest to him and reached him first, but just as he got to him, and was leaning over from his horse, to strike the dead man, the animal shied at the body, swerving to one side, and he failed to touch it. The horse ridden by the other Pawnee ran right over the Sioux, and his rider leaned down and touched him.

Baptiste claimed the *coup*—although acknowledging that he had not actually touched the man—on the ground that he had exposed himself to all the danger, and would have hit the man if his horse had not swerved as it did from the body; but the Pawnees would not allow it, and all gave the credit of the *coup* to the other boy, because he had actually touched the enemy.

On another occasion three or four young men started on the warpath from the Pawnee village. When they came near to Spotted Tail's camp on the Platte River, they crossed the stream, took some horses, and got them safely across the river. Then one of the boys recrossed, went back to the camp, and cut loose another horse. He had almost got this one out of the camp, when an Indian came out of a lodge near by, and sat down. The Pawnee shot the Sioux, counted *coup* on him, scalped him, and then hurried across the river with the whole Sioux camp in pursuit. When the party returned to the Pawnee village, this boy was the only one who received credit for a *coup*.

Among the Blackfeet the capture of a shield, bow, gun, war bonnet, war shirt, or medicine pipe was deemed a *coup*.

Nothing gave a man a higher place in the estimation of the people than the counting of *coups*, for, I repeat, personal bravery is of all qualities the most highly respected by Indians. On special occasions, as has been said, men counted over again in public their *coups*. This served to gratify personal vanity, and also to incite the young men to the performance of similar brave deeds. Besides this, they often made a more enduring record of these acts, by reproducing them pictographically on robes, cowskins, and other hides. There is now in my possession an illuminated cowskin, presented to me by Mr. J. Kipp, which contains the record of the *coups* and the most striking events in the life of Red Crane, a Blackfoot warrior, painted by himself. These pictographs are very rude and are drawn after the style common among Plains Indians, but no doubt they were sufficiently lifelike to call up to the mind of the artist each detail of the stirring events which they record.

The Indian warrior who stood up to relate some brave deed which he had performed was almost always in a position to prove the truth of his statements. Either he had the enemy's scalp, or some trophy captured from him, to produce as evidence, or else he had a witness of his feat in some companion. A man seldom boasted of any deed unless he was able to prove his story, and false statements about exploits against the enemy were most unusual. Temporary peace was often made between tribes usually at war, and, at the friendly meetings which took place during such times of peace, former battles were talked over, the performances of various individuals discussed, and the acts of particular men in the different fights commented on. In this way, if any man had falsely claimed to have done brave deeds, he would be detected.

An example of this occurred many years ago among the Cheyennes. At that time, there was a celebrated chief of the Skidi tribe of the Pawnee Nation whose name was Big Eagle. He was very brave, and the Cheyennes greatly feared him, and it was agreed among them that the man who could count *coup* on Big Eagle should be made war chief of the Cheyennes. After a fight on the Loup River, a Cheyenne warrior claimed to have counted *coup* on Big Eagle by thrusting a lance through his buttocks. On the strength of the claim, this man was made war chief of the Cheyennes. Some years later, during a friendly visit made by the Pawnees to the Cheyennes, this incident was mentioned. Big Eagle was present at the time, and, after inquiring into the matter, he rose in council, denied that he had ever been struck as claimed, and, throwing aside his robe, called on the Cheyennes present to examine his body and to point out the scars left by the lance. None were found. It was seen that Big Eagle spoke the truth; and the lying Cheyenne, from the proud position of war chief, sank to a point where he was an object of contempt to the meanest Indian in his tribe.

Among the Blackfeet a war party usually, or often, had its origin in a dream. Some man who has a dream, after he awakes tells of it. Perhaps he may say: "I dreamed that on a certain stream is a herd of horses that have been given to me, and that I am going away to get. I am going to war. I shall go to that place and get my band of horses." Then the men who know him, who believe that his medicine is strong and that he will have good luck, make up their minds to follow him. As soon as he has stated what he intends to do, his women and his female relations begin to make moccasins for him, and the old men among his relations begin to give him arrows and powder and ball to fit him out for war. The relations of those who are going with him do the same for them.

The leader notifies the young men who are going with him on what day and at what hour he intends to start. He determines the time for himself, but does not let the whole camp know it in advance. Of late years, large war parties have not been desirable. They have preferred to go out in small bodies.

Just before a war party sets out, its members get together and sing the "peeling a stick song," which is a wolf song. Then they build a sweat lodge and go into it, and with them goes in an old man, a medicine-pipe man, who has been a good warrior. They fill the pipe and ask him to pray for them, that they may have good luck, and may accomplish what they desire. The medicine-pipe man prays and sings and pours water on the hot stones, and the warriors with their knives slice bits of skin and flesh from their bodies,—their arms and breasts and sometimes from the tip of the tongue,—which they offer to the Sun. Then, after the ceremony is over, all dripping with perspiration from their vapor bath, the men go down to the river and plunge in.

In starting out, a war party often marches in the daytime, but sometimes they travel at night from the beginning. Often they may make an all night march across a wide prairie, in passing over which they might be seen if they travelled in the day. They journey on foot, always. The older men carry their arms, while the boys bear the moccasins, the ropes, and the food, which usually consists of dried meat or pemmican. They carry also coats and blankets and their war bonnets and otter skin medicine. The leader has but little physical labor to perform. His mind is occupied in planning the movements of his party. He is treated with the greatest respect. The others mend his moccasins, and give him the best of the food which they carry.

After they get away from the main camp, the leader selects the strongest of the young men, and sends him ahead to some designated butte, saying, "Go to that place, and look carefully over the country, and if you see nothing, make signals to us to come on." This scout goes on ahead, travelling in the ravines and coulées, and keeps himself well hidden. After he has reconnoitred and made signs that he sees nothing, the party proceeds straight toward him.

The party usually starts early in the morning and travels all day, making camp at sundown. During the day, if they happen to come upon an antelope or a buffalo, they kill it, if possible, and take some of the meat with them. They try in every way to economize their pemmican. They always endeavor to make camp in the thick timber, where they cannot be seen; and here, when it is necessary, on account of bad weather or for other reasons, they build a war lodge. Taking four young cotton-woods or aspens, on which the leaves are left, and lashing them together like lodge poles, but with the butts up, about these they place other similar trees, also butts up and untrimmed. The leaves keep the rain off, and prevent the light of the fire which is built in the lodge from showing through. Sometimes, when on the prairie, where there is no wood, in stormy weather they will build a shelter of rocks. When the party has come close to the enemy, or into a country where the enemy are likely to be found, they build no more fires, but eat their food uncooked.

When they see fresh tracks of people, or signs that enemies are in the country, they stop travelling in the daytime and move altogether by night, until they come to some good place for hiding, and here they stop and sleep. When day comes, the leader sends out young men to the different buttes, to look over the country and see if they can discover the enemy. If some one of the scouts reports that he has seen a camp, and that the enemy have been found, the leader directs his men to paint themselves and put on their war bonnets. This last is a figure of speech, since the war bonnets, having of late years been usually ornamented with brass bells, could not be worn in a secret attack, on account of the noise they would make. Before painting themselves, therefore, they untie their war bonnets, and spread them out on the ground, as if they were about to be worn, and then when they have finished painting themselves, tie them up again. When it begins to get dark, they start on the run for the enemy's camp. They leave their food in camp, but carry their ropes slung over the shoulder and under the arm, whips stuck in belts, guns and blankets.

After they have crept up close to the lodges, the leader chooses certain men that have strong hearts, and takes them with him into the camp to cut loose the horses. The rest of the party remain outside the camp, and look about its outskirts, driving in any horses that may be feeding about, not tied up. Of those who have gone into the camp, some cut loose one horse, while others cut all that may be tied about a lodge. Some go only once into the camp, and some go twice to get the horses. When they have secured the horses, they drive them off a little way from the camp, at first going slowly, and then mount and ride off fast. Generally, they travel two nights and one day before sleeping.

This is the usual method of procedure of an ordinary expedition to capture horses, and I have given it very nearly in the language of the men who explained it to me.

In their hostile encounters, the Blackfeet have much that is common to many Plains tribes, and also some customs that are peculiar to themselves. Like most Indians, they are subject to sudden, apparently causeless, panics, while at other times they display a courage that is heroic. They are firm believers in luck, and will follow a leader who is fortunate in his expeditions into almost any danger. On the other hand, if the leader of a war party loses his young men, or any of them, the people in the camp think that he is unlucky, and does not know how to lead a war party. Young men will not follow him as a leader, and he is obliged to go as a servant or scout under another leader. He is likely never again to lead a war party, having learned to distrust his luck.

If a war party meets the enemy, and kills several of them, losing in the battle one of its own number, it is likely, as the phrase is, to "cover" the slain Blackfoot with all the dead enemies save one, and to have a scalp dance over that remaining one. If a party had killed six of the enemy and lost a man, it might "cover" the slain Blackfoot with five of the enemy. In other words, the five dead enemies would pay for the one which the war party had lost. So far, matters would be even, and they would feel at liberty to rejoice over the victory gained over the one that is left.

The Blackfeet sometimes cut to pieces an enemy killed in battle. If a Blackfoot had a relation killed by a member of another tribe, and afterward killed one of this tribe, he was likely to cut him all to pieces "to get even," that is, to gratify his spite—to obtain revenge. Sometimes, after they had killed an enemy, they dragged his body into camp, so as to give the children an opportunity to count *coup* on it. Often they cut the feet and hands off the dead, and took them away and danced over them for a long time. Sometimes they cut off an arm or a leg, and often the head, and danced and rejoiced over this trophy.

Women and children of hostile tribes were often captured, and adopted into the Blackfoot tribes with all the rights and privileges of indigenous members. Men were rarely captured. When they were taken, they were sometimes killed in cold blood, especially if they had made a desperate resistance before being captured. At other times, the captive would be kept for a time, and then the chief would take him off away from the camp, and give him provisions, clothing, arms, and a horse, and let him go. The captive man always had a hard time at first. When he was brought into the camp, the women and children threw dirt on him and counted *coups* on him, pounding him with sticks and clubs. He was rarely tied, but was always watched. Often the man who had taken him prisoner had great trouble to keep his tribesmen from killing him.

In the very early days of this century, war parties used commonly to start out in the spring, going south to the land where horses were abundant, being absent all summer and the next winter, and returning the following summer or autumn, with great bands of horses. Sometimes they were gone two years. They say that on such journeys they used to go to *Spai'yu ksah'ku,* which means the Spanish lands— *Spai'yu* being a recently made word, no doubt from the French *espagnol.* That they did get as far as Mexico, or at least New Mexico, is indicated by the fact that they brought back branded horses and a few branded mules; for in these early days there was no stock upon the Plains, and animals bearing brands were found only in the Spanish American settlements. The Blackfeet did not know what these marks meant. From their raids into these distant lands, they sometimes brought back arms of strange make, lances, axes, and swords, of a form unlike any that they had seen. The lances had broad heads; some of the axes, as described, were evidently the old "T. Gray" trade axes of the Southwest. A sword, described as having a long, slender, straight blade, inlaid with a flower pattern of yellow metal along the back, was probably an old Spanish rapier.

In telling of these journeys to Spanish lands, they say of the very long reeds which grow there, that they are very large at the butt, are jointed, very hard, and very tall; they grow in marshy places; and the water there has a strange, mouldy smell.

It is said, too, that there have been war parties who have crossed the mountains and gone so far to the west that they have seen the big salt water which lies beyond, or west of, the Great Salt Lake. Journeys as far south as Salt Lake were not uncommon, and Hugh Monroe has told me of a war party he accompanied which went as far as this.

THE BLACKFOOT GENESIS

ALL animals of the Plains at one time heard and knew him, and all birds of the air heard and knew him. All things that he had made understood him, when he spoke to them,—the birds, the animals and the people.

Old Man was travelling about, south of here, making the people. He came from the south, travelling north, making animals and birds as he passed along. He made the mountains, prairies, timber, and brush first. So he went along, travelling northward, making things as he went, putting rivers here and there, and falls on them, putting red paint here and there in the ground,—fixing up the world as we see it to-day. He made the Milk River (the Teton) and crossed it, and, being tired, went up on a little hill and lay down to rest. As he lay on his back, stretched out on the ground, with arms extended, he marked himself out with stones,—the shape of his body, head, legs, arms, and everything. There you can see those rocks to-day. After he had rested, he went on northward, and stumbled over a knoll and fell down on his knees. Then he said, "You are a bad thing to be stumbling against"; so he raised up two large buttes there, and named them the Knees, and they are called so to this day. He went on further north, and with some of the rocks he carried with him he built the Sweet Grass Hills.

Old Man covered the plains with grass for the animals to feed on. He marked off a piece of ground, and in it he made to grow all kinds of roots and berries,—camas, wild carrots, wild turnips, sweet-root, bitter-root, sarvis berries, bull berries, cherries, plums, and rosebuds. He put trees in the ground. He put all kinds of animals on the ground. When he made the bighorn with its big head and horns, he made it out on the prairie. It did not seem to travel easily on the prairie; it was awkward and could not go fast. So he took it by one of its horns, and led it up into the mountains, and turned it loose; and it skipped about among the rocks, and went up fearful places with ease. So he said, "This is the place that suits you; this is what you are fitted for, the rocks and the mountains." While he was in the mountains, he made the antelope out of dirt, and turned it loose, to see how it would go. It ran so fast that it fell over some rocks and hurt itself. He saw that this would not do, and took the antelope down on the prairie, and turned it loose; and it ran away fast and gracefully, and he said, "This is what you are suited to."

One day Old Man determined that he would make a woman and a child; so he formed them both—the woman and the child, her son—of clay. After he had moulded the clay in human shape, he said to the clay, "You must be people," and then he covered it up and left it, and went away. The next morning he went to the place and took the covering off, and saw that the clay shapes had changed a little. The second morning there was still more change, and the third still more. The fourth morning he went to the place, took the covering off, looked at the images, and told them to rise and walk; and they did so. They walked down to the river with their Maker, and then he told them that his name was *Na'pi*, Old Man.

As they were standing by the river, the woman said to him, "How is it? will we always live, will there be no end to it?" He said: "I have never thought of that. We will have to decide it. I will take this buffalo chip and throw it in the river. If it floats, when people die, in four days they will become alive again; they will die for only four days. But if it sinks, there will be an end to them." He threw the chip into the river, and it floated. The woman turned and picked up a stone, and said: "No, I will throw this stone in the river; if it floats we will always live, if it sinks people must die, that they may always be sorry for each other." The woman threw the stone into the water, and it sank. "There," said Old Man, "you have chosen. There will be an end to them."

It was not many nights after, that the woman's child died, and she cried a great deal for it. She said to Old Man: "Let us change this. The law that you first made, let that be a law." He said: "Not so. What is made law must be law. We will undo nothing that we have done. The child is dead, but it cannot be changed. People will have to die."

That is how we came to be people. It is he who made us.

The first people were poor and naked, and did not know how to get a living. Old Man showed them the roots and berries, and told them that they could eat them; that in a certain month of the year they could peel the bark off some trees and eat it, that it was good. He told the people that the animals should be their food, and gave them to the people, saying, "These are your herds." He said: "All these little animals that live in the ground—rats, squirrels, skunks, beavers—are good to eat. You need not fear to eat of their flesh." He made all the birds that fly, and told the people that there was no harm in their flesh, that it could be eaten. The first people that he created he used to take about through the timber and swamps and over the prairies, and show them the different plants. Of a certain plant he would say, "the root of this plant, if gathered in a certain month of the year, is good for a certain sickness." So they learned the power of all herbs.

In those days there were buffalo. Now the people had no arms, but those black animals with long beards were armed; and once, as the people were moving about, the buffalo saw them, and ran after them, and hooked them, and killed and ate them. One day, as the Maker of the people was travelling over the country, he saw some of his children, that he had made, lying dead, torn to pieces and partly eaten by the buffalo. When he saw this he was very sad. He said: "This will not do. I will change this. The people shall eat the buffalo."

He went to some of the people who were left, and said to them, "How is it that you people do nothing to these animals that are killing you?" The people said: "What can we do? We have no way to kill these animals, while they are armed and can kill us." Then said the Maker: "That is not hard. I will make you a weapon that will kill these animals." So he went out, and cut some sarvis berry shoots, and brought them in, and peeled the bark off them. He took a larger piece of wood, and flattened it, and tied a string to it, and made a bow. Now, as he was the master of all birds and could do with them as he wished, he went out and caught one, and took feathers from its wing, and split them, and tied them to the shaft of wood. He tied four feathers along the shaft, and tried the arrow at a mark, and found that it did not fly well. He took these feathers off, and put on three; and when he tried it again, he found that it was good. He went out and began to break sharp pieces off the stones. He tried them, and found that the black flint stones made the best arrow points, and some white flints. Then he taught the people how to use these things.

Then he said: "The next time you go out, take these things with you, and use them as I tell you, and do not run from these animals. When they run at you, as soon as they get pretty close, shoot the arrows at them, as I have taught you; and you will see that they will run from you or will run in a circle around you."

Now, as people became plenty, one day three men went out on to the plain to see the buffalo, but they had no arms. They saw the animals, but when the buffalo saw the men, they ran after them and killed two of them, but one got away. One day after this, the people went on a little hill to look about, and the buffalo saw them, and said, "*Saiyah*, there is some more of our food," and they rushed on them. This time the people did not run. They began to shoot at the buffalo with the bows and arrows *Na'pi* had given them, and the buffalo began to fall; but in the fight a person was killed.

At this time these people had flint knives given them, and they cut up the bodies of the dead buffalo. It is not healthful to eat the meat raw, so Old Man gathered soft dry rotten driftwood and made punk of it, and then got a piece of hard wood, and drilled a hole in it with an arrow point, and gave them a pointed piece of hard wood, and taught them how to make a fire with fire sticks, and to cook the flesh of these animals and eat it.

They got a kind of stone that was in the land, and then took another harder stone and worked one upon the other, and hollowed out the softer one, and made a kettle of it. This was the fashion of their dishes.

Also Old Man said to the people: "Now, if you are overcome, you may go and sleep, and get power. Something will come to you in your dream, that will help you. Whatever these animals tell you to do, you must obey them, as they appear to you in your sleep. Be guided by them. If anybody wants help, if you are alone and travelling, and cry aloud for help, your prayer will be answered. It may be by the eagles, perhaps by the buffalo, or by the bears. Whatever animal answers your prayer, you must listen to him."

That was how the first people got through the world, by the power of their dreams.

After this, Old Man kept on, travelling north. Many of the animals that he had made followed him as he went. The animals understood him when he spoke to them, and he used them as his servants. When he got to the north point of the Porcupine Mountains, there he made some more mud images of people, and blew breath upon them, and they became people. He made men and women. They asked him, "What are we to eat?" He made many images of clay, in the form of buffalo. Then he blew breath on these, and they stood up; and when he made signs to them, they started to run. Then he said to the people, "Those are your food." They said to him, "Well, now, we have those animals; how are we to kill them?" "I will show you," he said. He took them to the cliff, and made them build rock piles like this, > ; and he made the people hide behind these piles of rock, and said, "When I lead the buffalo this way, as I bring them opposite to you, rise up."

After he had told them how to act, he started on toward a herd of buffalo. He began to call them, and the buffalo started to run toward him, and they followed him until they were inside the lines. Then he dropped back; and as the people rose up, the buffalo ran in a straight line and jumped over the cliff. He told the people to go and take the flesh of those animals. They tried to tear the limbs apart, but they could not. They tried to bite pieces out, and could not. So Old Man went to the edge of the cliff, and broke some pieces of stone with sharp edges, and told them to cut the flesh with these. When they had taken the skins from these animals, they set up some poles and put the hides on them, and so made a shelter to sleep under. There were some of these buffalo that went over the cliff that were not dead. Their legs were broken, but they were still alive. The people cut strips of green hide, and tied stones in the middle, and made large mauls, and broke in the skulls of the buffalo, and killed them.

After he had taught those people these things, he started off again, travelling north, until he came to where Bow and Elbow rivers meet. There he made some more people, and taught them the same things. From here he again went on northward. When he had come nearly to the Red Deer's River, he reached the hill where the Old Man sleeps. There he lay down and rested himself. The form of his body is to be seen there yet.

When he awoke from his sleep, he travelled further northward and came to a fine high hill. He climbed to the top of it, and there sat down to rest. He looked over the country below him, and it pleased him. Before him the hill was steep, and he said to himself, "Well, this is a fine place for sliding; I will have some fun," and he began to slide down the hill. The marks where he slid down are to be seen yet, and the place is known to all people as the "Old Man's Sliding Ground."

This is as far as the Blackfeet followed Old Man. The Crees know what he did further north.

In later times once, *Na'pi* said, "Here I will mark you off a piece of ground," and he did so. Then he said: "There is your land, and it is full of all kinds of animals, and many things grow in this land. Let no other people come into it. This is for you five tribes (Blackfeet, Bloods, Piegans, Gros Ventres, Sarcees). When people come to cross the line, take your bows and arrows, your lances and your battle axes, and give them battle and keep them out. If they gain a footing, trouble will come to you."

Our forefathers gave battle to all people who came to cross these lines, and kept them out. Of late years we have let our friends, the white people, come in, and you know the result. We, his children, have failed to obey his laws.

LODGE TALES

THE PEACE WITH THE SNAKES

I

In those days there was a Piegan chief named Owl Bear. He was a great chief, very brave and generous. One night he had a dream: he saw many dead bodies of the enemy lying about, scalped, and he knew that he must go to war. So he called out for a feast, and after the people had eaten, he said:—

"I had a strong dream last night. I went to war against the Snakes, and killed many of their warriors. So the signs are good, and I feel that I must go. Let us have a big party now, and I will be the leader. We will start to-morrow night."

Then he told two old men to go out in the camp and shout the news, so that all might know. A big party was made up. Two hundred men, they say, went with this chief to war. The first night they travelled only a little way, for they were not used to walking, and soon got tired.

In the morning the chief got up early and went and made a sacrifice, and when he came back to the others, some said, "Come now, tell us your dream of this night."

"I dreamed good," said Owl Bear. "I had a good dream. We will have good luck."

But many others said they had bad dreams. They saw blood running from their bodies.

Night came, and the party started on, travelling south, and keeping near the foot-hills; and when daylight came, they stopped in thick pine woods and built war lodges. They put up poles as for a lodge, and covered them very thick with pine boughs, so they could build fires and cook, and no one would see the light and smoke; and they all ate some of the food they carried, and then went to sleep.

Again the chief had a good dream, but the others all had bad dreams, and some talked about turning back; but Owl Bear laughed at them, and when night came, all started on. So they travelled for some nights, and all kept dreaming bad except the chief. He always had good dreams. One day after a sleep, a person again asked Owl Bear if he dreamed good. "Yes," he replied. "I have again dreamed of good luck."

"We still dream bad," the person said, "and now some of us are going to turn back. We will go no further, for bad luck is surely ahead."

"Go back! go back!" said Owl Bear. "I think you are cowards; I want no cowards with me." They did not speak again. Many of them turned around, and started north, toward home.

Two more days' travel. Owl Bear and his warriors went on, and then another party turned back, for they still had bad dreams. All the men now left with him were his relations. All the others had turned back.

They travelled on, and travelled on, always having bad dreams, until they came close to the Elk River. Then the oldest relation said, "Come, my chief, let us all turn back. We still have bad dreams. We cannot have good luck."

"No," replied Owl Bear, "I will not turn back."

Then they were going to seize him and tie his hands, for they had talked of this before. They thought to tie him and make him go back with them. Then the chief got very angry. He put an arrow on his bow, and said: "Do not touch me. You are my relations; but if any of you try to tie me, I will kill you. Now I am ashamed. My relations are cowards and will turn back. I have told you I have always dreamed good, and that we would have good luck. Now I don't care; I am covered with shame. I am going now to the Snake camp and will give them my body. I am ashamed. Go! go! and when you get home put on women's dresses. You are no longer men."

They said no more. They turned back homeward, and the chief was all alone. His heart was very sad as he travelled on, and he was much ashamed, for his relations had left him.

II

Night was coming on. The sun had set and rain was beginning to fall. Owl Bear looked around for some place where he could sleep dry. Close by he saw a hole in the rocks. He got down on his hands and knees and crept in. Here it was very dark. He could see nothing, so he crept very slowly, feeling as he went. All at once his hand touched something strange. He felt of it. It was a person's foot, and there was a moccasin on it. He stopped, and sat still. Then he felt a little further. Yes, it was a person's leg. He could feel the cowskin legging. Now he did not know what to do. He thought perhaps it was a dead person; and again, he thought it might be one of his relations, who had become ashamed and turned back after him.

Pretty soon he put his hand on the leg again and felt along up. He touched the person's belly. It was warm. He felt of the breast, and could feel it rise and fall as the breath came and went; and the heart was beating fast. Still the person did not move. Maybe he was afraid. Perhaps he thought that was a ghost feeling of him.

Owl Bear now knew this person was not dead. He thought he would try if he could learn who the man was, for he was not afraid. His heart was sad. His people and his relations had left him, and he had made up his mind to give his body to the Snakes. So he began and felt all over the man,—of his face, hair, robe, leggings, belt, weapons; and by and by he stopped feeling of him. He could not tell whether it was one of his people or not.

Pretty soon the strange person sat up and felt all over Owl Bear; and when he had finished, he took the Piegan's hand and opened it and held it up, waving it from side to side, saying by signs, "Who are you?"

Owl Bear put his closed hand against the person's cheek and rubbed it; he said in signs, "Piegan!" and then he asked the person who he was. A finger was placed against his breast and moved across it zigzag. It was the sign for "Snake."

"*Hai yah!*" thought Owl Bear, "a Snake, my enemy." For a long time he sat still, thinking. By and by he drew his knife from his belt and placed it in the Snake's hand, and signed, "Kill me!" He waited. He thought soon his heart would be cut. He wanted to die. Why live? His people had left him.

Then the Snake took Owl Bear's hand and put a knife in it and motioned that Owl Bear should cut his heart, but the Piegan would not do it. He lay down, and the Snake lay down beside him. Maybe they slept. Likely not.

So the night went and morning came. It was light, and they crawled out of the cave, and talked a long time together by signs. Owl Bear told the Snake where he had come from, how his party had dreamed bad and left him, and that he was going alone to give his body to the Snakes.

Then the Snake said: "I was going to war, too. I was going against the Piegans. Now I am done. Are you a chief?"

"I am the head chief," replied Owl Bear. "I lead. All the others follow."

"I am the same as you," said the Snake. "I am the chief. I like you. You are brave. You gave me your knife to kill you with. How is your heart? Shall the Snakes and the Piegans make peace?"

"Your words are good," replied Owl Bear. "I am glad."

"How many nights will it take you to go home and come back here with your people?" asked the Snake.

Owl Bear thought and counted. "In twenty-five nights," he replied, "the Piegans will camp down by that creek."

"My trail," said the Snake, "goes across the mountains. I will try to be here in twenty-five nights, but I will camp with my people just behind that first mountain. When you get here with the Piegans, come with one of your wives and stay all night with me. In the morning the Snakes will move and put up their lodges beside the Piegans."

"As you say," replied the chief, "so it shall be done." Then they built a fire and cooked some meat and ate together.

"I am ashamed to go home," said Owl Bear. "I have taken no horses, no scalps. Let me cut off your side locks?"

"Take them," said the Snake.

Owl Bear cut off the chief's braids close to his head, and then the Snake cut off the Piegan's braids. Then they exchanged clothes and weapons and started out, the Piegan north, the Snake south.

III

"Owl Bear has come! Owl Bear has come!" the people were shouting.

The warriors rushed to his lodge. *Whish!* how quickly it was filled! Hundreds stood outside, waiting to hear the news.

For a long time the chief did not speak. He was still angry with his people. An old man was talking, telling the news of the camp. Owl Bear did not look at him. He ate some food and rested. Many were in the lodge who had started to war with him. They were now ashamed. They did not speak, either, but kept looking at the fire. After a long time the chief said: "I travelled on alone. I met a Snake. I took his scalp and clothes, and his weapons. See, here is his scalp!" And he held up the two braids of hair.

No one spoke, but the chief saw them nudge each other and smile a little; and soon they went out and said to one another: "What a lie! That is not an enemy's scalp; there is no flesh on it. He has robbed some dead person."

Some one told the chief what they said, but he only laughed and replied:—

"I do not care. They were too much afraid even to go on and rob a dead person. They should wear women's dresses."

Near sunset, Owl Bear called for a horse, and rode all through camp so every one could hear, shouting out: "Listen! Listen! To-morrow we move camp. We travel south. The Piegans and Snakes are going to make peace. If any one refuses to go, I will kill him. All must go."

Then an old medicine man came up to him and said: "*Kyi*, Owl Bear! listen to me. Why talk like this? You know we are not afraid of the Snakes. Have we not fought them and driven them out of this country? Do you think we are afraid to go and meet them? No. We will go and make peace with them as you say, and if they want to fight, we will fight. Now you are angry with those who started to war with you. Don't be angry. Dreams belong to the Sun. He gave them to us, so that we can see ahead and know what will happen. The Piegans are not cowards. Their dreams told them to turn back. So do not be angry with them any more."

"There is truth in what you say, old man," replied Owl Bear; "I will take your words."

IV

In those days the Piegans were a great tribe. When they travelled, if you were with the head ones, you could not see the last ones, they were so far back. They had more horses than they could count, so they used fresh horses every day and travelled very fast. On the twenty-fourth day they reached the place where Owl Bear had told the Snake they would camp, and put up their lodges along the creek. Soon some young men came in, and said they had seen some fresh horse trails up toward the mountain.

"It must be the Snakes," said the chief; "they have already arrived, although there is yet one night." So he called one of his wives, and getting on their horses they set out to find the Snake camp. They took the trail up over the mountain, and soon came in sight of the lodges. It was a big camp. Every open place in the valley was covered with lodges, and the hills were dotted with horses; for the Snakes had a great many more horses than the Piegans.

Some of the Snakes saw the Piegans coming, and they ran to the chief, saying: "Two strangers are in sight, coming this way. What shall be done?"

"Do not harm them," replied the chief. "They are friends of mine. I have been expecting them." Then the Snakes wondered, for the chief had told them nothing about his war trip.

Now when Owl Bear had come to the camp, he asked in signs for the chief's lodge, and they pointed him to one in the middle. It was small and old. The Piegan got off his horse, and the Snake chief came out and hugged him and kissed him, and said: "I am glad you have come to-day to my lodge. So are my people. You are tired. Enter my lodge and we will eat." So they went inside and many of the Snakes came in, and they had a great feast.

Then the Snake chief told his people how he had met the Piegan, and how brave he was, and that now they were going to make a great peace; and he sent some men to tell the people, so that they would be ready to move camp in the morning. Evening came. Everywhere people were shouting out for feasts, and the chief took Owl Bear to them. It was very late when they returned. Then the Snake had one of his wives make a bed at the back of the lodge; and when it was ready he said: "Now, my friend, there is your bed. This is now your lodge; also the woman who made the bed, she is now your wife; also everything in this lodge is yours. The parfleches, saddles, food, robes, bowls, everything is yours. I give them to you because you are my friend and a brave man."

"You give me too much," replied Owl Bear. "I am ashamed, but I take your words. I have nothing with me but one wife. She is yours."

Next morning camp was broken early. The horses were driven in, and the Snake chief gave Owl Bear his whole band,—two hundred head, all large, powerful horses.

All were now ready, and the chiefs started ahead. Close behind them were all the warriors, hundreds and hundreds, and last came the women and children, and the young men driving the loose horses. As they came in sight of the Piegan camp, all the warriors started out to meet them, dressed in their war costumes and singing the great war song. There was no wind, and the sound came across the valley and up the hill like the noise of thunder. Then the Snakes began to sing, and thus the two parties advanced. At last they met. The Piegans turned and rode beside them, and so they came to the camp. Then they got off their horses and kissed each other. Every Piegan asked a Snake into his lodge to eat and rest, and the Snake women put up their lodges beside the Piegan lodges. So the great peace was made.

V

In Owl Bear's lodge there was a great feast, and when they had finished he said to his people: "Here is the man whose scalp I took. Did I say I killed him? No. I gave him my knife and told him to kill me. He would not do it; and he gave me his knife, but I would not kill him. So we talked together what we should do, and now we have made peace. And now (turning to the Snake) this is your lodge, also all the things in it. My horses, too, I give you. All are yours."

So it was. The Piegan took the Snake's wife, lodge, and horses, and the Snake took the Piegan's, and they camped side by side. All the people camped together, and feasted each other and made presents. So the peace was made.

For many days they camped side by side. The young men kept hunting, and the women were always busy drying meat and tanning robes and cowskins. Buffalo were always close, and after a while the people had all the meat and robes they could carry. Then, one day, the Snake chief said to Owl Bear: "Now, my friend, we have camped a long time together, and I am glad we have made peace. We have dug a hole in the ground, and in it we have put our anger and covered it up, so there is no more war between us. And now I think it time to go. To-morrow morning the Snakes break camp and go back south."

"Your words are good," replied Owl Bear. "I too am glad we have made this peace. You say you must go south, and I feel lonesome. I would like you to go with us so we could camp together a long time, but as you say, so it shall be done. To-morrow you will start south. I too shall break camp, for I would be lonesome here without you; and the Piegans will start in the home direction."

The lodges were being taken down and packed. The men sat about the fireplaces, taking a last smoke together. They were now great friends. Many Snakes had married Piegan women, and many Piegans had married Snake women. At last all was ready. The great chiefs mounted their horses and started out, and soon both parties were strung out on the trail.

Some young men, however, stayed behind to gamble a while. It was yet early in the morning, and by riding fast it would not take them long to catch up with their camps. All day they kept playing; and sometimes the Piegans would win, and sometimes the Snakes.

It was now almost sunset. "Let us have one horse race," they said, "and we will stop." Each side had a good horse, and they ran their best; but they came in so close together it could not be told who won. The Snakes claimed that their horse won, and the Piegans would not allow it. So they got angry and began to quarrel, and pretty soon they began to fight and to shoot at each other, and some were killed.

Since that time the Snakes and Piegans have never been at peace.

HEAVY COLLAR
AND THE GHOST WOMAN

The Blood camp was on Old Man's River, where Fort McLeod now stands. A party of seven men started to war toward the Cypress Hills. Heavy Collar was the leader. They went around the Cypress Mountains, but found no enemies and started back toward their camp. On their homeward way, Heavy Collar used to take the lead. He would go out far ahead on the high hills, and look over the country, acting as scout for the party. At length they came to the south branch of the Saskatchewan River, above Seven Persons' Creek. In those days there were many war parties about, and this party travelled concealed as much as possible in the coulées and low places.

As they were following up the river, they saw at a distance three old bulls lying down close to a cut bank. Heavy Collar left his party, and went out to kill one of these bulls, and when he had come close to them, he shot one and killed it right there. He cut it up, and, as he was hungry, he went down into a ravine below him, to roast a piece of meat; for he had left his party a long way behind, and night was now coming on. As he was roasting the meat, he thought,—for he was very tired,—"It is a pity I did not bring one of my young men with me. He could go up on that hill and get some hair from that bull's head, and I could wipe out my gun." While he sat there thinking this, and talking to himself, a bunch of this hair came over him through the air, and fell on the ground right in front of him. When this happened, it frightened him a little; for he thought that perhaps some of his enemies were close by, and had thrown the bunch of hair at him. After a little while, he took the hair, and cleaned his gun and loaded it, and then sat and watched for a time. He was uneasy, and at length decided that he would go on further up the river, to see what he could discover. He went on, up the stream, until he came to the mouth of the St. Mary's River. It was now very late in the night, and he was very tired, so he crept into a large bunch of rye-grass to hide and sleep for the night.

The summer before this, the Blackfeet (*Sik-si-kau*) had been camped on this bottom, and a woman had been killed in this same patch of rye-grass where Heavy Collar had lain down to rest. He did not know this, but still he seemed to be troubled that night. He could not sleep. He could always hear something, but what it was he could not make out. He tried to go to sleep, but as soon as he dozed off he kept thinking he heard something in the distance. He spent the night there, and in the morning when it became light, there he saw right beside him the skeleton of the woman who had been killed the summer before.

That morning he went on, following up the stream to Belly River. All day long as he was travelling, he kept thinking about his having slept by this woman's bones. It troubled him. He could not forget it. At the same time he was very tired, because he had walked so far and had slept so little. As night came on, he crossed over to an island, and determined to camp for the night. At the upper end of the island was a large tree that had drifted down and lodged, and in a fork of this tree he built his fire, and got in a crotch of one of the forks, and sat with his back to the fire, warming himself, but all the time he was thinking about the woman he had slept beside the night before. As he sat there, all at once he heard over beyond the tree, on the other side of the fire, a sound as if something were being dragged toward him along the ground. It sounded as if a piece of a lodge were being dragged over the grass. It came closer and closer.

Heavy Collar was scared. He was afraid to turn his head and look back to see what it was that was coming. He heard the noise come up to the tree in which his fire was built, and then it stopped, and all at once he heard some one whistling a tune. He turned around and looked toward the sound, and there, sitting on the other fork of the tree, right opposite to him, was the pile of bones by which he had slept, only now all together in the shape of a skeleton. This ghost had on it a lodge covering. The string, which is tied to the pole, was fastened about the ghost's neck; the wings of the lodge stood out on either side of its head, and behind it the lodge could be seen, stretched out and fading away into the darkness. The ghost sat on the old dead limb and whistled its tune, and as it whistled, it swung its legs in time to the tune.

When Heavy Collar saw this, his heart almost melted away. At length he mustered up courage, and said: "Oh ghost, go away, and do not trouble me. I am very tired; I want to rest." The ghost paid no attention to him, but kept on whistling, swinging its legs in time to the tune. Four times he prayed to her, saying: "Oh ghost, take pity on me! Go away and leave me alone. I am tired; I want to rest." The more he prayed, the more the ghost whistled and seemed pleased, swinging her legs, and turning her head from side to side, sometimes looking down at him, and sometimes up at the stars, and all the time whistling.

When he saw that she took no notice of what he said, Heavy Collar got angry at heart, and said, "Well, ghost, you do not listen to my prayers, and I shall have to shoot you to drive you away." With that he seized his gun, and throwing it to his shoulder, shot right at the ghost. When he shot at her, she fell over backward into the darkness, screaming out: "Oh Heavy Collar, you have shot me, you have killed me! You dog, Heavy Collar! there is no place on this earth where you can go that I will not find you; no place where you can hide that I will not come."

As she fell back and said this, Heavy Collar sprang to his feet, and ran away as fast as he could. She called after him: "I have been killed once, and now you are trying to kill me again. Oh Heavy Collar!" As he ran away, he could still hear her angry words following him, until at last they died away in the distance. He ran all night long, and whenever he stopped to breathe and listen, he seemed to hear in the distance the echoes of her voice. All he could hear was, "Oh Heavy Collar!" and then he would rush away again. He ran until he was all tired out, and by this time it was daylight. He was now quite a long way below Fort McLeod. He was very sleepy, but dared not lie down, for he remembered that the ghost had said that she would follow him. He kept walking on for some time, and then sat down to rest, and at once feel asleep.

Before he had left his party, Heavy Collar had said to his young men: "Now remember, if any one of us should get separated from the party, let him always travel to the Belly River Buttes. There will be our meeting-place." When their leader did not return to them, the party started across the country and went toward the Belly River Buttes. Heavy Collar had followed the river up, and had gone a long distance out of his way; and when he awoke from his sleep, he too started straight for the Belly River Buttes, as he had said he would.

When his party reached the Buttes, one of them went up on top of the hill to watch. After a time, as he looked down the river, he saw two persons coming, and as they came nearer, he saw that one of them was Heavy Collar, and by his side was a woman. The watcher called up the rest of the party, and said to them: "Here comes our chief. He has had luck. He is bringing a woman with him. If he brings her into camp, we will take her away from him." And they all laughed. They supposed that he had captured her. They went down to the camp, and sat about the fire, looking at the two people coming, and laughing among themselves at the idea of their chief bringing in a woman. When the two persons had come close, they could see that Heavy Collar was walking fast, and the woman would walk by his side a little way, trying to keep up, and then would fall behind, and then trot along to catch up to him again. Just before the pair reached camp there was a deep ravine that they had to cross. They went down into this side by side, and then Heavy Collar came up out of it alone, and came on into the camp.

When he got there, all the young men began to laugh at him and to call out, "Heavy Collar, where is your woman?" He looked at them for a moment, and then said: "Why, I have no woman. I do not understand what you are talking about." One of them said: "Oh, he has hidden her in that ravine. He was afraid to bring her into camp." Another said, "Where did you capture her, and what tribe does she belong to?" Heavy Collar looked from one to another, and said: "I think you are all crazy. I have taken no woman. What do you mean?" The young man said: "Why, that woman that you had with you just now: where did you get her, and where did you leave her? Is she down in the coulée? We all saw her, and it is no use to deny that she was with you. Come now, where is she?" When they said this, Heavy Collar's heart grew very heavy, for he knew that it must have been the ghost woman; and he told them the story. Some of the young men could not believe this, and they ran down to the ravine, where they had last seen the woman. There they saw in the soft dirt the tracks made by Heavy Collar, when he went down into the ravine, but there were no other tracks near his, where they had seen the woman walking. When they found that it was a ghost that had come along with Heavy Collar, they resolved to go back to their main camp. The party had been out so long that their moccasins were all worn out, and some of them were footsore, so that they could not travel fast, but at last they came to the cut banks, and there found their camp—seven lodges.

That night, after they had reached camp, they were inviting each other to feasts. It was getting pretty late in the night, and the moon was shining brightly, when one of the Bloods called out for Heavy Collar to come and eat with him. Heavy Collar shouted, "Yes, I will be there pretty soon." He got up and went out of the lodge, and went a little way from it, and sat down. While he was sitting there, a big bear walked out of the brush close to him. Heavy Collar felt around him for a stone to throw at the bear, so as to scare it away, for he thought it had not seen him. As he was feeling about, his hand came upon a piece of bone, and he threw this over at the bear, and hit it. Then the bear spoke, and said: "Well, well, well, Heavy Collar; you have killed me once, and now here you are hitting me. Where is there a place in this world where you can hide from me?

137

I will find you, I don't care where you may go." When Heavy Collar heard this, he knew it was the ghost woman, and he jumped up and ran toward his lodge, calling out, "Run, run! a ghost bear is upon us!"

All the people in the camp ran to his lodge, so that it was crowded full of people. There was a big fire in the lodge, and the wind was blowing hard from the west. Men, women, and children were huddled together in the lodge, and were very much afraid of the ghost. They could hear her walking toward the lodge grumbling, and saying: "I will kill all these dogs. Not one of them shall get away." The sounds kept coming closer and closer, until they were right at the lodge door. Then she said, "I will smoke you to death." And as she said this, she moved the poles, so that the wings of the lodge turned toward the west, and the wind could blow in freely through the smoke hole. All this time she was threatening terrible things against them. The lodge began to get full of smoke, and the children were crying, and all were in great distress—almost suffocating. So they said, "Let us lift one man up here inside, and let him try to fix the ears, so that the lodge will get clear of smoke." They raised a man up, and he was standing on the shoulders of the others, and, blinded and half strangled by the smoke, was trying to turn the wings. While he was doing this, the ghost suddenly hit the lodge a blow, and said, "*Un!*" and this scared the people who were holding the man, and they jumped and let him go, and he fell down. Then the people were in despair, and said, "It is no use; she is resolved to smoke us to death." All the time the smoke was getting thicker in the lodge.

Heavy Collar said: "Is it possible that she can destroy us? Is there no one here who has some strong dream power that can overcome this ghost?"

His mother said: "I will try to do something. I am older than any of you, and I will see what I can do." So she got down her medicine bundle and painted herself, and got out a pipe and filled it and lighted it, and stuck the stem out through the lodge door, and sat there and began to pray to the ghost woman. She said: "Oh ghost, take pity on us, and go away. We have never wronged you, but you are troubling us and frightening our children. Accept what I offer you, and leave us alone."

A voice came from behind the lodge and said: "No, no, no; you dogs, I will not listen to you. Every one of you must die."

The old woman repeated her prayer: "Ghost, take pity on us. Accept this smoke and go away."

Then the ghost said: "How can you expect me to smoke, when I am way back here? Bring that pipe out here. I have no long bill to reach round the lodge." So the old woman went out of the lodge door, and reached out the stem of the pipe as far as she could reach around toward the back of the lodge. The ghost said: "No, I do not wish to go around there to where you have that pipe. If you want me to smoke it, you must bring it here." The old woman went around the lodge toward her, and the ghost woman began to back away, and said, "No, I do not smoke that kind of a pipe." And when the ghost started away, the old woman followed her, and she could not help herself.

She called out, "Oh my children, the ghost is carrying me off!" Heavy Collar rushed out, and called to the others, "Come, and help me take my mother from the ghost." He grasped his mother about the waist and held her, and another man took him by the waist, and another him, until they were all strung out, one behind the other, and all following the old woman, who was following the ghost woman, who was walking away.

All at once the old woman let go of the pipe, and fell over dead. The ghost disappeared, and they were troubled no more by the ghost woman.

SCARFACE

ORIGIN OF THE MEDICINE LODGE

I

In the earliest times there was no war. All the tribes were at peace. In those days there was a man who had a daughter, a very beautiful girl. Many young men wanted to marry her, but every time she was asked, she only shook her head and said she did not want a husband.

"How is this?" asked her father. "Some of these young men are rich, handsome, and brave."

"Why should I marry?" replied the girl. "I have a rich father and mother. Our lodge is good. The parfleches are never empty. There are plenty of tanned robes and soft furs for winter. Why worry me, then?"

The Raven Bearers held a dance; they all dressed carefully and wore their ornaments, and each one tried to dance the best. Afterwards some of them asked for this girl, but still she said no. Then the Bulls, the Kit-foxes, and others of the *I-kun-uh'-kah-tsi* held their dances, and all those who were rich, many great warriors, asked this man for his daughter, but to every one of them she said no. Then her father was angry, and said: "Why, now, this way? All the best men have asked for you, and still you say no. I believe you have a secret lover."

"Ah!" said her mother. "What shame for us should a child be born and our daughter still unmarried!" "Father! mother!" replied the girl, "pity me. I have no secret lover, but now hear the truth. That Above Person, the Sun, told me, 'Do not marry any of those men, for you are mine; thus you shall be happy, and live to great age'; and again he said, 'Take heed. You must not marry. You are mine.'"

"Ah!" replied her father. "It must always be as he says." And they talked no more about it.

There was a poor young man, very poor. His father, mother, all his relations, had gone to the Sand Hills. He had no lodge, no wife to tan his robes or sew his moccasins. He stopped in one lodge to-day, and to-morrow he ate and slept in another; thus he lived. He was a good-looking young man, except that on his cheek he had a scar, and his clothes were always old and poor.

After those dances some of the young men met this poor Scarface, and they laughed at him, and said: "Why don't you ask that girl to marry you? You are so rich and handsome!" Scarface did not laugh; he replied: "Ah! I will do as you say. I will go and ask her." All the young men thought this was funny. They laughed a great deal. But Scarface went down by the river. He waited by the river, where the women came to get water, and by and by the girl came along. "Girl," he said, "wait. I want to speak with you. Not as a designing person do I ask you, but openly where the Sun looks down, and all may see."

"Speak then," said the girl.

"I have seen the days," continued the young man. "You have refused those who are young, and rich, and brave. Now, to-day, they laughed and said to me, 'Why do you not ask her?' I am poor, very poor. I have no lodge, no food, no clothes, no robes and warm furs. I have no relations; all have gone to the Sand Hills; yet, now, to-day, I ask you, take pity, be my wife."

The girl hid her face in her robe and brushed the ground with the point of her moccasin, back and forth, back and forth; for she was thinking. After a time she said: "True. I have refused all those rich young men, yet now the poor one asks me, and I am glad. I will be your wife, and my people will be happy. You are poor, but it does not matter. My father will give you dogs. My mother will make us a lodge. My people will give us robes and furs. You will be poor no longer."

Then the young man was happy, and he started to kiss her, but she held him back, and said: "Wait! The Sun has spoken to me. He says I may not marry; that I belong to him. He says if I listen to him, I shall live to great age. But now I say: Go to the Sun. Tell him, 'She whom you spoke with heeds your words. She has never done wrong, but now she wants to marry. I want her for my wife.' Ask him to take that scar from your face. That will be his sign. I will know he is pleased. But if he refuses, or if you fail to find his lodge, then do not return to me."

"Oh!" cried the young man, "at first your words were good. I was glad. But now it is dark. My heart is dead. Where is that far-off lodge? where the trail, which no one yet has travelled?"

"Take courage, take courage!" said the girl; and she went to her lodge.

II

Scarface was very sad. He sat down and covered his head with his robe and tried to think what to do. After a while he got up, and went to an old woman who had been kind to him. "Pity me," he said. "I am very poor. I am going away now on a long journey. Make me some moccasins."

"Where are you going?" asked the old woman. "There is no war; we are very peaceful here."

"I do not know where I shall go," replied Scarface. "I am in trouble, but I cannot tell you now what it is."

So the old woman made him some moccasins, seven pairs, with parfleche soles, and also she gave him a sack of food,—pemmican of berries, pounded meat, and dried back fat; for this old woman had a good heart. She liked the young man.

All alone, and with a sad heart, he climbed the bluffs and stopped to take a last look at the camp. He wondered if he would ever see his sweetheart and the people again. "*Hai'-yu!* Pity me, O Sun," he prayed, and turning, he started to find the trail.

For many days he travelled on, over great prairies, along timbered rivers and among the mountains, and every day his sack of food grew lighter; but he saved it as much as he could, and ate berries, and roots, and sometimes he killed an animal of some kind. One night he stopped by the home of a wolf. "*Hai-yah!*" said that one; "what is my brother doing so far from home?"

"Ah!" replied Scarface, "I seek the place where the Sun lives; I am sent to speak with him."

"I have travelled far," said the wolf. "I know all the prairies, the valleys, and the mountains, but I have never seen the Sun's home. Wait; I know one who is very wise. Ask the bear. He may tell you."

The next day the man travelled on again, stopping now and then to pick a few berries, and when night came he arrived at the bear's lodge.

"Where is your home?" asked the bear. "Why are you travelling alone, my brother?"

"Help me! Pity me!" replied the young man; "because of her words I seek the Sun. I go to ask him for her."

"I know not where he stops," replied the bear. "I have travelled by many rivers, and I know the mountains, yet I have never seen his lodge. There is some one beyond, that striped-face, who is very smart. Go and ask him."

The badger was in his hole. Stooping over, the young man shouted: "Oh, cunning striped-face! Oh, generous animal! I wish to speak with you."

"What do you want?" said the badger, poking his head out of the hole.

"I want to find the Sun's home," replied Scarface. "I want to speak with him."

"I do not know where he lives," replied the badger. "I never travel very far. Over there in the timber is a wolverine. He is always travelling around, and is of much knowledge. Maybe he can tell you."

Then Scarface went to the woods and looked all around for the wolverine, but could not find him. So he sat down to rest. "*Hai'-yu! Hai'-yu!*" he cried. "Wolverine, take pity on me. My food is gone, my moccasins worn out. Now I must die."

"What is it, my brother?" he heard, and looking around, he saw the animal sitting near.

"She whom I would marry," said Scarface, "belongs to the Sun; I am trying to find where he lives, to ask him for her."

"Ah!" said the wolverine. "I know where he lives. Wait; it is nearly night. To-morrow I will show you the trail to the big water. He lives on the other side of it."

Early in the morning, the wolverine showed him the trail, and Scarface followed it until he came to the water's edge. He looked out over it, and his heart almost stopped. Never before had any one seen

143

such a big water. The other side could not be seen, and there was no end to it. Scarface sat down on the shore. His food was all gone, his moccasins worn out. His heart was sick. "I cannot cross this big water," he said. "I cannot return to the people. Here, by this water, I shall die."

Not so. His Helpers were there. Two swans came swimming up to the shore. "Why have you come here?" they asked him. "What are you doing? It is very far to the place where your people live."

"I am here," replied Scarface, "to die. Far away, in my country, is a beautiful girl. I want to marry her, but she belongs to the Sun. So I started to find him and ask for her. I have travelled many days. My food is gone. I cannot go back. I cannot cross this big water, so I am going to die."

"No," said the swans; "it shall not be so. Across this water is the home of that Above Person. Get on our backs, and we will take you there."

Scarface quickly arose. He felt strong again. He waded out into the water and lay down on the swans' backs, and they started off. Very deep and black is that fearful water. Strange people live there, mighty animals which often seize and drown a person. The swans carried him safely, and took him to the other side. Here was a broad hard trail leading back from the water's edge.

"*Kyi*," said the swans. "You are now close to the Sun's lodge. Follow that trail, and you will soon see it."

III

Scarface started up the trail, and pretty soon he came to some beautiful things, lying in it. There was a war shirt, a shield, and a bow and arrows. He had never seen such pretty weapons; but he did not touch them. He walked carefully around them, and travelled on. A little way further on, he met a young man, the handsomest person he had ever seen. His hair was very long, and he wore clothing made of strange skins. His moccasins were sewn with bright colored feathers. The young man said to him, "Did you see some weapons lying on the trail?"

"Yes," replied Scarface; "I saw them."

"But did you not touch them?" asked the young man.

"No; I thought some one had left them there, so I did not take them."

"You are not a thief," said the young man. "What is your name?"

"Scarface."

"Where are you going?"

"To the Sun."

"My name," said the young man, "is A-pi-su'-ahts. The Sun is my father; come, I will take you to our lodge. My father is not now at home, but he will come in at night."

Soon they came to the lodge. It was very large and handsome; strange medicine animals were painted on it. Behind, on a tripod, were strange weapons and beautiful clothes—the Sun's. Scarface was ashamed to go in, but Morning Star said, "Do not be afraid, my friend; we are glad you have come."

They entered. One person was sitting there, Ko-ko-mik'-e-is, the Sun's wife, Morning Star's mother. She spoke to Scarface kindly, and gave him something to eat. "Why have you come so far from your people?" she asked.

Then Scarface told her about the beautiful girl he wanted to marry. "She belongs to the Sun," he said. "I have come to ask him for her."

When it was time for the Sun to come home, the Moon hid Scarface under a pile of robes. As soon as the Sun got to the doorway, he stopped, and said, "I smell a person."

"Yes, father," said Morning Star; "a good young man has come to see you. I know he is good, for he found some of my things on the trail and did not touch them."

Then Scarface came out from under the robes, and the Sun entered and sat down. "I am glad you have come to our lodge," he said. "Stay with us as long as you think best. My son is lonesome sometimes; be his friend."

The next day the Moon called Scarface out of the lodge, and said to him: "Go with Morning Star where you please, but never hunt near that big water; do not let him go there. It is the home of great birds which have long sharp bills; they kill people. I have had many sons, but these birds have killed them all. Morning Star is the only one left."

So Scarface stayed there a long time and hunted with Morning Star. One day they came near the water, and saw the big birds.

"Come," said Morning Star; "let us go and kill those birds."

"No, no!" replied Scarface; "we must not go there. Those are very terrible birds; they will kill us."

Morning Star would not listen. He ran towards the water, and Scarface followed. He knew that he must kill the birds and save the boy. If not, the Sun would be angry and might kill him. He ran ahead and met the birds, which were coming towards him to fight, and killed every one of them with his spear: not one was left. Then the young men cut off their heads, and carried them home. Morning Star's mother was glad when they told her what they had done, and showed her the birds' heads. She cried, and called Scarface "my son." When the Sun came home at night, she told him about it, and he too was glad. "My son," he said to Scarface, "I will not forget what you have this day done for me. Tell me now, what can I do for you?"

"*Hai'-yu*," replied Scarface. "*Hai'-yu*, pity me. I am here to ask you for that girl. I want to marry her. I asked her, and she was glad; but she says you own her, that you told her not to marry."

"What you say is true," said the Sun. "I have watched the days, so I know it. Now, then, I give her to you; she is yours. I am glad she has been wise. I know she has never done wrong. The Sun pities good women. They shall live a long time. So shall their husbands and children. Now you will soon go home. Let me tell you something. Be wise and listen: I am the only chief. Everything is mine. I made the earth, the mountains, prairies, rivers, and forests. I made the people and all the animals. This is why I say I alone am the chief. I can never die. True, the winter makes me old and weak, but every summer I grow young again."

Then said the Sun: "What one of all animals is smartest? The raven is, for he always finds food. He is never hungry. Which one of all the animals is most *Nat-o'-ye*? The buffalo is. Of all animals, I like him best. He is for the people. He is your food and your shelter. What part of his body is sacred? The tongue is. That is mine. What else is

The Blackfeet

sacred? Berries are. They are mine too. Come with me and see the
world." He took Scarface to the edge of the sky, and they looked
down and saw it. It is round and flat, and all around the edge is
the jumping-off place [or walls straight down]. Then said the Sun:
"When any man is sick or in danger, his wife may promise to build me
a lodge, if he recovers. If the woman is pure and true, then I will be
pleased and help the man. But if she is bad, if she lies, then I will be
angry. You shall build the lodge like the world, round, with walls, but
first you must build a sweat house of a hundred sticks. It shall be like
the sky [a hemisphere], and half of it shall be painted red. That is
me. The other half you will paint black. That is the night."

Further said the Sun: "Which is the best, the heart or the brain?
The brain is. The heart often lies, the brain never." Then he told
Scarface everything about making the Medicine Lodge, and when he
had finished, he rubbed a powerful medicine on his face, and the scar
disappeared. Then he gave him two raven feathers saying: "These are
the sign for the girl, that I give her to you. They must always be
worn by the husband of the woman who builds a Medicine Lodge."

The young man was now ready to return home. Morning Star and
the Sun gave him many beautiful presents. The Moon cried and
kissed him, and called him "my son." Then the Sun showed him the
short trail. It was the Wolf Road (Milky Way). He followed it, and
soon reached the ground.

IV

It was a very hot day. All the lodge skins were raised, and the
people sat in the shade. There was a chief, a very generous man, and
all day long people kept coming to his lodge to feast and smoke with
him. Early in the morning this chief saw a person sitting out on a
butte near by, close wrapped in his robe. The chief's friends came and
went, the sun reached the middle, and passed on, down towards the
mountains. Still this person did not move. When it was almost night,
the chief said: "Why does that person sit there so long? The heat has
been strong, but he has never eaten nor drunk. He may be a stranger;
go and ask him in."

So some young men went up to him, and said: "Why do you sit

147

here in the great heat all day? Come to the shade of the lodges. The chief asks you to feast with him."

Then the person arose and threw off his robe, and they were surprised. He wore beautiful clothes. His bow, shield, and other weapons were of strange make. But they knew his face, although the scar was gone, and they ran ahead, shouting, "The scarface poor young man has come. He is poor no longer. The scar on his face is gone."

All the people rushed out to see him. "Where have you been?" they asked. "Where did you get all these pretty things?" He did not answer. There in the crowd stood that young woman; and taking the two raven feathers from his head, he gave them to her, and said: "The trail was very long, and I nearly died, but by those Helpers, I found his lodge. He is glad. He sends these feathers to you. They are the sign."

Great was her gladness then. They were married, and made the first Medicine Lodge, as the Sun had said. The Sun was glad. He gave them great age. They were never sick. When they were very old, one morning, their children said: "Awake! Rise and eat." They did not move. In the night, in sleep, without pain, their shadows had departed for the Sand Hills.

THE GHOSTS' BUFFALO

A LONG time ago there were four Blackfeet, who went to war against the Crees. They travelled a long way, and at last their horses gave out, and they started back toward their homes. As they were going along they came to the Sand Hills; and while they were passing through them, they saw in the sand a fresh travois trail, where people had been travelling.

One of the men said: "Let us follow this trail until we come up with some of our people. Then we will camp with them." They followed the trail for a long way, and at length one of the Blackfeet, named E-kūs'-kini,—a very powerful person,—said to the others: "Why follow this longer? It is just nothing." The others said: "Not so. These are our people. We will go on and camp with them." They went on, and toward evening, one of them found a stone maul and a dog travois. He said: "Look at these things. I know this maul and this travois. They belonged to my mother, who died. They were buried with her. This is strange." He took the things. When night overtook the men, they camped.

Early in the morning, they heard, all about them, sounds as if a camp of people were there. They heard a young man shouting a sort of war cry, as young men do; women chopping wood; a man calling for a feast, asking people to come to his lodge and smoke,—all the different sounds of the camp. They looked about, but could see nothing; and then they were frightened and covered their heads with their robes. At last they took courage, and started to look around and see what they could learn about this strange thing. For a little while they saw nothing, but pretty soon one of them said: "Look over there. See that pis'kun. Let us go over and look at it." As they were going toward it, one of them picked up a stone pointed arrow. He said: "Look at this. It belonged to my father. This is his place." They started to go on toward the pis'kun, but suddenly they could see no pis'kun. It had disappeared all at once.

A little while after this, one of them spoke up, and said: "Look over there. There is my father running buffalo. There! he has killed. Let us go over to him." They all looked where this man pointed, and they could see a person on a white horse, running buffalo. While they were looking, the person killed the buffalo, and got off his horse to butcher it. They started to go over toward him, and saw him at work butchering, and saw him turn the buffalo over on its back; but before they got to the place where he was, the person got on his horse and rode off, and when they got to where he had been skinning the buffalo, they saw lying on the ground only a dead mouse. There was no buffalo there. By the side of the mouse was a buffalo chip, and lying on it was an arrow painted red. The man said: "That is my father's arrow. That is the way he painted them." He took it up in his hands; and when he held it in his hands, he saw that it was not an arrow but a blade of spear grass. Then he laid it down, and it was an arrow again.

Another Blackfoot found a buffalo rock, I-nis'-kim.

Some time after this, the men got home to their camp. The man who had taken the maul and the dog travois, when he got home and smelled the smoke from the fire, died, and so did his horse. It seems that the shadow of the person who owned the things was angry at him and followed him home. Two others of these Blackfeet have since died, killed in war; but E-kūs'-kini is alive yet. He took a stone and an iron arrow point that had belonged to his father, and always carried them about with him. That is why he has lived so long. The man who took the stone arrow point found near the pis'kun, which had belonged to his father, took it home with him. This was his medicine. After that he was badly wounded in two fights, but he was not killed; he got well.

The one who took the buffalo rock, I-nis'-kim, it afterward made strong to call the buffalo into the pis'kun. He would take the rock and put it in his lodge close to the fire, where he could look at it, and would pray over it and make medicine. Sometimes he would ask for a hundred buffalo to jump into the pis'kun, and the next day a hundred would jump in. He was powerful.

OLD MAN STORIES

UNDER the name Na'pi, Old Man, have been confused two wholly different persons talked of by the Blackfeet. The Sun, the creator of the universe, giver of light, heat, and life, and reverenced by every one, is often called Old Man, but there is another personality who bears the same name, but who is very different in his character. This last Na'pi is a mixture of wisdom and foolishness; he is malicious, selfish, childish, and weak. He delights in tormenting people. Yet the mean things he does are so foolish that he is constantly getting himself into scrapes, and is often obliged to ask the animals to help him out of his troubles. His bad deeds almost always bring their own punishment.

Interpreters commonly translate this word Na'pi as Old Man, but it is also the term for white man; and the Cheyenne and Arapahoe tribes tell just such stories about a similar person whom they also call "white man." Tribes of Dakota stock tell of a similar person whom they call "the spider."

The stories about this Old Man are told by the Blackfeet for entertainment rather than with any serious purpose, and when that part of the story is reached where Old Man is in some difficulty which he cannot get out of, the man who is telling the story, and those who are listening to it, laugh delightedly.

Some stories of this kind are these:

THE RACE

ONCE Old Man was travelling around, when he heard some very queer singing. He had never heard anything like this before, and looked all around to see who it was. At last he saw it was the cottontail rabbits, singing and making medicine. They had built a fire, and got a lot of hot ashes, and they would lie down in these ashes and sing while one covered them up. They would stay there only a short time though, for the ashes were very hot.

"Little Brothers," said Old Man, "that is very wonderful, how you lie in those hot ashes and coals without burning. I wish you would teach me how to do it."

"Come on, Old Man," said the rabbits, "we will show you how to do it. You must sing our song, and only stay in the ashes a short time." So Old Man began to sing, and he lay down, and they covered him with coals and ashes, and they did not burn him at all.

"That is very nice," he said. "You have powerful medicine. Now I want to know it all, so you lie down and let me cover you up."

So the rabbits all lay down in the ashes, and Old Man covered them up, and then he put the whole fire over them. One old rabbit got out, and Old Man was about to put her back when she said, "Pity me, my children are about to be born."

"All right," replied Old Man. "I will let you go, so there will be some more rabbits; but I will roast these nicely and have a feast." And he put more wood on the fire. When the rabbits were cooked, he cut some red willow brush and laid them on it to cool. The grease soaked into these branches, so, even to-day if you hold red willow over a fire, you will see the grease on the bark. You can see, too, that ever since, the rabbits have a burnt place on their backs, where the one that got away was singed.

Old Man sat down, and was waiting for the rabbits to cool a little, when a coyote came along, limping very badly. "Pity me, Old Man," he said, "you have lots of cooked rabbits; give me one of them."

"Go away," exclaimed Old Man. "If you are too lazy to catch your food, I will not help you."

"My leg is broken," said the coyote. "I can't catch anything, and I am starving. Just give me half a rabbit."

"I don't care if you die," replied Old Man. "I worked hard to cook all these rabbits, and I will not give any away. But I will tell you what we will do. We will run a race to that butte, way out there, and if you beat me you can have a rabbit."

"All right," said the coyote. So they started. Old Man ran very fast, and the coyote limped along behind, but close to him, until they got near to the butte. Then the coyote turned round and ran back very fast, for he was not lame at all. It took Old Man a long time to go back, and just before he got to the fire, the coyote swallowed the last rabbit, and trotted off over the prairie.

THE ROCK

ONCE Old Man was travelling, and becoming tired he sat down on a rock to rest. After a while he started to go on, and because the sun was hot he threw his robe over the rock, saying: "Here, I give you my robe, because you are poor and have let me rest on you. Always keep it."

He had not gone very far, when it began to rain, and meeting a coyote he said: "Little brother, run back to that rock, and ask him to lend me his robe. We will cover ourselves with it and keep dry." So the coyote ran back to the rock, but returned without the robe. "Where is the robe?" asked Old Man. "*Sai-yah!*" replied the coyote. "The rock said you gave him the robe, and he was going to keep it."

Then Old Man was very angry, and went back to the rock and jerked the robe off it, saying: "I only wanted to borrow this robe until the rain was over, but now that you have acted so mean about it, I will keep it. You don't need a robe anyhow. You have been out in the rain and snow all your life, and it will not hurt you to live so always."

With the coyote he went off into a coulée, and sat down. The rain was falling, and they covered themselves with the robe and were very comfortable. Pretty soon they heard a loud noise, and Old Man told the coyote to go up on the hill and see what it was. Soon he came running back, saying, "Run! run! the big rock is coming"; and they both ran away as fast as they could. The coyote tried to crawl into a badger hole, but it was too small for him and he stuck fast, and before he could get out, the rock rolled over him and crushed his hind parts. Old Man was scared, and as he ran he threw off his robe and what clothes he could, so that he might run faster. The rock kept gaining on him all the time.

Not far off was a band of buffalo bulls, and Old Man cried out to them, saying, "Oh my brothers, help me, help me. Stop that rock." The bulls ran and tried to stop it, but it crushed their heads. Some deer and antelope tried to help Old Man, but they were killed, too. A lot of rattlesnakes formed themselves into a lariat, and tried to catch it; but those at the noose end were all cut to pieces. The rock was now close to Old Man, so close that it began to hit his heels; and he was about to give up, when he saw a flock of bull bats circling over his head. "Oh my little brothers," he cried, "help me. I am almost dead." Then the bull bats flew down, one after another, against the rock; and every time one of them hit it he chipped off a piece, and at last one hit it fair in the middle and broke it into two pieces.

Then Old Man was very glad. He went to where there was a nest of bull bats, and made the young ones' mouths very wide and pinched off their bills, to make them pretty and queer looking. That is the reason they look so to-day.

THE THEFT FROM THE SUN

ONCE Old Man was travelling around, when he came to the Sun's lodge, and the Sun asked him to stay a while. Old Man was very glad to do so.

One day the meat was all gone, and the Sun said, *"Kyi!* Old Man, what say you if we go and kill some deer?"

"You speak well," replied Old Man. "I like deer meat."

The Sun took down a bag and pulled out a beautiful pair of leggings. They were embroidered with porcupine quills and bright feathers. "These," said the Sun, "are my hunting leggings. They are great medicine. All I have to do is to put them on and walk around a patch of brush, when the leggings set it on fire and drive the deer out so that I can shoot them."

"Hai-yah!" exclaimed Old Man. "How wonderful!" He made up his mind he would have those leggings, if he had to steal them.

They went out to hunt, and the first patch of brush they came to, the Sun set on fire with his hunting leggings. A lot of white-tail deer ran out, and they each shot one.

That night, when they went to bed, the Sun pulled off his leggings and placed them to one side. Old Man saw where he put them, and in the middle of the night, when every one was asleep, he stole them and went off. He travelled a long time, until he had gone far and was very tired, and then, making a pillow of the leggings, lay down and slept. In the morning, he heard some one talking. The Sun was saying, "Old Man, why are my leggings under your head?" He looked around, and saw he was in the Sun's lodge, and thought he must have wandered around and got lost, and returned there. Again the Sun spoke and said, "What are you doing with my leggings?" "Oh," replied Old Man, "I couldn't find anything for a pillow, so I just put these under my head."

Night came again, and again Old Man stole the leggings and ran off. This time he did not walk at all; he just kept running until pretty near morning, and then lay down and slept. You see what a fool he was. He did not know that the whole world is the Sun's lodge. He did not know that, no matter how far he ran, he could not get out of the Sun's sight. When morning came, he found himself still in the Sun's lodge. But this time the Sun said: "Old Man, since you like my leggings so much, I will give them to you. Keep them." Then Old Man was very glad and went away.

One day his food was all gone, so he put on the medicine leggings and set fire to a piece of brush. He was just going to kill some deer that were running out, when he saw that the fire was getting close to him. He ran away as fast as he could, but the fire gained on him and began to burn his legs. His leggings were all on fire. He came to a river and jumped in, and pulled off the leggings as soon as he could. They were burned to pieces.

Perhaps the Sun did this to him because he tried to steal the leggings.

THE FOX

ONE day Old Man went out hunting and took the fox with him. They hunted for several days, but killed nothing. It was nice warm weather in the late fall. After they had become very hungry, as they were going along one day, Old Man went up over a ridge and on the other side he saw four big buffalo bulls lying down; but there was no way by which they could get near them. He dodged back out of sight and told the fox what he had seen, and they thought for a long time, to see if there was no way by which these bulls might be killed.

At last Old Man said to the fox: "My little brother, I can think of only one way to get these bulls. This is my plan, if you agree to it. I will pluck all the fur off you except one tuft on the end of your tail. Then you go over the hill and walk up and down in sight of the bulls, and you will seem so funny to them that they will laugh themselves to death."

The fox did not like to do this, but he could think of nothing better, so he agreed to what Old Man proposed. Old Man plucked him perfectly bare, except the end of his tail, and the fox went over the ridge and walked up and down. When he had come close to the bulls, he played around and walked on his hind legs and went through all sorts of antics. When the bulls first saw him, they got up on their feet, and looked at him. They did not know what to make of him. Then they began to laugh, and the more they looked at him, the more they laughed, until at last one by one they fell down exhausted and died. Then Old Man came over the hill, and went down to the bulls, and began to butcher them. By this time it had grown a little colder.

"Ah, little brother," said Old Man to the fox, "you did splendidly. I do not wonder that the bulls laughed themselves to death. I nearly died myself as I watched you from the hill. You looked very funny." While he was saying this, he was working away skinning off the hides and getting the meat ready to carry to camp, all the time talking to the fox, who stood about, his back humped up and his teeth chattering with the cold. Now a wind sprang up from the north and a few snowflakes were flying in the air. It was growing colder and colder. Old Man kept on talking, and every now and then he would say something to the fox, who was sitting behind him perfectly still, with his jaw shoved out and his teeth shining.

At last Old Man had the bulls all skinned and the meat cut up, and as he rose up he said: "It is getting pretty cold, isn't it? Well, we do not care for the cold. We have got all our winter's meat, and we will have nothing to do but feast and dance and sing until spring." The fox made no answer. Then Old Man got angry, and called out: "Why don't you answer me? Don't you hear me talking to you?" The fox said nothing. Then Old Man was mad, and he said, "Can't you speak?" and stepped up to the fox and gave him a push with his foot, and the fox fell over. He was dead, frozen stiff with the cold.

THE CHEYENNES

GRINNELL MEETS THE CHEYENNES

My first meeting with the Cheyenne Indians was hostile, and after that, though often in the country of the Cheyennes, I never knew them until their wars were over.

My first visit to their camp was in 1890 when, at the invitation of my old schoolmate and friend, Lieut. Edward W. Casey, 22d Infantry, who had enlisted a troop of Cheyenne scouts, I visited him at Fort Keogh and made their acquaintance. Lieutenant Casey was killed in January, 1891, and his scouts were disbanded a little later.

From that time on, no year has passed without my seeing the Cheyennes in the North or in the South, or in both camps. I have been fortunate enough to have had, as interpreters in the North, William Rowland, who married into the tribe in the year 1850, and later his sons, James and Willis. In the South, Ben Clark helped me; and until his death in 1918 George Bent, an educated half-breed born at Bent's Old Fort in 1843, who lived his life with his people, was my friend and assistant. He was the son of Owl Woman and Col. William Bent, a man of excellent intelligence and of extraordinary memory.

After a few years' acquaintance, the Indians began to give me their confidence, and I have been able to some extent to penetrate into the secrets of their life. On the other hand, I am constantly impressed by the number of things about the Indians that I do not know.

In describing the life, the ways, and the beliefs of the Cheyennes, I have gone into details which may sometimes appear superfluous; but after all, if one is to understand the viewpoint of the Cheyennes, this seems necessary. These primitive people in certain ways live more in accordance with custom and form than we do, and a comprehension of the motives which govern their acts cannot be had without these details.

I have never been able to regard the Indian as a mere object for study—a museum specimen. A half-century spent in rubbing shoulders with them, during which I have had a share in almost every phase of their old-time life, forbids me to think of them except as acquaint-

159

ances, comrades, and friends. While their culture differs from ours in some respects, fundamentally they are like ourselves, except in so far as their environment has obliged them to adopt a mode of life and of reasoning that is not quite our own, and which, without experience, we do not readily understand.

It is impossible for me to acknowledge all the kindness that I have received during my long association with the Cheyennes. My Indian friends have always been cordial and helpful. To my interpreters, Ben Clark, George Bent, William Rowland and his sons, as well as to Mr. and Mrs. J. R. Eddy and to Mr. and Mrs. A. C. Stohr, I owe much.

THE CHEYENNES

THE Cheyennes are one of three groups of Indians of the Western plains belonging to the Algonquian family. They are recent immigrants to the region. According to the statement of Black Moccasin, who was long regarded as their most reliable historian—the man with the best memory—some of them reached the Missouri River about 1676, two hundred and four winters before 1880, when the statement was made. Before this they had lived for a time on the river bearing their name, which runs into the Red River of the North from the west, and on which one of their old village sites still exists. Earlier still they were in Minnesota. They have traditions of long journeyings before they reached there.

For a number of years after coming to the Missouri the Cheyennes lived on its banks, cultivating the ground, and occupying earth lodges not unlike those used up to recent times by the Rees and the Mandans. Gradually they drifted out on the plains, gave up their sedentary habits and began to move about over the prairie, dwelling in skin lodges and following the buffalo. As recently as 1850 they tilled the soil to some extent, and men have described to me their mothers' corn patches on the Little Missouri at about that date.

The people whom we know as Cheyennes are made up of two related tribes, Tsĭs tsĭs'tăs and Sūh'tāī. The latter have been absorbed by the former, and have left hardly any trace. They were the tribe known to early writers as Stā ĭ tăn', *i. e.*, Sūh'tāī hē' tan ē—a man of the Suhtai.

I have known many Cheyennes who remembered old people who were Suhtai—born in the separate Suhtai camp. They agree that the Suhtai language differed somewhat from the Cheyennes, "it sounded funny to them," and that the Suhtai had many customs of their own which later were laughed at, because unusual. In 1831, at the time when Bent's Fort was completed, the Suhtai still camped apart by themselves—were still a separate tribe.

The name Cheyenne is not in use by the tribe. They call themselves Tsĭs tsĭs' tăs, a word variously translated which Rev. R. Pettér, our authority on the Cheyenne language, believes to mean "similarly bred." If this is its meaning, it resembles so many other Indian tribal names which are explained to mean variously, "the people," "the real people," etc., and perhaps actually mean *the* people," *i. e.*, "the folks," "our folks," "us." Tsĭs tsĭs'tăs might also mean the cut or gashed people, and the tribal sign signifies cut or gashed, though often explained as referring to striped feathers sometimes, but by no means always, used in feathering the arrows. The word Cheyenne is frequently explained as coming from the French *chien* in allusion to the Dog Soldiers, but it is, in fact, a Sioux term Shā hĭ'ē la, or Sha hĭ'e na, people speaking language not understood.

The Sioux speak of those who talk intelligibly to them as "white talkers," and call those who speak a language not understood "red talkers." I'ā or ĭ'ē is to talk intelligibly. Iē'skā used as a verb means to speak fluently and intelligently. As a substantive the word means an interpreter. In speaking of one who talks their language the Dakotas use the verb Skā ē'ā to talk white. Of one whose language they cannot understand and who cannot understand them they say Shā ē'ā, to talk red; that is, unintelligibly. The name given by the Sioux to the Cheyennes, Shā hĭ'ē la, means red words, or red speech—speaking a foreign tongue.

Partly as a result of long association with the village tribes of the Missouri—Rees, Mandans, and Hidatsa—the Cheyennes have among them a strong infusion of foreign blood. A still greater mingling of alien blood comes from their warlike character, so pronounced during many years of the last century, which resulted in the capture from their enemies of great numbers of children of both sexes who in due course were adopted into the tribe, grew up as Cheyennes, and married and reared children. Old Cheyennes have told me that it is difficult to find any Cheyennes without a strain of foreign blood, and as I think over my acquaintances I can recall hardly any whose ancestry can be traced far back wholly in the Cheyenne tribe. In another book I have given a list of twenty-eight tribes from which captives had been taken by the Cheyennes.

When the Cheyennes first met the white people they were shy and timid, and endeavored to avoid the newcomers. Lewis and Clark speak of this, and old men among the Cheyennes say that they have always been told that in former times the chiefs advised that the white strangers be avoided. This may have some reference to the speech attributed to the Cheyenne Culture Hero, in which he prophesied a meeting with a people whose skins were white and whose ways were different, and predicted that misfortune to his people would follow their knowledge of these strangers.

The late Ben Clark, in the manuscript prepared at the request of General Sheridan, declared that the Cheyennes were called the Kite Indians, because perpetually on the move—always seen at a distance and fleeing.

Among the tribes of the plains the Cheyennes have had one ally on whose fidelity they could always depend. These were the Arapahoes, who for many generations have been associated with the Cheyennes on terms of the closest friendship, camping with them for long periods, uniting with them in their wars, or at other times being the medium through whom have come proposals for peace from hostile tribes.

The tradition as to when the Arapahoes joined the Cheyennes is vague enough, and we know little about it, though much has been written on the subject. A milder and more easy-going people than the Cheyennes, they yet fought side by side with them in many a stubborn battle. There is a large infusion of Arapaho blood in the Cheyenne tribe, for many Cheyenne men married Arapaho women. On the other hand, it is my impression that comparatively few Cheyenne women have married Arapaho men.

The Cheyennes

Historical knowledge of the Cheyennes begins with the accounts of Lewis and Clark, though many years earlier the French trappers and traders had penetrated their country, which was on the plains near the Black Hills, and especially on the upper courses of certain streams which flow out of those hills. I think it very possible that long before this the Cheyennes had been met by the Verendryes, and that they may have been the tribe which the *Verendrye Journal* terms *Gens de l'arc*. Perhaps this can never be shown, but the name *Gens du serpent*, given to their enemies by the people of the Bow, suggests the Cheyenne term Shĭ shĭ′ nĭ wĭ hē tăn ĭū, snake men, the name given by the Cheyennes to the Comanches, who, the Cheyennes declare, occupied that country at the time when they reached the neighborhood of the Black Hills. The Cheyenne name for the tribes called Snakes by the whites is Sŭs′sŏn ĭ.

Although the books constantly speak of the Cheyennes as at war with the Sioux, I do not find among them any tradition that they ever had serious quarrels with the plains people whom we know and speak of as Sioux. On the other hand, they were at bitter enmity with the northern Dakota or Assiniboines, and traditions of their wars with them run back a long way. Later enemies were the Kiowas, the Comanches, and the Crows, all of whom they gradually expelled from the country that they had invaded. The Cheyennes were long at war with the Pawnees and with the Shoshoni, and these hostilities endured up to the time when intertribal wars ceased.

Early in the nineteenth century they were at peace with the Kiowas and Comanches, and in the *Journal of Jacob Fowler* for November, 1821, are found references to Kiowa Comanches, Kiowa Apaches, Cheyennes and "Snakes" (Comanches?) travelling together in more or less amity. Cheyenne tradition speaks of the Kiowas as peaceable co-occupants with them of the Little Missouri country long after the Spaniards had come up there from the southwest to trade and before the Cheyennes had ever seen the French or English whites. The last great battle with the Kiowas, Comanches, and Apaches took place in 1838. Two years later a peace was made which has not since been broken.

The Cheyennes were long at war with the Utes. At the time of the first settlement of western Colorado, after gold had been discovered, miners had come into the country, and villages and towns had been established on the flanks of the mountains in that territory, war journeys by Cheyennes and Utes against each other were constantly taking place. The reports from officials of the Indian Service during the years 1862 to 1865 frequently complain of the trouble given to the settlers by the Cheyennes and Arapahoes in their war journeys against the Utes and by the Utes when they went against the Cheyennes.

Farther to the northward the Cheyennes had other enemies in the Crows, on whose territory they had begun to encroach after they had crossed the Missouri River and moved westward toward the mountains. Their battles with the Crows lasted at least seventy years, and perhaps longer, but were interrupted by a truce which perhaps endured from 1851 to 1854 or thereabouts.

With the Blackfeet, still farther to the north, the Cheyennes did not often come in contact, though occasionally they met, and when they met they fought.

The village tribes of the Missouri—Mandan, Arikara, and Hidatsa—were commonly on good terms with the Cheyennes. This is what we should expect from the fact that these were the first tribes that they met in friendship on the plains and since they lived with or near them for a long time. Still there were occasional quarrels even with these people. Maximilian tells of stories of battles with the Cheyennes that he heard from the Mandans, while the Cheyennes give accounts of fights that they had with the Arikaras.

On their way west, perhaps long before they reached the country of the Red River, the Cheyennes met the Assiniboines—the Ho hé. It is related that the two tribes came together when each was trying to surround a herd of buffalo. They quarrelled over this and came to blows. Old Assiniboines have told me that at this time the Cheyennes were armed only with clubs and with sharpened sticks, and this is precisely what the Cheyennes themselves say. The Assiniboines, however, had guns and killed a number of the Cheyennes and scalped them.

The sound of the guns and their dreadful power terrified the Cheyennes and they fled. As they had never before been attacked by enemies, the Cheyennes did not know what to make of the situation, but after a time one of them stood up and harangued the people and said: "Now we have fought with these people; they attacked us and have killed some of us. After this let us fight with all people we meet, and we shall become great men." So they began to fight all tribes wherever they met them and it did make great men of them. They came to be great warriors and took many prisoners.

However, there is a tradition of a time when the Cheyennes and their kindred, the Sūh'tāī, lived in the far northeast—long before the battles with the Ho hé—when those two tribes fought with one another. During their last great fight they discovered that they spoke a similar language and that they were related, and then made a peace which was never broken.

Not a few traditions are handed down of the battles of the Cheyennes and the Ho hé, in which the Cheyennes were always defeated. Some Cheyenne authorities include the Ojibwa among the Ho hé. It was the practise of the Ho hé to come at night to attack the Cheyenne camps. They carried horns made of the hollow stems of some plant, with which they signalled to each other, making a call like that of the buffalo in spring, so that, if the Cheyennes heard them approaching, they might suppose buffalo were coming and thus not be on the lookout for the enemy. They slew many Cheyennes.

An oft-told story explains how a dog saved a family from death by the Ho hé.

In those days a man, his wife, and well-grown son were camped apart from the tribe. They had a dog, whose puppies were in the lodge. One night the mother dog went out to look for food for the puppies, and returning to them after a time began to cry over them and lick them. The man saw what she was doing and wondered. He spoke to the dog and said: "Why do you do this? If you know that something bad is going to happen, tell me what it is. We do not wish to die. If we are in danger, help us, and we will save your puppies. Try in some way to help us."

After he had spoken thus to the dog, she went out of the lodge and was gone for some time, and then came back and stood in the lodge looking toward the door. The man's wife told him to take up the puppies. He put them in his robe on his back, and they all made ready to go out, but first the man made up a large fire in the lodge, so that any one who saw it would suppose the people were still there.

The dog left the lodge and they followed her, and she led them down to the river and straight across. After a time they heard guns sounding all around their camp, and they knew that the Ho hé were attacking the lodge with the fire burning in it. They went on to another camp where Cheyennes were living and told them that the Ho hé had attacked their lodge, so the Cheyennes moved away and all escaped. The story of how the dog saved her master has been told in the camp since that time.

For a long time the Cheyennes possessed no arms that they could use in fighting the Ho hé. They talk much about those dreadful days, and tell of the terror that they felt of these enemies, of the triumph when on rare occasions and through some accident they succeeded in killing one, of the care with which their camping-places were chosen to avoid attack, and of how finally, through the ready wit of an old woman, they succeeded in obtaining a few guns.

In those days, long before they had horses, they travelled from place to place, packing some of their property on dogs and carrying the rest on their backs. Once the people were camped in their earth lodges and were chasing buffalo on foot. They had hunted for three or four days and now had abundant meat. They left this camp and moved a short distance down the stream. One old woman, however, who was busy making grease, remained at the old camp. She said: "I shall stay here for a time, because I wish to finish pounding up my bones, and boiling them, and skimming off the grease."

The night was dark and the old woman was alone in the camp. She was still boiling her bones and skimming the grease from the pot. She had made a torch and tied it to a stick and thrust the stick down her back, between her dress and her body, so that the torch stood above her head, and threw light on the pot. She was blowing the grease off the water when a person entered the lodge and sat down by the head of her bed. She did not look up, but kept blowing the grease from the water. Then, one after another, walked into the lodge about fifty great, tall Assiniboines.

There was plenty of food hanging in the lodge, and at one side was some pounded meat. The Assiniboines said to each other: "We will get something to eat first, and then we will kill her." They made signs to her that they were hungry, and to each one she gave some pounded meat, and then began to roast some fresh meat.

The old woman was badly frightened. She kept saying to herself: "They will surely kill me. What can I do to save myself?" Hanging up in the lodge was a great sheet of back fat—tallow—and the old woman took it down to roast it so that the visitors might eat it with their meat. She put it on a stick and hung it over the fire until it had begun to cook and the hot grease was dropping from it. Then, lifting it as if to turn it, she took it from the stick and gave it a mighty swing around her head, throwing the hot fat in the faces of the Assiniboines sitting around the circle, and all jumped back burned. Then she rushed out of the lodge.

Not far in front of the lodge was a high cut bank above the river, with rocks below. The Assiniboines, furious with their burns, rushed after the old woman, following the torch that she carried over her head. She ran fast toward the bank and when close to it threw her torch ahead of her and turned sharp to one side, running along the edge of the bank. The Assiniboines followed the blazing light, and all ran over the bank and, falling on the rocks below, were hurt or killed. The old woman hurried away after the Cheyenne camp and overtook it. She told of the Assiniboines who had come to her lodge, and of what she had done, saying: "I could hear them fall over the cliff; I think all fell over." The next morning the men returned to the old camp, and here under the bank they found the fifty Ho hé, some of them dead, some with broken backs, some with broken legs, and some with broken arms, creeping about. They killed them all and secured their guns.

The Cheyennes were driven by the Assiniboines in a southwesterly direction until they reached the Missouri River, not far from where Fort Pierre now is. Here for a long time they remained, living with the Mandans and the Arikaras in earth lodges, raising their crops, and making journeys away from the village to secure game or to catch fish; to gather the eggs and young of water-birds in summer, or to collect skunks in the autumn when they were fat.

Later they wandered out on the plains after buffalo.

VILLAGE LIFE

INCIDENTS OF A DAY

IF in imagination we can carry ourselves back sixty or seventy years, to the time when the Indians wandered free and before their lives had been greatly modified by the influence of civilization, we may picture some of the features of the daily life of the Cheyennes in the days of the buffalo.

The camp was pitched in a broad bottom, and the lodges stood in a great circle whose diameter was half a mile or more—three arrow flights from a strong bow, and as far as a man can throw an arrow by hand. It was summer, and most of the women had renewed their lodges, so that they stood white in the dim light of the early morning. The sun had not yet risen, but already the fires were kindled, and from the lodges gray columns of smoke were rising through the still air. From all quarters of the camp women were hurrying down to the stream, or coming from it, carrying to the lodges water for the morning use; for the Cheyennes did not use water that had stood all night —they called it dead, and said that they wished to drink living water. As the light grew stronger, men and boys—some of them little fellows just able to walk—came from the lodges and hurried down to the stream, to plunge into it; for the early morning bath was a regular practice. This was done by all at most seasons of the year; but some of them omitted the bath in winter when the streams were frozen, while others broke the ice and bathed in the cold water. This was for good health, to make them hardy, and also to wash away all sickness. The custom was peculiar to the men; women did not do it. The practice was similar to that of the Blackfeet.

The rising sun looked down upon a camp full of moving people. The women were cooking the meals, the men and boys were returning to the lodges. The pot was removed from the fire, and with a sharpened stick the meat taken from it and put in wooden bowls, or in dishes made of buffalo-horn. Before eating, most of the boys rode out into the hills, and drove in the herds of horses, from which certain ones were selected to be tied in front of the lodges, to be at hand for any use, while those—usually the most valuable ones—which during the night had been tethered there, were turned loose and taken to the hills to graze, under the charge of a son or a nephew of the lodge, or perhaps of some poor orphan who lived there, receiving his food and clothing and in return performing the various small services that all boys were expected to render to older persons.

The morning meal ended, many of the men saddled their horses and started out to hunt; but before this the voice of the old crier was heard, shouting out to the camp the commands of the chiefs, the order of the day, or perhaps only some items of personal news. He commenced at the opening of the circle, which always faced the rising sun, and riding around, within but close to the lodges, first to the south, then to the west, then to the north, and so back to the east again, called out the news, repeating his announcement at frequent intervals. Perhaps it was that the camp was to remain in this place for one, two, or three days; perhaps that men were not to disturb the buffalo; perhaps that some soldier band was to have a dance that night; or merely that some warrior or chief had lost a piece of property, and people were notified of its ownership. At first the crier's voice came to the distant lodges merely as a faint, droning shout, without words, but it told the people that he was coming, and as he drew nearer, they began to listen, to distinguish what he was saying. A woman, eager for news, stepped out of her lodge to hear the better, and exchanged with some interested neighbor comments on the announcement.

Now, some woman who was making a new lodge carried out and spread on the ground the dressed skins to be used in its construction. Before day came, she had sent a messenger to call her friends to come and help her sew it, and the lodge cutter was already standing over the skins, preparing them for the sewing. The women who were to help in the work, some of them carrying their bundles of sinew thread, began to arrive from various quarters of the camp. Many hands made light work, and before night the sewing of the lodge was completed.

Long before this the children had scattered out to play. Some of the tiniest, unless they had older sisters or cousins to take charge of them, stayed close by their mothers; but the older ones scattered to the river, where the boys were swimming and diving in the warm water, or were running races on the sandbars, or perhaps burying each other, all except the head, in the sand, already heated by the strengthening sun. Other lads were busy near a mud-bank, modeling images of animals and people and lodges from the tenacious clay, and setting them in the sun to dry.

Some of the older boys and young men were practicing at shooting with the bow, or at throwing arrows, or were playing one of the wheel games, or sliding their slender, straight throwing-sticks far along the smooth ground.

Big girls, not yet old enough to work at dressing hides, gathered in groups to play football.

During the morning parties of women and young girls started off to get wood, perhaps only two or three together, perhaps fifteen or twenty. They were a merry group, laughing, joking, and playing tricks on one another. When the place was reached where they were to get wood, some gathered the sticks lying on the ground; others climbed up into the trees, breaking off and throwing down the dead branches, while those below trimmed and made them ready for the ropes. The wood was divided into even loads, and when all these were prepared, each woman took hers on her back, and, in single file, they set out for the camp, separating as they reached it, each turning off to her own lodge. In winter when there was snow on the ground, the companies of women made hard-beaten roads to and from the timber, where they gathered their fuel.

Other groups of women and young girls went out into the hills to gather roots, and were seen walking across the wide prairie, armed with their root-diggers, and then climbing the hills, and at last—mere dots in the distance—scattering out and occupied in their work.

The men left in the camp sat about in the shade of the lodges. Some smoked and gossiped; others worked at different implements which they were fashioning, a bow, arrows, a pipe, a pipestem, a whetstone, or what not. Old men discussed the happenings of past years, their war journeys, their meetings with other tribes, visits that they had received from white people, or mysterious events that had taken place within their knowledge. Sometimes, near groups of these old men might be seen two or three growing boys, seated at a little distance behind them, eagerly drinking in the talk that flowed from the lips of these wise elders.

Some young men devoted much time to their personal appearance, plucking out the hairs from eyebrows, lips, and cheeks, combing and braiding their hair, and painting their faces. After this had been done to the dandy's satisfaction, he dressed himself in his finest clothing, and a little later rode about the camp so that people might admire him.

For plucking out the hair, a pair of tweezers was used, called the "eyebrow plucker," from which we might infer that the Cheyennes practiced plucking the eyebrows before they removed the hair from the face by the same process. This last custom is still very generally practiced, although some men now allow the eyebrows and lashes to remain, more especially the eyelashes. At present some Cheyenne young men shave instead of plucking the hair from the face.

Before this some old women dragged out their green hides, and spread them on the ground, and were hard at work over them. Others pounded berries under a shade; others still sewed clothing.

As midday approached, and the sun grew hotter, many of the people retired to the lodges; the lodge-skins were raised all about and they sat there in the shade, while a warm breeze blew through the lodge.

As the afternoon advanced, men were seen returning from the hunt, riding horses laden with meat. Each dismounted before his lodge, and his women took the load from the horse, and either turned the animal loose, or, if it was a fine running horse, took it down to the stream and washed from it the blood and dirt with which it was likely to be covered.

Suddenly, from a near-by hill, sounded the war-cry, and there was a little stir among the growing men of the camp. The women and girls who had been off to dig roots were announcing their return and signaling with their blankets, and a crowd of men rushed out to try to rob them of some of their spoils, while the women in the camp hurried out of the lodges to see the fun.

As they were returning to the camp, the girls who went out to dig bear-roots and turnips tied their roots in small bundles of five or six. Often some girl who was slow at digging, and had secured but few roots, might propose that they should divide into two parties and gamble for the bunches of roots. If all agreed, one of the women threw her root-digger as far as she could, and the others stood in a row and threw their root-diggers at the first one. If a woman's missile touched the mark, her side won. If a root-digger from each side hit it, the game was a draw, while if none of the root-diggers thrown hit the mark, it also was a draw. They competed as well by throwing the short root-diggers so that they should strike on one end and keep turning over, end for end, as they went. The farthest throw won. Some root-diggers would not go at all; they perhaps just stood in the ground, or bounded off to one side. In these contests, they tied the small roots in bunches of five or ten, and wagered these bunches, or a number of them.

In the same way, and for the same purpose, they threw the front marrow-bone of a buffalo, the metacarpal. It was thrown on the ground, so as to strike on its end, and then bound, turning over and over, end for end, to go as far as possible. Often, before betting, a woman might throw the bone, and then go to it and put her foot on it, and say, "If you do not win for me, you shall be pounded up and used to get grease from." This was a jocular threat, the expression of a hope that she might win.

Now, when the women were returning to camp with their roots, and when they had come within sight of the camp, they sat down in a line, and each woman put her roots a little way in front of her on the ground. Then some woman shouted the war-cry, and signaled to the camp with a blanket, as if a war-party were returning. When the people saw this, some of the young men took the parfleches used under the stone anvils on which meat and berries were pounded, and carried them as shields, while some had already made imitation shields of willow twigs. These young men mounted the oldest, laziest, ugliest horses they could find, and charged out on the women, who were busily gathering sticks and buffalo-chips with which to defend themselves.

When the two parties were close together, the girls pelted the men, who dodged and protected themselves behind their shields, and there was much confusion. Only a man who had been wounded in war, or had had his horse shot under him in real warfare, was permitted to take the roots away from the girls. Such men might do so, though before they secured their plunder they received a plentiful pelting. A man who was hit by a missile was supposed to be wounded, and out of the game. Other men might not dismount. However, after a time the men got some roots, and they retired to some hill to eat them, while the girls went on to camp with those they had saved.

The parties who had been gathering roots were made up of little girls, grown girls, married women, and old women. They were not so attacked when they went for berries or cherries, but only when they went for *pomme blanche*.

Among the Southern Cheyennes it is said that mounted men used to steal upon and surprise the women, and after counting a coup to take their roots. If the women discovered the men coming, they sounded an alarm, and all rushed together to defend themselves. With a root-digger they drew on the ground before them a little furrow to represent breastworks. It was understood that no man might pass that furrow to take roots, unless he had counted a coup or killed an enemy within breastworks. If none of the men had performed this feat, none might enter, and they rode about outside the circle, while the women hooted at and derided them. A man who had counted a coup within breastworks, however, dismounted and entered the circle, told of his coup, and took what roots he wished, sometimes loading himself down with them.

As the sun fell, and it grew cooler, people came out of their lodges, and the scene grew more active. Now the feast shout was heard, and children were seen going to and fro across the circle, carrying messages of invitation. Working women and working men had long ago put away their tasks; the evening meal was being prepared. From the hills, horses were driven in, and, followed by great clouds of dust, rushed down the bluffs and into the camp, where, after some had been caught, the others turned about and returned to the hills.

As darkness settled down, the bright firelight shone through the yellow lodge-skins; sparks came from each smoke-hole, as the fire was mended or fresh wood thrown upon it. For three or four hours the camp was a busy place. People were passing back and forth in all directions. Music began to be heard: songs for dancing from some lodge where young men and women were having a social dance; the quicker, more lively music of the gambling songs, from some home where the game of "hiding" was being played; the droning, minor chant of a doctor, whose song was a prayer to the favorable spirits for help; or the love notes of some boy, who was playing his flute on a hill away from the camp. To most of the songs time was kept by drumming; it might be on a large drum, for the dancers, or on a small hand drum, for the doctor; or perhaps only on a parfleche or on the ground, by the gamblers. Over all the camp there was the hum which always accompanied the assembling of a number of people, and this was broken by the neigh of a colt, the barking of dogs, the yelp of some sportive boy, the shout of some old man calling a friend to a feast, the musical laughter of the women, and in the distance the shrill howl of coyotes. Then suddenly the people seemed to grow fewer; one by one the fires burned down, and at last the camp was as silent as the prairie had been before the people moved in.

Long after the people had gone to bed, young people might be awake and stirring, and perhaps doing reckless things. One night, many years ago, Buffalo Wallow Woman, then a young girl, in company with another girl, her special friend, went out of the lodge late, after all the people were asleep. Lying on the ground near the lodge was a three-year-old colt that had never been ridden. He was fast asleep and his nose was resting on the ground. Buffalo Wallow Woman said to her friend, "I could ride that colt."

"Do not be foolish," said the other girl; "he would throw you off." Buffalo Wallow Woman gathered her blanket close about her, began to sing a song, and then jumped on the colt's back. She remembers how it sprang to its feet, and the first few bucks, but after that she must have lost her wits, and just clung to the horse.

The animal rushed about through the camp and frightened all the horses, which stampeded with a great noise. The people awoke and rushed from their lodges, and the horses dashed out of camp toward the hills. The next thing that Buffalo Wallow Woman remembers is that the colt stopped at the edge of a cut bank, while she flew over its head and alighted in the willows below. She was frightened, and under the cover of the bluff and the darkness crept back into the camp. It took the people a long time to gather their horses.

At the breaking up of any large gathering, as the camp at the Medicine Lodge, or at the renewing of the arrows, there was a general presenting of gifts, chiefly of women's things. The women relations of a young married man presented to his wife or to his mother-in-law food, dishes, shawls, or blankets, which the wife or mother-in-law distributed among the girl's female relations. These, on their part, were likely the next day to bring similar gifts—sometimes even lodges and lodge-poles—which they presented to the girl or to her mother, and which by them were given to those relations of the husband who had made the other presents. At these large gatherings the well-to-do young men usually possessed large new lodges, like those owned by the chiefs and the heads of the soldier bands. Such lodges were especially visited by parties of serenaders who were looking for presents.

NAMES OF THE CHEYENNE MONTHS

Here are incorporated the names of the Cheyenne moons or months, with their respective meanings, the first list being that given by Wolf Chief, the other by Big Knife.

Ok sēy′ ē shĭ hĭs, Hoop-and-stick game moon; January.

Măk ōk sēy′ ĭ shĭ, Big hoop-and-stick game moon; February.

Pŭn ŭ mă ĕs′ sĭ nĭ, Light snow moon; also called *Shi iv i ne*, Dusty moon; March.

Măt sĭ′ ŏ mĭ ĭsh′ ĭ, Spring moon; April.

There is no name for May and June, but they are referred to as "the time when the horses get fat."

Hĭvĭ ŭts ĭ′ ĭ shĭ, Moon when the buffalo bulls are rutting; July.

The Cheyennes have no name for August, but it is referred to as "the time when the cherries are ripe."

Tō nō′ ĭsh ĭ, Cool moon; September.

Sē′ ĭn ĕ, Moon when the water begins to freeze on the edge of the streams; October.

Hĭk′ ŏ mĭn ĭ, Freezing moon; November.

Māk hĭk ŏ mĭn ĭ, Big freezing moon; December.

Kā ŭhk tsĭ′ ŭt sĭ, January.

Māh kŏhk tsĭ′ ŭt sĭ, February. Big wheel moon. A few buffalo calves and colts appear, but it is still cold.

Pō ō tăn ĕ′ ĭshĭ, March. Buffalo-and-horses-begin-to-fill-out moon.

Māhk ē ō mĕ′ shĭ, April fat moon.

Hŏhk tsĭ′ ĕt sĭ, April moon, when they play wheels. When high water comes, the wheels and the sticks are thrown into the stream and carried off by the water.

Ō ăssĭ′ ŏ wāh′ tŭt′, May moon, shiny, or bright; ball game month; because during this month the sun shines bright.

June, July, and August moons are just summer; green grass is up, the hot weather comes, and they do not count the moons until the plums get ripe.

Wāh′ kă nŭn ē ĭshĭ, September moon. Plum moon.

Hĭs′ sĭ kē vĭn hĭs′, October. Dust or dirt in the face, from the dry dust blowing.

Hē kōn ĭn hĭst′, November. Hard face, referring to the cold. Leaves falling, and a little ice formed at the edge of the rivers.

Māhk hē kōn ĭn′ ĭ, December. Big hard face. Strong cold.

CERTAIN CAMP CUSTOMS

In the ordinary life of the camp there is much of custom and ceremonial, all of it interesting, but so great in volume that it is impossible to learn any great part of it, or, within any ordinary limits, to set down even the part that one has learned.

A good part of the life of home and camp was conducted after established forms which were supposed to be known to everyone, and the failure to observe these conventions was formerly regarded by Indians as an extraordinary proceeding, much, in fact, as a breach of good manners would be looked at by well-reared people in civilized society.

The Cheyennes

Thus, in the old days it was a common remark among Indians that white men did not seem to know how to act—how to conduct themselves. Of course, in these later times, a long experience of the white man's ignorance and disregard of their methods and ways of life has more or less accustomed them to such violations, and they no longer feel their former sense of injury and indignation at what they regard as his bad manners.

In entering the lodge the visitor turned to the right, and paused or sat down. The owner was sitting on his bed at the back of the lodge—the west side, or perhaps farther to the south—and when he welcomed the person entering, he asked him to come back and sit down. The place of honor was at the left of and next to the owner, who with his family lived to the left of the door, though his sleeping place might be at the back of the lodge. It was not etiquette to go to that part of the lodge occupied by the family, nor to pass between the fire and the owner of the lodge; nor, indeed, was it good manners to pass between anyone sitting in the lodge and the fire. Well-bred people passed behind the sitters, who leaned forward to give them room.

In the lodge, as a member of the owner's family, there was often a boy or a young man who was not related to it. Boys from ten to fifteen years of age, orphans or young relatives who had no one to care for them, often lived in a man's lodge and herded his horses, and performed other small services. The lad received his food and clothing, and after a time, when the lodge owner thought best, he gave him a pony. When the boy was fifteen or sixteen years of age, he perhaps went on the war-path. If on this first war-path he did well, showed courage, or was so fortunate as to capture horses or to count a coup, he no longer herded horses when he returned, but he still lived in the lodge, hunted, and turned in his meat there, and remained a member of the family. Such boys did not make the fires, but they cut the tobacco, lighted pipes, and carried messages. The fires were lighted by the women.

In old times smoking was an important ceremony, which different men practiced in different ways. In some cases no one might leave or enter a lodge while the owner was smoking. Some men went so far as to tie up the door of the lodge. No one must stand up or walk about in the lodge. Certain men, who were very particular, when about to smoke took down everything that was hanging up in the lodge, on the back-rests or to the lodge-poles. When they smoked they began by ceremonially pointing the pipestem to the sky, to the ground, and to the four directions, in order, and saying: "Spirit Above, smoke. Earth, smoke. Four cardinal points, smoke." Then the man made his prayer for help. The smokes to the four cardinal points were offered to the spirits who dwell in those quarters.

The pipe when passed always went with the sun, from right to left, starting from the owner of the lodge. When the man sitting next to the door had smoked, the pipe might not be passed across the door-way, but was handed back all around the circle—no one smoking—to the man on the opposite side of the door. He smoked, and then the man on his left, and so the pipe went on to the owner, or until it was smoked out. In primitive times they had a native tobacco that they cultivated and used for smoking.

At present, in the South, they mix dried leaves of the sumach with the tobacco they smoke. In old times they put a little buffalo grease with this. In the North they use "red-willow" (cornel) bark with tobacco.

The Cheyennes think it unlucky to touch anything with the stem of the pipe while smoking. The pipe must be held straight up as it is passing from man to man, not passed across the body the stem or bowl first, but held upright, the bowl down. Still there are various individual ways of passing the pipe. Some hold it so that the neighbor can take hold of the top of the stem; others, so that he can grasp the lower part. Others point the stem downward, and others still—and this is more usual—rest the bowl of the pipe on the ground as it passes. Many men will not receive the pipe unless it is passed to them in what they con-sider the proper way.

Often they make a prayer as they take the first smoke—sometimes a very long prayer. In old times some men would not smoke unless a little powdered buffalo-chip was scattered on top of the tobacco when lighting it. This was only to make the first catch more readily. Some would not smoke unless alone. Nowadays, old men when cleaning the pipe empty the ashes carefully into a little tin can, on which the cover is replaced. None will scatter their ashes after smoking, but keep them carefully in a little pile near the edge of the fire. This has some relation to the sacredness or solemnity of the act of smoking. When old men are smoking, nothing must be beaten in the lodge. There must be no sudden noise. No one must tap on a stick. Dishes must not be knocked together. No one should walk in front of the smoker; that is to say, between him and the fire. In old times, as a rule, only the older men smoked. Young men were advised not to do so, as it would make them short-winded, so that they could not run long and far. In old times many men would not smoke if a woman was in the lodge.

In buffalo days men were continually calling to the feast. The crier was asked to go out and call the names of those invited, mentioning each man's name, and bidding him to the lodge of the host. If it was not a formal feast given to a large number, but only two or three men were invited, the host might send a boy or even a little child, who would go to the man's lodge and say, "My father calls you." The meal usually consisted of roasted ribs or boiled hump ribs, or boiled tongue, of the buffalo.

A feast was begun and ended with prayer, and before eating, a little from each kettle was offered to the spirits, the food being held up to the sky and then placed on the ground at the edge of the fire. Private persons did the same when eating, in the lodge or elsewhere. The food offered lay where it had been deposited by the fire till the lodge was swept. When it had been held up to the sky and then placed on the ground, it was supposed to be consumed and no longer to be of any value.

At feasts were often related the stories and traditions of the tribe. A person might make a feast and ask a certain man or woman to come and tell a particular story. After the guests had eaten, he or she would tell the story, and at its close might possibly present the story to some individual in the lodge, and after this had been done that person might tell it. At such gatherings people who were well known as story-tellers were in great demand.

When a man desired to have stories told in his lodge for entertainment at night he sent to some old man well known as a story-teller a message asking him to come to his lodge and eat. A comfortable place was fixed for the guest to sit and lie, and food was prepared, but not cooked. Meantime the news that such a man was to tell stories at this lodge had gone through the camp and very likely many people gathered there to listen.

When the old man came in and sat down, a pipe was offered him, and he smoked. When he received the pipe he raised and lowered it four times, touching the bowl of the pipe to the ground four times, and after he had finished smoking he went through the ceremonial motions of passing hands over legs, arms, and head. This was a promise to tell the truth—that is, to relate the stories as he had heard them—and a prayer for help to do this. Then food was cooked and set by the side of the fire.

Many of the stories told by the Cheyennes were the property of particular families, and might be related only by members of these families, grandparents and parents carefully teaching the children these tales of the past. Such stories were often personal property, and only those to whom they had been presented might repeat them.

Certain stories were told in sections. A short story might be told, and at a certain point the narrator stopped and after a pause said, "I will tie another one to it." Then there was a long pause; the pipe was perhaps lighted and smoked, and a little conversation was had; then the story-teller began again, and told another section of the tale, ending as before. Such stories were often told in groups of four or six, and might last all night. At less formal gatherings a man might tell a story, and when it was finished might say: "The story is ended. Can anyone tie another to it?" Another man might then relate a story, ending it with the same words, and so stories might be told all about the lodge.

When a sacred story was to be told the people were called into the lodge, the door was closed, and everyone sat quite still. No one was permitted to enter or go out while the narrator was speaking. Playing children were told to keep away, because if any noise were made in or near the lodge, something bad would happen—someone might get sick or die, or might be killed. Sacred stories were told only at night, for if they were related in the daytime, the narrator would become hunch-backed.

Speech-making, story-telling, and conversation were the usual forms of entertainment among the Cheyennes at their more or less formal feasts; but on some occasions feasts were given which were attended by the members of two of the soldier bands, for the purpose of determining which band had among its members the most men who had performed brave deeds.

When a competition of this sort took place, the two bands were ranged on opposite sides of the lodge, facing each other. Those present did not at first speak, except when asked. Some elderly man was chosen to preside, one who had no special affiliation with either party, and so was disinterested. He sat at the back of the lodge with the pipe lying on the ground before him, the bowl pointing to the south. The umpire had already thought over the list of brave deeds to be brought up. Before him were a number of counters, consisting of small sharpened sticks, which he thrust upright into the ground for the purpose of marking what had been related—the points gained by either party.

When all were ready to begin, he passed a counter to the man sitting at one end of the line. The counter passed from hand to hand until it reached the man for whom it was intended, and then the umpire asked, perhaps, "Which one of you ever counted coup on a man who carried a gun?" If the man holding the stick had not done this, he passed it to his next neighbor; and so it went from hand to hand until it reached one who had done this thing, when he narrated the circumstance, perhaps mentioning the name of some witness to the deed.

Sometimes most unlikely things were suggested by the umpire, as when the stick was passed for a man who, riding a spotted horse, had touched an enemy carrying a gun. Without a word the stick passed from hand to hand until it reached a man on the north side of the lodge, who said: "At such a time and such a place, when riding a spotted horse, I touched a Ute. He held his gun in one hand, and was trying hard to get away."

"Ah," said the umpire—Woman's Heart, a Kiowa,—"that will not do. He must have shot at you." So the stick went on, and no one claimed the deed. When one side had counted a coup, and received credit for it, the stick was passed again to that side. A man who had more than once performed the feat mentioned might ask to have a second or a third stick passed to him, receiving them up to the number of his coups of the kind in question. When the coup had been related, the stick which had been passed for it was returned to the umpire, who thrust it in the ground to his right or left hand, according as the winning was by the party to his right or left.

In case neither side had been able to count the coup suggested, or if both sides had counted it, so that they were even, the stick was passed alternately to one side and the other. After four passings of the stick, someone might suggest that the pipe be lighted, and for a time smoking and conversation followed. The partaking of this pipe was a pledge of the smokers' truthfulness; and the purpose of the pipe lying on the ground before the umpire was also to insure truth-telling. No one would venture to lie or to exaggerate under such circumstances.

After the pipe had been smoked out, the contest began again, and with intermissions for smoking was likely to last all night. Whichever side had the most sticks received a feast the next day from the losing side.

Young men who had not done much in war never took part in such a competition. It was participated in chiefly by those who had been to war many times.

Among the Cheyennes, just as among all people, civilized and savage, the belief prevailed that personal suffering was acceptable to the supernatural powers, and would be likely to secure their favor. Just as the devout Christian in a civilized community may, during certain seasons of the year, wear a hair shirt, refrain from eating meat or using tobacco, or may give up going to the theatre, in the belief that this sacrifice of self is acceptable to God, so the Cheyenne who wished for good fortune—for success in his undertakings, or to avert an evil chance—cut strips of skin from his body, or starved, or swung to the pole, believing that by this sacrifice of self he would gain the favor of the *Ma i yūn'*, those mysterious powers which controlled the affairs of men, and brought good fortune or bad, according as they were reverenced or neglected. It has been said elsewhere that in old times men going on the war-path used to slice bits of skin from their arms in sacrifice, and in earlier days—at the time when they wore nose-rings—men used to take narrow cross-strips of skin from the arms, frequently from shoulder to wrist, and sometimes cut similar strips from the legs. These were offered in sacrifice—a part of the body given to *Hĕ' ămmă wi' hio*, to bring good fortune. Sometimes, in the same way, a narrow strip of skin was cut out, running in a spiral from the middle of the chest around over its surface, as large as a dinner plate. Besides this, there were many other forms of personal sacrifice, of which the suffering in the Medicine Lodge is that best known.

Many years ago, when they went on the war-path, and felt that they were in danger, young men used to promise the spirits that if they were saved from danger they would cause themselves to suffer.

In those old times, young men used to go off on the hills and fast for four nights. This was called *a wū wŭn'*, starving. They did this in order that they might be fortunate, and might not be hit in battle. When they slept, they lay on their faces, with their heads toward the east; they had no shelter and no covering. They might smoke three times each day—at sunrise, at noon, and at the going down of the sun.

The young man might ask an instructor to take him up on a high hill, on the right-hand side of a river; that is to say, either on the south or the west side; or to a point of rocks on the right-hand side of a lake. The young man must lie there for four days without eating or drinking. Usually such young men took up with them white sage, to lie on as a bed, and a filled pipe. Sometimes, if the sun was very hot, the man stuck a bush in the ground to give him a little shade. Usually he made an offering to Heammawihio, which he left there when he went away from the spot. These votaries did not choose places which were especially dangerous, but went to the tops of hills, open to the view, from which they could see off over the prairie.

If the dreams which a man had during this ordeal were favorable, he usually remained for four days; but if unfavorable, he was likely to stop and to return to the camp. If he fasted to the end, after four days the old man went to him and brought him down to the camp. They did this only in summer. This is said to have been purely a sacrifice, and not an attempt to dream for power; but often those who lay there did have dreams, and what they dreamed surely came to pass. If the Maiyun came to the man and talked to him, and smoked the pipe, he would be successful. Not everyone starved, and to only a part of those who starved did the vision come.

In another form of personal sacrifice the suffering was more acute, though shorter lived. When a young man intended to sacrifice himself in this way, he went out in the afternoon and cut a stout pole to take up on the hill with him. To the top of this pole a rope was tied.

At daylight the next morning the young man filled a pipe and went to the home of a man who had done what he now intended to do. He entered this man's lodge and offered the pipe to him. The man took the pipe and smoked. When he had finished smoking, he said to the young man, "Well, friend, what is it?" The young man replied, "I wish you to go up on the hills with me."

When they started, the young man took with him the pole he had cut, and when they reached the place the old man dug a hole in the ground and planted the pole there. He then took hold of the rope, and tested the pole to see that it was firm in the ground, and that there was plenty of room for the young man to swing.

The young man sat down, facing the east, holding his shoulders well back, and his arms and wrists at his side. The old man pinched up the skin of the breast on either side, ran a knife through it, and then taking two skewers, about three and a half inches long, he passed one through the cut on each side of the breast. From a knot tied in each end of the rope, two flat ends of hide ran out, and from these ends hung heavy deerskin strings, slit like a buttonhole. The eyelets of each string were slipped over each end of either skewer. Then the old man stepped behind the young man, lifted him up and drew him back, so as to see if the rope was tight and the pull on its two branches even. After that the old man said, "Now, walk up that way [to the right, *i.e.*, south] and back four times." He walked about one-quarter of a circle to the right four times and back. He might then walk one-quarter of a circle to the left, walking a half-circle in all. The pipe was left at the end of the quarter-circle to the right (at the southern limit of his walk), and it was there that he smoked three times during the day. All the time that he was walking, the man was sagging back on the rope, trying to tear the skewers through the skin of the breast. He never succeeded in doing this, however; the skin is too tough.

The man who had given the instruction then went back to the camp, and at sundown came again, and with a knife cut the skin across behind each skewer, so as to free it. The skin cut off was placed, with a prayer, on the ground at the foot of the pole and left there. He then untied the rope from the pole, rolled it up, and returned to his lodge, taking the young man with him. At the left of the back of the lodge the young man found his food in a bowl, and some water. The old man offered these to him, and first he drank his water, then ate.

Men suffered in this way in order that they might be fortunate in war—might take horses, or might count a coup—or it might be done as the result of a dream. It was often done just before going on the war-path. The same man might do it several times.

Sometimes this sacrifice was made in the night, in which case assistance was asked of some old man who had suffered in the night time. The boy or young man was obliged to find out for himself the name of one who had done this same thing at night. The sufferer was made fast to the pole just as the sun was setting, and was set free just as the sun rose.

If done at night, the young man contemplated the spirits, and often during these sufferings he saw wonderful visions. Men were pierced and swung to the pole at night in the same way as during the day. There were different opinions as to which form of suffering was the more acceptable to the Maiyun.

Sometimes in the day a young man might have several buffalo-skulls attached to slits cut in the skin of the back, over the shoulder blades, and drag the skulls up and down over the course where he walked. This was sometimes done at the camp, and after the circle of the lodges had been put up the young man might start at the opening of and within the circle, and go all around the circle to the point from which he had started. There the old man awaited him, and took off the skulls, which were placed in line in the opening of the circle, facing inward. In taking off the skulls, the drawn-out skin was cut off, and the old man held each piece to the sun, and down to the ground, and toward the four directions, and then buried it in the ground. This might be done at any time when the young man wished to pay his vow. Often it was done at the time of the Medicine Lodge, but might be done at any time.

Besides offering the pipe to the instructor, the young man was obliged to make him a liberal payment.

Sometimes when the Medicine Lodge was being made, a young man might have a slit cut in his shoulder, and tie to the shoulder a shield, which he wore through the ceremony.

When, at the Medicine Lodge or at any other time, men swung to the pole in this way, if they broke away, then they stopped and retired.

Sometimes a young man might take a buffalo-skull to the top of a hill, and from sunrise to sunset stand on it without eating or drinking, all the time looking at the sun. Sometimes, toward evening, friends would go up to the place to bring him down to the camp, and would find him so stiff from standing on the skull all day in one position that he could hardly move. When he did this, he stood facing the east in the morning, and turned, following the sun until it disappeared in the west.

The young man might stand in the same way on the ground, motionless, except as he turned with the sun. He might rest four times during the day, sitting down for a little while. This was regarded as an easy thing to do.

A young man might ask an old man if he knew how to stand in the water. The old man, if he assented, took him to a stream, and led him into the water until it was about up to his chest, and there he must stand all night. While standing there, the man might see some good sign, or something that was bad. If what he saw portended evil, he usually gave up, and left the water.

Once in a Medicine Lodge ceremony the father of Stacey Riggs, looking at the top of the center-pole, saw there himself. His fingers were cut, and his head hair gone; he stopped dancing. His wife asked him why he had stopped, and he told her what he had seen. Afterward, when he was killed by the Utes—in 1864, not far from Bent's stockade, on the Purgatoire River—he was scalped, and his fingers were cut, just as he had seen himself in the Medicine Lodge.

Old Whirlwind, as a young man, sleeping on a high hill for four nights, without food or drink, had a vision in which he saw himself, but with gray hair. This was a sign to him that he should live until he was old—until his hair was gray. He did live until his hair turned gray, and died an old man. He was in the Sauk and Fox fight, and was in great danger there.

A friend who starved himself twice, once lying down and once standing up, prayed that he might be helped through his life, might live to old age, and that whenever they had war he might kill an enemy. It has been so up to this time. When he went up on the hill to perform this sacrifice, he was told to stand up, but that just at noon he might sit down for a short time. After he had been standing for nearly twenty-four hours he was so stiff and sore he could hardly sit down. Each man who went out to perform this sacrifice was instructed in what he must do by older persons who knew—who themselves had been taught, and had made this sacrifice. Such instructors were not necessarily possessed of spiritual powers.

THE BOY AND THE GIRL

PEOPLE who know of the Indian only from books think of him solely as a warrior. As they have heard of him chiefly when he is at war, they do not realize that this phase of his life occupies but a small part of his existence, or that aside from this he has a communal and family life on which his well-being depends. He has a wife and little ones whom he loves as we do ours; parents and grandparents whom he respects for their experience and the wisdom derived from it; chiefs and rulers to whose words he listens and whose advice he follows, and spiritual directors, who tell him about the powers which rule the earth, the air, and the waters, and advise him in his relation to the forces of the unseen world. In other words, his is a complex life, not devoted solely to one pursuit, but full of varied and diverse interests. He must provide food for his family, must maintain his position in the camp, and must uphold the standing of the tribe in its relations to other peoples. All these duties call for the exercise of a discretion and self-restraint in his living which can be acquired only as a result of some system of education.

Even those who have had much to do with Indians hardly realize that their children are taught. They see the little boys constantly playing about the camp, engaged in sham battles, or swimming in the stream, or, in winter, sliding down hill on sleds made of buffalo-ribs, or throwing their javelin-like darts, or practicing with the bow and arrow, or stealthily hunting small birds or rabbits; and, contrasting this life of freedom with that of the white child, who spends much of his time in the schoolhouse, they assume that the Indian child grows up without instruction and without guidance. Yet no group of people could possibly live together in peace and harmony if each member of it followed his own inclinations without regard to the wishes and rights of his fellows. Like other people, the Indians have sufficient care for their own comfort to see to it that no member of the tribe shall unduly interfere with this, or infringe on the rights of others.

Among the Cheyennes the men were energetic, brave, and hardy; the women virtuous, devoted, and masterful. Though they were savages of the stone age, their code of sexual morality was that held by the most civilized peoples. Such fathers and such mothers were likely to produce and rear children like themselves: impatient of control or restraint, perhaps, and fierce and cruel in taking revenge for injuries, yet after all possessing many of the qualities which we wish to see in our children: courage, independence, perseverance—manliness. These qualities they inherited, but how were they brought out?

The Indian child was carefully trained, and from early childhood. Its training began before it walked, and continued through its child life. The training consisted almost wholly of advice and counsel, and the child was told to do, or warned to refrain from doing, certain things, not because they were right or wrong, but because the act or failure to act was for his advantage or disadvantage in after life. He was told that to pursue a certain course would benefit him, and for that reason was advised to follow it. His pride and ambition were appealed to, and worthy examples among living men in the tribe were pointed out for emulation. Of abstract principles of right and wrong, as we understand them, the Indian knew nothing. He had never been told of them. The instructor of the Indian child did not attempt to entice him to do right by presenting the hope of heaven, nor to frighten him from evil by the fear of hell; instead, he pointed out that the respect and approbation of one's fellow men were to be desired, while their condemnation and contempt were to be dreaded. The Indian lived in public. He was constantly under the eyes of the members of his tribe, and most of his doings were known to them. As he was eager for the approval of his fellows, and greedy of their praise, so public opinion promised the reward he hoped for and threatened the punishment he feared.

Indians never whip their children, nor punish them in any way. Sometimes a mother, irritated by the resistance of a yelling child, will give it an impatient shake by one arm as she drags it along, but I have never witnessed anything in the nature of the punishment of a child by a parent.

When a Cheyenne baby was born it was warmly wrapped up, and for a time carefully protected from the weather. During the first two or three months of its existence, if the weather was cold or stormy, the child was carried about in its mother's arms, and was not laced on a baby-board or cradle until it had become so hardy as to be able to endure some degree of exposure. Old people say that in earlier days, when the tribe lived in lodges, and moved about over the prairie, a large proportion of the children born in winter died. It can readily be understood that while living this nomadic life it might have been very difficult to protect new-born children from the cold.

As soon as the child had become strong and hardy enough, and the weather had grown milder, it was lashed on the cradle or baby-board. During a good part of the time it was carried about on its board, which, when the mother put it down, was sometimes hung up to a lodge-pole, or leaned against the side of the lodge in the camp. When the child was not on the board, and was not scrambling about on the ground, it was carried on its mother's back, her blanket or robe holding the little body close to hers, passing around her shoulders, and being held by her in front. The child's head was a little higher than the mother's; its hips lay between her shoulders, its heels showing through the blanket just above her loins. In such a position the child seemed perfectly comfortable and at home. It ate, if the mother passed food to it over her shoulder, or slept, its head rolling about on its neck, as its mother moved, like a toy Chinese mandarin.

The mothers played with their babies, and tried to keep them amused and quiet.

When the camp moved, the women carried the babies on their

backs, or hung the boards on saddles or travois poles, while the little boys old enough to look out for themselves ran along on foot, or rode colts or horses, as the case might be. The little girls rode by twos or threes on top of the packs. Many children, however,—too young to be allowed to go without the guidance of some older person, yet too old and big to be carried by an overworked woman who was busy driving and minding half a dozen pack-ponies—were carried on a travois, confined in a cage made of willow twigs and shaped like a sweat-house. The flat bottom rested across the travois, which was hauled by some steady old packhorse. In old times, when many children were carried in travois hauled by dogs, runaways sometimes occurred, though not often. A dog, tempted by the sudden appearance of game, might start off in pursuit, and, tipping over the travois, leave the child howling on the prairie, to be recovered by the alarmed mother. Usually, however, the mother led the dog that hauled her baby.

When a little baby reached the age of from three to six months, it was time for its ears to be pierced. At the next Medicine Lodge, therefore, or at any great dance or gathering of the people, the mother took the child to the place of the meeting; and the father requested the old crier to call out and ask a certain named person to pierce the child's ears. The person invited to do this might actually pierce the ears, or might merely pierce them ceremonially—*i.e.*, make the motions of piercing them. Before doing either, he counted a coup, telling of some important act performed in war. If the man merely performed the operation ceremonially, the ears might afterward be pierced in fact by anyone, without ceremony. As an acknowledgment of the service, the father presented the person with from one to three horses, and perhaps other good presents. If a man should have his child's ears pierced without this ceremony, it would create a scandal in the camp. People would say that he had no affection for his child.

In ancient times the person who actually pierced the child's ears made a long cut in the outer margin of the ear, from the top nearly to the lobe, and the strip on the outside was wound with beads or with brass wire.

A father who was very fond of his child, and could afford it, might have the child's ears pierced several times. He might give a horse each to two or three different men for the same service. In one reported case, a man gave eight horses for this purpose. Such liberality showed the man's affection for his child, and caused him to be talked about and praised.

Wealthy people sometimes had their child's ears pierced even before birth, making up an image on the occasion of some great dance, and having the ears ceremonially pierced. This was an old-time way.

Occasionally, among tribes on the buffalo plains, we find accounts of cases where a father himself has been obliged to care for and bring up an unweaned babe, without a woman's help. I have heard of such instances among the Cheyennes. Young Woman, who was born in 1830—three years before the stars fell—has told me that she was so reared. Her mother was an Arapaho, and her father half Cheyenne and half Arapaho.

When her father was a young man returning from the war-path, he learned that his wife had run off with another man. Instead of returning to the camp, he sent a friend to it to get his little baby, and when it was brought to him, he carried it from where they were camped, on the head of the Platte River, south to Bent's Fort, on the Arkansas. The baby was unweaned, and to support it he killed cows which had calves and cutting out the udders gave them to the child to suck. In the same way he killed female deer and antelope, and let the child suck the udders. So he nourished her until he reached the Cheyenne camp, where a woman took charge of the child. Afterward she lived among the Northern Cheyennes. A like case was that of Arapaho Chief, a Northern Cheyenne.

At first children are called only by pet names. *Mŏk′ sō ĭs*, meaning "pot belly," is a term of endearment for a little boy; *Mŏk′ sĭ ĭs′* is a term for a little girl.

Such names were used only for very small children. When a child reached the age of five or six years, a more formal name was given it. A boy might be named after his father's brother, or after his grandfather. A good name was always chosen, though he might have also a nickname by which he was commonly called. A woman's daughter might not be named after the relations of the mother, but after some relative of the father. In fact, children were almost always named after their father's relatives.

Formal names were always given to children by the time they were six or seven years of age, and sometimes much earlier. Not long after a child was born, the father's brother-in-law or father might send for the baby, and when it was brought to him might take it in his arms and give it his name, and a horse. He would say, "I give him my name," —Na vĭ′ hĭsht nāt′ ă mĭt′′ "my name I give to him"—or the order might be reversed. Then he specified which one of his names he wished given.

If the uncle did not send for the child, the father was very likely to give the child the name of one of its uncles; or if it had no uncle, of its grandfather. A cousin, or some near relative, notified the man whose name had been given to the child, and he was expected to present to it a horse. The name having been given and the horse received, the same horse was given away when the child's ears were pierced.

In the case of a girl, the same thing happened. The father's sister very likely made a cradle for the baby, whom she herself wrapped up and put in the cradle, and then gave her a name and a pony. After a time the man gave his sister a horse in return for the cradle. If the sister did not offer to name the child, the mother might choose a sister-in-law's name, and she was expected to give a horse. The child might be named after a brother or a sister killed in battle. Then, of course, no horse was given. Names thus remained in families. Such a name the child retained until he had made a journey to war.

The infant's education began at an early age, its mother teaching it first to keep quiet, in order that it should not disturb the older people in the lodge. Crying babies were hushed, or, if they did not cease their noise, were taken out of the lodge and off into the brush, where their screams would not disturb anyone. If older people were talking, and a tiny child entered the lodge and began to talk to its mother, she held up her finger warningly, and it ceased to talk, or else whispered its wants to her. Thus the first lesson that the child learned was one of self-control—self-effacement in the presence of its elders. It remembered this all through life.

This lesson learned, it was not taught much more until old enough, if a boy, to have given him a bow and arrows, or if a girl, to have a doll, made of deerskin, which she took about with her everywhere.

Perhaps her mother or aunt made for her a tiny board or cradle for the doll, and on this she commonly carried it about on her back, after the precise fashion in which the women carried their babies. She treated her doll as all children do theirs, dressing and undressing it, singing lullabies to it, lacing it on its board, and, as time passed, making for it various required articles of feminine clothing. Often as a doll she had one of the tiny puppies so common in Indian camps, taking it when its eyes were scarcely open, and keeping it until the dog had grown too active and too much disposed to wander to be longer companionable.

As soon as she was old enough to walk for considerable distances, the little girl followed her mother everywhere, trotting along behind her, or at her side, when she went for water or for wood. In all things she imitated her parent. Even when only three or four years of age, she might be seen marching proudly along, bowed forward under the apparent weight of a backload of slender twigs, which she carried in exact imitation of her mother, who staggered under a heavy burden of stout sticks.

Boys learned to ride almost as soon as they learned to walk. From earliest babyhood infants were familiar with horses and their motions, and children two or three years of age often rode in front of or behind their mothers, clinging to them or to the horses' manes. They thus gained confidence, learned balance, and became riders, just as they learned to walk—by practice. They did not fear a horse, nor dread a fall, for they began to ride old gentle pack-ponies, which never made unexpected motions; and by the time they were five or six years of age, the boys were riding young colts bareback. Soon after this they began to go into the hills to herd the ponies. They early became expert in the use of the rope for catching horses.

Little girls, too, learned to ride at an early age, and while they did not have the practice that boys had, they became good horsewomen, and in case of need could ride hard and far.

In summer little girls as well as little boys spent much time in the water, and all were good swimmers. The courage of such children in the water is shown by an incident in the lives of three old women who in 1912 were still alive on the Tongue River Indian Reservation. When ten or twelve years of age, these children had been sent down to the stream to get some water. Their mothers were at work fleshing buffalo-hides and had so many to work on that the hides were beginning to get dry. The little girls were sent to get water to keep the hides damp until their mothers could flesh them. They went to the stream, and one of them proposed that before carrying up the water they should take a swim. They took off their clothes and ran out onto a fallen tree that projected over the water; and, when about to dive in, one of them noticed a hole in the bank deep under the water, and proposed that they should see where it led to. They swam under the water into the hole. It was dark and nothing could be seen; but the little girls felt something large and soft pass by them, going out of the hole as they were going in. They went on a few feet and saw a little light and, raising their heads, found themselves in a beaver's house. A little frightened by the creature that they had met in the water, which was of course a beaver, they did not like to go back and, seeing the opening at the top of the house through which light filtered, they readily broke a hole through the roof and crept out onto the bottom. Here they found themselves in the midst of a thick growth of wild roses and had a very difficult time, and were much scratched up in getting out of the bushes. This must have taken place perhaps between 1850 and 1860, and the women were Buffalo Wallow Woman, Omaha Woman, and the wife of Big Head, who was sister to White Bull.

Little companies of small boys and girls often went off camping. The little girls packed the dogs, and moved a little way from the camp and there put up their little lodges—made and sewed for them by their mothers—arranging them in a circle just as did the old people in the big camp. In all that they did they imitated their elders. The little boys who accompanied them were the men of the mimic camp.

In the children's play camps the little girls used tiny lodge-poles—often the tall weed-stalks that are used for windbreaks about the lodge—and the boys sometimes acted as horses and dragged the lodge-poles, or hauled travois with the little babies on them. To the sticks they rode as horses, as well as on the dogs, they sometimes fixed travois.

When the lodges were put up the boys used to stand in line, and the older girls asked them to choose their mothers. Each boy selected the girl who should be his mother, and they played together. The girls played in this way until they were pretty well grown, fourteen or fifteen years of age; but the boys gave it up when they were younger, for they strove to be men early, and usually soon after they had reached their twelfth year they began to try to hunt buffalo, killing calves as soon as they could ride well and were strong enough to bend the bow.

Sometimes two camps of children, one representing some hostile tribe, were established near each other. The boys of one camp would go on the war-path against those of the other, and they fought like seasoned men, taking captives and counting coups. They tied bunches of buffalo-hair to poles for scalps, and after the fight the successful party held dances of rejoicing. They carried lances made of willow branches, shields made of bent willow shoots with the leafy twigs hanging down like feathers, and little bows and arrows, the latter usually slender, straight weed-stalks, often with a prickly-pear thorn for a point. After the camp had been pitched, another party of boys might attack it, and while its men were fighting and charging the enemy, trying to drive them back, its women, if they thought the battle was going against them, would pull down the lodges, pack up their possessions, and begin to run away. In such a battle the men might often shoot each other, and when the wounded fell, men and women rushed out and dragged them back, so that the enemy should not touch them and count a coup. If the village was captured, all the food its people had was taken from them. This often consisted chiefly of roots gathered by the women, and tender grass-shoots, of which they often gathered a great deal.

The little boys when playing at going to war rode sticks for horses, and each one also led or dragged another stick, which represented another horse, the boy's war-horse. If an attack was threatened by a pretended war-party, those attacked changed horses, and leaving their common horses and their things together in one place, they rode out to meet the enemy and the battle began. The opposing forces charged and retreated forward and backward, just as in a real battle. Each party knew or suspected where the others had left their things, and if one group drove back the other, it might capture its opponent's horses and other property and thus win a great victory.

In their pretended buffalo hunts also the boys rode sticks for horses, and lashed them with their quirts to make them run fast. Sometimes, when buffalo were close by and the real hunters of the big camp killed them near at hand, the little boys rode their stick horses out to the killing ground and returned to the play camp with loads of actual meat tied behind them on their horses. Some boys merely picked up pieces of the meat that had been thrown away, but often a good-natured hunter would give the lads pieces of meat to use in their camp.

If there were no buffalo about, perhaps some children went out from the camp, and returning by a roundabout way, pretended to be buffalo. Others in the camp, discovering them, prepared to go out to surround them. The children representing the buffalo went out on the prairie in a company; they were both boys and girls—bulls and cows. Some pretended to be eating grass, and some were lying down.

The boys who were to run buffalo had small bows and arrows. Those who represented the buffalo carried sticks three or four feet long, sharpened at one end. On this sharp end was impaled the flat leaf of a prickly-pear, which still bore its thorns. In the middle of the leaf, on either side, was rubbed a little spot of dirt. This leaf had two meanings: it represented the buffalo's horn or weapon of defense, but, besides this, the little spot of dirt represented the buffalo's heart. If an arrow pierced this, the buffalo fell down and died.

Some of the boy buffalo runners started out on the hunt far ahead of the others, so as to get beyond the pretended buffalo and cut off their flight. The others formed a wide crescent when making the charge. When the proper time came, the hunters rushed toward the herd, which in turn ran away. The larger boys, who represented the bulls, ran slowly behind the herd, and the hunters avoided them, because, if wounded, they might turn to fight, and chase those who were pursuing them; and if they overtook the pursuers, might strike them with the prickly-pear leaves which they held on the sticks, and fill the hunters' skin with thorns. If this happened, it was told through the camp, "A bull has hooked and hurt" so-and-so. If the dirt-marked center of the prickly-pear leaf was hit, and the buffalo who carried it dropped to the ground dead, the hunters pretended to butcher it, and to carry the meat home.

With their dog travois, the little girls followed the hunters out to the killing ground.

Often some of the buffalo proved too fast for the hunters and ran a long way off, and then stood on the prairie and looked back. The hunters could not overtake them.

Perhaps a number of the boys might appear on the prairie not far from camp and pretend to be wild horses, and others started out from camp on their stick horses to chase and try to catch them, throwing ropes over those that they overtook.

The little girls often had trouble with their pack-dogs, just as did their mothers in real life. Many old and gentle dogs stayed about with them, but others, younger and more playful, were hard to catch when they wished to move camp, or might even run away and go back to the real camp.

Food must be had for the mimic camp, and the children went down to the creek to get fish. They thrust straight twigs in the mud of the bottom, across the stream in a half circle, the concavity being upstream. The sticks were so close together that the fish could not pass between them. In the middle of the stream, in what would be the center of the circle, if it were complete, a taller twig was thrust into the stream-bed, to the base of which a piece of meat was tied. Above the half-circle, on one bank, was fastened a flexible fence or gate of willow twigs closely strung together on sinew, and made like a mattress or a back-rest. It was long enough to reach from one bank to the other.

When all preparations had been made, the boys went a long way up the stream, and entering it, formed a line across it, and came down, wading through the water, beating it with sticks, making a great noise, and so driving the fish before them. If the water was roily, the girls who remained below near the trap perhaps saw no fish, but if there were many there, they tugged at the meat and shook the willow twig which stood alone. Then the girls quickly entered the stream, and stretched the flexible fence or gate across it, making it impossible for the fish to pass up the stream. All now plunged into the water, and with their hands caught and threw out on the bank the fish that were confined between the half-circle of twigs and the fence about it. In this way they caught many fish, and these they cooked and ate.

The children did not stay out all night, but during the day they pretended that it was night, and went to bed. During the day they moved the camp often; even every hour or two.

These children imitated the regular family life, pretending to be man and wife, and the tiny babies—who were their brothers and sisters—served them for children. Little boys courted little girls; a boy sent to the girl's lodge sticks to represent horses, and if his offer was accepted received with her other sticks and gifts in return. Babies able to sit up were taken out into these camps, but not those that were too young. Sometimes a baby might get hungry and cry, and its little sister who was caring for it was obliged to carry it home to her mother, so that the baby might nurse.

Soon after the little boy was able to run about easily, a small bow and some arrows were made for him by his father, uncle, or elder brother, and he was encouraged to use them. When he went out of the lodge to play, his mother said to him, "Now, be careful; do nothing bad; do not strike anyone; do not shoot anyone with your arrow." He was likely to remember these oft-repeated injunctions.

After that, much of his time was spent in practice with the bow. He strove constantly to shoot more accurately at a mark, to send the shaft farther and farther, and to drop his arrow nearer and nearer to a given spot. As he grew more accustomed to the use of the bow, he hunted sparrows and other small birds among the sagebrush and in the thickets along the streams, with other little fellows of his own age; and as his strength and skill increased, began to make excursions on the prairie for rabbits, grouse, and even turkeys. Little boys eight or ten years of age killed numbers of small birds with their arrows, and sometimes even killed them on the wing.

Though he keenly enjoyed the pursuit, the Cheyenne boy did not hunt merely for pleasure. To him it was serious work. He was encouraged to hunt by his parents and relatives, and was told that he must try hard to be a good hunter, so that hereafter he might be able to furnish food for the lodge, and might help to support his mother and sisters. When successful, he was praised; and if he brought in a little bird, it was cooked and eaten as a matter of course, quite as seriously as any other food was treated. The first large bird, or the first rabbit, killed by the boy, he exhibited to the family with no little pride, in which all shared.

In their hunting, these tiny urchins displayed immense caution and patience, creeping stealthily about through the underbrush of the river bottom, or among the sagebrush on the prairie, striving to approach the woodpeckers climbing the trunk of a cottonwood tree, or the blackbirds swinging on the top of a bush, or the meadow larks stalking about in the grass. The care with which they twisted and wound in and out of cover when approaching the game, taking advantage of every inequality in the ground, of the brush, and of the clumps of rye grass, was precisely what they would have to practice when hunting later in life. At first, to be sure, they missed most of their shots, but they did not become discouraged, and now and then they killed a bird.

As a boy grew older and more skillful, he often took with him two or three little boys when he set out to kill small birds. The bigger boy shot the birds with blunt arrows, and the little fellows gathered them up and carried them, by passing the heads under the gee-string, about the waist. Sometimes when the boys had enough birds, they chose a place for camping and built a fire. They picked and dressed the birds, and roasted them on the coals.

The older boys often set out in companies of four or five, and traveling across the prairie, a bow-shot apart, beat a considerable width of country. If game was detected, they strove to approach within shot before startling it, and often succeeded. Jackrabbits, however, were likely to bounce up under their feet, and to scurry away, pursued by a flight of arrows. If the animal escaped, the boys watched it, if possible, until it had stopped for the last time, taken its last look about, and settled down to hide. Then, having closely marked the spot, they very slowly and cautiously approached it in a half-circle, scanning the ground with the utmost care. If one discovered the rabbit squatting close, he indicated its position to the others, and they tried to surround and, if possible, to shoot it, before it started to run. They were often very successful in this hunting. Sometimes in the spring they succeeded in killing a kid antelope or two—a great prize.

While engaged in this hunting, the boys not only learned how to approach and secure game, but also unconsciously picked up a knowledge of many other things incidental to success in life. They came to understand the signs of the prairie, to know the habits of wild animals, learned how to observe, how to become trackers, where the different birds and animals were found, and how they acted under different conditions; and were training themselves to habits of endurance and patience.

As little boys grew larger they were often warned by their parents and uncles always to be quiet when older people were about, not to be noisy, not to play in the lodge, not to run in front of anyone. In the lodge they were not allowed to pound or knock on anything, and especially not to tap or hack with a knife any stick in the lodge, and above all not to tap on a stick in the fire. To do this might cause bad luck; a boy who did any of these things might even cut off his finger.

If by an unlucky chance a boy at play threw a stone or a piece of dirt or a mud ball against the lodge of a priest—a medicine man—it was necessary, to avert bad luck, that he should be purified by the medicine man, who unwrapped his sacred bundle, and with long ceremony and much passing of hands over the offender, and wiping him off with white sagebrush, prayed that his error might be pardoned. Unless this were done, the medicine would be broken, and many evil things might happen. Perhaps the lad might be struck by lightning.

From the beginning the boy was taught that his chief duty in life was to be brave, and to go to war and fight. He was treated always with great consideration, for it was remembered that he might not be long with his people, that in his first fight he might be killed; and, therefore, while he was with them they wished to treat him well—to make him comfortable and happy. For this reason, a boy was better treated than a girl. He had a good bed, often at the back of the lodge. For a lad to bring in a stick of wood or a bucket of water was considered unfitting. If he did a thing like this, it was talked of in the camp as something to be regretted, as more or less of a scandal.

When a boy was about twelve years of age, some old grandfather began to talk with him, and advise him as to how he should live. He was instructed in manly duties. He was told that when older people spoke to him, he must listen and must do as they told him. If anyone directed him to go after horses, he should start at once. He should do nothing bad in the camp, and should not quarrel with his fellows. He should get up early; should never let the sun find him in bed, but must be early out in the hills looking for the horses. These were his especial charge, and he must watch them, never lose them, and see that they had water always. He was told that when he grew older it was his duty to hunt and support his mother and sisters. A man must take good care of his arms and keep them in good order. He must never boast. To go about bragging of the brave things that he might intend to do was not manly. If he performed brave deeds, he himself should not speak of them; his comrades would do that. It was predicted that if he listened to the advice given him he would grow up to be a good man, and would amount to something. In this way their fathers, uncles, and grandfathers talked to the boys, and often wise old men harangued little groups who were playing about the camp.

A boy had usually reached his twelfth, thirteenth, or fourteenth year when he first went out to hunt buffalo. Before this he had been instructed in the theory of buffalo running, and had been told how and where to ride, and where to hit the buffalo if he was to be success-ful. If on his first chase a boy killed a calf, his father was greatly pleased, and, if a well-to-do-man, he might present a good horse to some poor man, and in addition might give a feast and invite poor people to come and eat with him. Perhaps he might be still more generous, and at the end of the feast give to his guests presents of robes or blankets. As soon as the boy reached home and his success was known, the father called out from his lodge something like this: "My son has killed a little calf, and I give the best horse that I have to Blue Hawk." If he gave a feast, he explained again, saying: "My little boy has killed a calf. He is going to be a good man and a good hunter. We have had good luck." The man to whom the horse had been presented rode about the camp to show it to the people, and as he rode he sang a song, mentioning the name of the donor and telling why the horse had been given to him.

Bird Bear, whose boy name was Crow Bed, told me that as a child his father talked to him but little, while his grandfather gave him much advice. This was natural enough, since at that age the father was still engaged in war and hunting, which occupied most of his time, while the older man had passed the period of active life.

Crow Bed was quite young when he went on his first buffalo chase, but he had a good horse, and was soon among the buffalo and close up alongside of a little calf. He was excited and shot a good many arrows into it, but he kept shooting until the animal fell. After he had killed the calf he felt glad and proud. He dismounted and butchered the calf, and with much labor put it on his horse and took the whole animal home, not cutting the meat from the bones and leaving the skeleton on the ground, as a man would have done. When he reached his lodge, his people laughed at him a little for bringing it all home, but his father praised him and said that he had done well. "After a little while," he said, "you will get to killing larger ones, and pretty soon you will kill big buffalo."

His father then shouted out, calling a certain man named White Thunder to come to the lodge and see what his son had done; that he had brought meat into the camp. After White Thunder had come to the lodge, his father presented to White Thunder the horse the boy had ridden and the pack of meat that he had brought in. The incident was discussed all through the village, so that everyone knew of Crow Bed's success.

A year or two later, when a party was made up to go to war against the Snakes, his grandfather advised Crow Bed to go with it. Before they started out the old man said to him: "Now, when the party is about to make a charge on the enemy, do not be afraid. Do as the others do. When you fight, try to kill. When you meet the enemy, if you are brave and kill and count a coup, it will make a man of you, and the people will look on you as a man. Do not fear anything. It is not a disgrace to be killed in a fight."

When Crow Bed started, his father gave away the best horse that he had, because his son was starting on his first war-path. He cried out, asking any poor person in the village who needed a horse to come and see his son starting to war for the first time. He did the same thing when Crow Bed returned from the war-path, although on this first war journey the party had traveled for many days without finding enemies, and returned to the village without accomplishing anything.

My friend, Shell,—who died years ago, more than eighty years of age,—told me that his instruction came chiefly from his father, who gave much advice to him and to the other boys of the family. He remembered especially the father's warning to his children to be truthful and honest, never to lie. His father was a chief, and almost every night there were many people in his lodge, talking about different things, and the children listened to the conversation of their elders, and learned much. Shell was thirteen years of age the summer when he went on his first buffalo hunt. His father was a skillful arrow-maker, and the boy had plenty of arrows; and as he was riding a good horse, he killed three calves on this first chase. After the hunt was over, his father, who also had been running buffalo, came back and asked the boy if he had killed anything. Shell pointed out the three calves, and his father got off and cut up the meat. When they reached the camp, his father called out to a certain man to come and see what his son had done. When the man reached the lodge, his father gave him the horse Shell had ridden, and the pack of meat which it bore.

As Shell and his brothers grew older, his father used to teach them all good things, but especially that when they went to war they must be brave. That is why the Cheyennes used to fight so hard. They were taught it from childhood.

His father used to tell him never to associate with women, and, above all, never to run off with one. He would say: "Whenever you find a woman that you love, give horses and marry her. Then you will be married in the right way. Whenever a man runs off with a woman, both are talked about, and this is bad for both."

Older men gave much advice to their grandsons, sons, and nephews, and tried constantly to warn them against mistakes and to make life easier for them. A well-brought-up man was likely to advise his grown son that occasionally, when he killed a good fat buffalo, he should seek out some old man who possessed spiritual power and offer him the meat, in order to secure his friendliness and the benefit of his prayers. If the old man accepted the present the carcass was pulled around on its belly until the head faced the east. The old man slit the animal down its back, took out the right kidney, and handed it to the young man, who pointed it toward the east, south, west, and north, then up to the sky, and down to the ground, and placed it on a buffalo-chip. The old man was likely to say to the young man: "May you live to be as old as I am, and always have good luck in your hunting. May you and your family live long and always have abundance." As the old man went back to camp with the meat, he called aloud the name of the young man, so that all might know he had given him a buffalo. This was an ancient custom.

The training of the little girls was looked after even more carefully than that of the boys. Their mothers, aunts, and grandmothers constantly gave them good advice. They recommended them especially to stay at home, not to run about the camp, and this was so frequently impressed on them that it became a matter of course for them to remain near the lodge, or to go away from it only in company. Both mothers and fathers talked to their daughters, and quite as much to their sons, but in a different way. The mother said: "Daughter, when you grow up to be a young woman, if you see anyone whom you like, you must not be foolish and run off with him. You must marry decently. If you do so, you will become a good woman, and will be a help to your brothers and to your cousins." They warned girls not to be foolish, and the advice was repeated over and over again.

As a girl grew larger she was sent for water, and when still older she took a rope and went for wood, carrying it on her back. The old women early began to teach the girls how to cut moccasins, and how to apply quills and to make beadwork. As they grew older they learned how to cook, and to dress hides, but girls were not put regularly to dressing hides until they were old enough to marry.

Boys and girls alike had each some special friend of their own sex to whom they were devotedly attached, and each pair of friends talked over the advice received from parents.

Children seldom or never quarreled or fought among themselves, and though, as they grew older, continually engaging in contests of strength, such as wrestling and kicking matches, and games somewhat like football, they rarely lost their temper. Two boys might be seen swaying to and fro in a wrestling bout, each encouraged by the shouts of his partisans among the onlookers, and each doing his best. When finally one was thrown all the spectators raised a great shout of laughter, but he who had been overcome arose laughing too, for he realized that the others were not ridiculing him, but were showing their enjoyment of the contest they had witnessed. The Cheyenne boys are naturally good-natured and pleasant, and the importance of living on good terms with their fellows having been drilled into them from earliest childhood, they accepted defeat and success with equal cheerfulness. Among a group of white children there would be much more bickering.

Usually, but by no means always, the Cheyenne boy learned to kill buffalo before he made his first journey to war. Sometimes—as in the case of Bald Faced Bull—the little fellow's ambition for glory, and ignorance of what war meant, led him to join a war-party at a very tender age. Little boys who did this received much consideration from the older members of the party, and were carefully looked after. They were taken in charge by some older man, and were kept apart from the younger members, who would be likely to tease and embarrass them, and in all ways the journey was made easy for them. Yet when the moment came to fight, they were given every opportunity to distinguish themselves, which meant to fight and to be killed. Because on the occasion referred to Bald Faced Bull was riding a very fast horse, he was chosen as one of ten to charge the camp of the enemy, the most dangerous work in the fight. While such little boys did not often accomplish any great feat, yet sometimes they did so, and returned to the village covered with glory, to the unspeakable delight and pride of their families, and to be objects of respect and admiration to their less ambitious and energetic playfellows. Even when they did nothing especially noteworthy, they were undergoing a training, were learning to know themselves, and to be steady under all conditions, and were hardening themselves to the toils which were to be their most important occupation for the next twenty-five years.

If on such a journey the boy performed any especially creditable act—if by some chance he killed an enemy, or counted a coup—some one of his near relations, his mother or aunt or an uncle, gave away a horse on the return of the party, and presented him with a new name. If the mother gave the horse, she selected a name that her brother had borne; if the aunt, she chose her brother's name; if the uncle, his brother's name. The name was always a good name—that of some brave man. The name before being given was discussed in the home and chosen with deliberation. If the name given was that of a living man, that man took another name, perhaps that of his father or of an uncle.

A result of all this training was that the best of the Cheyenne youths had for their highest ambition the wish to be brave and to fight well; and hence they desired always to be going to war. If a few of them were traveling over the prairie in time of war, and people were seen, there was immediate rejoicing. "Ha!" one would say to his neighbor, "there are some people at last. Now we are going to have a good time. Now we will have fun. Hurry! hurry! Get ready to fight!" Meantime, any loads carried on the saddles, all extra clothing, and often the saddles themselves, were stripped from the horses and thrown on the ground, and the party, laughing and chattering in the highest possible spirits at the prospect of a fight, set out in hot haste to attack the strangers. If these proved to be friends, the disappointment of the young men was great. I recall a case in which a party of Cheyennes, scouting for the Government, charged a group of about their own number, which they presently discovered to be other scouts of their own people under command of the late Lieut. Edward W. Casey. They were much cast down.

A boy's education by advice and admonition usually ended with his first journey to war. When he had made that, he was supposed to have reached years of discretion and to have acquired by practical experience enough discretion to decide for himself what he ought to do, or to consult with older men and ask their advice. The first war journey was often long and hard and without any results, the boy returning to the village with nothing to show for his trip, but with a store of practical knowledge which would be useful to him all his life long.

Some of the young Cheyenne boys were practical jokers and, like many practical jokes, theirs were sometimes thoughtless and cruel. Little Hawk, born between 1840 and 1850, was a practical joker about whom many stories were told. Sometimes he hid by the trail along which the women passed in going for water; and when a woman passed, carrying a skin full of water, Little Hawk shot an arrow through it, and laughed delightedly at the sight of the water spurting in two straight streams from the holes where the arrow had gone in and come out. The water-skin was ruined beyond repair.

As late as the middle of the last century, the Mexicans often came north to the Cheyenne camp to trade; and brought with them some foods that the Cheyennes were very fond of. Once when the Mexicans had come to the camp, and almost the whole tribe had gone out to where the Mexicans were, to get a taste of the food they brought to trade, Little Hawk went around among the lodges, and from every lodge that had no occupant he took from the quivers all the arrows, carried them to his own lodge and hid them behind its lining. That night an alarm was given that Pawnees were about and had already taken a bunch of horses. It was ordered that all should arm themselves and scatter out on the edge of the camp to guard it. The men seized their bows; but when they took them, there were no arrows in the cases. It was a time of great confusion; but at length someone shouted out that Little Hawk must have done this and, rushing to his lodge, they found their arrows. Some of the men cried out: "Divide them up now and let us start out to meet the enemy. We can exchange arrows tomorrow."

On another occasion, one night the people heard a loud shout saying, "The Mexicans have come to trade; they are camped here just outside the circle." All the women jumped out of bed, got together the things that they had to trade, and rushed off in the direction of the voice. When they got outside the circle they could see no camp, and looked around, not knowing what to do. Then from behind them on the other side of the camp came the shout, "The Mexicans are camped here, and have plenty of things to trade." At once the women, thinking they had made a mistake, turned about and ran in that direction; but when they reached the border of the camp on that side, no Mexicans were to be found. Then the cry sounded from still another direction, saying: "This is where the Mexicans are; come this way"; and some of the women started, but presently someone shouted out, "Oh, it must be Little Hawk who is calling us about from one place to another." It proved to be Little Hawk, and there were no Mexicans.

About the middle of the last century the Cheyennes still, to a large extent, made their war journeys on foot; and were extremely tough and enduring. Such men lived until a few years ago; and an example of this came out in a story told of an incident that happened to She Bear when a young man.

She Bear possessed a sense of humor which made him quite ready to laugh at a joke even if it were against himself. He said that when he was a young man he heard of a dance that was to be held in two or three days at a neighboring camp, distant from his home about seventy-five miles, and set out to walk to that camp to attend the dance.

He had gone about half the distance, and was walking along singing to himself and practicing his dancing steps as he walked. Presently someone behind him said: "You are dancing well; the girls will look at you"; and turning about he saw close to him Spotted Wolf, who also was on his way to the dance and had been watching She Bear from a place of concealment. She Bear told this as a joke on himself; but the interesting part of the story seemed to me that a young man should start off to walk seventy-five miles in order to attend a social dance.

THE CHEYENNES AND THEIR STORIES

FOR many years the Cheyennes have been separated into two groups known as Northern and Southern Cheyennes, the latter those in Oklahoma. These are merely two divisions of the same people, and the separation took place less than one hundred years ago. There is nothing permanent about it. Some people go to the south, live there for a few years or a generation, and then come back to the north; or, in some cases, one part of a family may live in the south and another part in the north. In the old days before the coming of the railroads there was frequent passing back and forth between Northern and Southern Cheyennes.

Since the Indians had no books and none of the usual forms of civilized diversions, their entertainment was derived largely from social intercourse, such as conversation, story telling, and speech making. They were great visitors and spent much of their time either in discussing the news of the camp or in talking of the events that had happened in the past.

Since they had no written characters their history was wholly traditional, handed down from one generation to another by word of mouth. The elder, who transmitted these accounts to younger people, solemnly impressed upon his hearers the importance of repeating the story just as it had been told to them.

The Cheyennes

Story telling was a favorite form of entertainment, and it was a common practice for hosts at feasts to invite some story teller to be a guest, and then, after all had eaten, to relate his stories. Men known as good story tellers were in demand, and were popular. The learning of these stories must have been a fine training for the memory of the young, who were frequently examined by their elders to see how completely they had assimilated the tales so often repeated to them.

Some of the stories were short, others were long, sometimes told in great detail, and even in sections. A short story might be told, and when it was finished the narrator stopped, and, after a pause, said, "I will tie another one to it." Then there was a long pause; the pipe was perhaps lighted and smoked, and a little conversation had; then the story teller began again and told another section of the tale, ending as before. Such stories were often told in groups of four or six, and might last all night. At formal gatherings a man might tell a story and when it was finished might say: "The story is ended. Can anyone tie another to it?" Another man might then relate one, ending it with the same words, and so stories might be told all about the lodge. Or a story might end with the words, "This cuts it off."

Of the tales of the past, those narrating the events of the warpath were perhaps the most popular; by listening to them a fairly clear notion may be had of the methods by which the tribal wars were carried on. Yet mystery, magic, and the performances of doctors and priests—men who possessed spiritual power—had their part, often an important part, in the narratives related by the older men. Sacred stories were told reverently, and with some ceremony. After the people had assembled in the lodge the door was closed and tied down and all sat still; there was no conversation; no one might go in or out; no noise might be made in or near the lodge during the telling of the story, lest the lack of reverence should bring misfortune. These sacred stories were to be told only at night. If related in the daytime the narrator might become hunchbacked.

The oral literature of the Cheyennes is extensive and the tales vary greatly in character. Some of them are well worth listening to, and others seem more or less trival. Of the older stories there are many variants. Some of the stories contain the same incidents, and it is not easy to separate them into groups. Many are very old, while, on the other hand, some of the war stories deal with matters of but a generation or two ago, and in certain cases the precise year is given.

The stories which the Indians narrate, covering a wide field of subjects, furnish to us concrete examples of their ways of thought. Besides their inherent interest, many of them have a direct relation to the early history of our country, and some tell of events happening on ground now occupied by great numbers of white people.

CREATION TALE

THE creation story of the Cheyennes tells of a being who was floating on the surface of the water. Water birds, swans, geese, ducks, and other birds that swim already existed, and these were all about him. The person called to these birds and asked them to bring him some earth. They were glad to do so, and agreed one after another to dive down through the water and see if they could find earth at the bottom. The larger birds dived in vain. They came up without anything, for they could not reach the bottom, but at last one small duck came to the surface with a little mud in its bill. The bird swam to the being and put the mud in his hand, and he took it and worked it with his fingers until it was dry, when he placed it in little piles on the surface of the water, and each little pile became land, and grew and grew and spread, until, as far as one could see, solid land was everywhere. Thus was created the earth we walk on.

After there was firm ground the creator took from his right side a rib and from it made a man. From the man's left side he took a rib and from that made a woman. These two persons were made at the same place, but after they had been made they were separated, and the woman was put far in the north, and the man in the south.

Another creation story told me long ago by Ben Clark, who had married a Cheyenne woman and lived long with the tribe, says that once the Cheyennes were all under the ground, living in darkness. One day a man saw far off a little spot of white. He approached it, and gradually it grew larger, and presently he found himself surrounded by the light, which blinded and frightened him. After a little time, however, he became used to this, and going back below the ground, as he had come, told his fellows, and a part of them also came out from under the ground, and thereafter lived on the earth's surface. This suggests a tale told of the beginnings of the Mandan Indians.

After the creator had made the two people, whom he placed far apart in the north and in the south, he stood between them with his back toward the rising sun. He said to them, "In that direction," pointing to the south, "you will find many sorts of animals and birds different from those which you will find in that direction," pointing to the north where the woman stood. "The birds that live in the south will go to the north in summer. Where the woman is it will be cold and the grass and trees will not grow well. There will be hardly any of them, but where the man is everything will grow; trees, bushes, grass."

The woman in the north, though she was gray-haired, was not old. She never seemed to grow any older. The man in the south was young. He did not grow older.

In the north lives *Ho ĭm' a ha*, the Winter Man, the power that brings cold and snow, and also brings sickness and death. He obeys the woman in the north. He is often spoken of in the stories and is said to have declared at a meeting of the supernatural beings that he would "take pity on no one." When at this meeting he spoke in this way, the Thunder, who represents the power of the south, declared that it would not do to let *Ho ĭm' a ha* have everything to say; so, with the help of the buffalo, the Thunder made fire, and taught one of the culture heroes how to do the same thing.

He said to Sweet Medicine, "Get a stick and I will teach you something by which your people can warm themselves, can cook food, and with which they can burn things." He showed Sweet Medicine how to rest the point of the stick in the middle of a dried buffalo chip, and then to rub it between his hands and twirl it fast. The young man did so, and after a time the chip caught fire. Thus, by the help of the Thunder the people were given something to use against the cold, something that would warm them.

The man and woman in the south and in the north appear to typify summer and winter, the man representing the sun or the Thunder, while the woman represents the power that wars against the sun.

Twice a year there is a conflict between the Thunder and the Winter Man. At the end of summer when the streams get low and the grass becomes yellow and dry, *Ho ĭm′ a ha* comes down from the north and says to the Thunder: "Move back, move back, to the place from which you came. I want to spread all over the earth and freeze things and cover everything with snow." Then the Thunder moves back. Toward spring, when the days begin to grow longer, the Thunder comes back from the south and says to *Ho ĭm′ a ha*, "Go back, go back, to the place from which you came; I wish to warm the earth and to make the grass grow, and all things to turn green." Then the Winter Man moves back and the Thunder comes, bringing the rain; the grass grows and all the earth is green. So there is a struggle between these two powers. They follow each other back and forth.

The two first people, the man in the south and the woman in the north, never came together, but later other people were created and from them the earth was populated.

TWO STORIES OF MYSTERY

THE STOLEN GIRL

THERE was once a young girl who had many men coming to court her. She was the daughter of a chief, and his lodge was pitched in the center of the circle. Many young men came to see her, but she refused them all. She did not care for any of them. She wanted a young man that she could love.

One evening as she sat in the lodge, she perceived a very pleasant smell in the air, and wondered what it came from. She wanted to look out and see, but did not wish to go to the door and herself be seen; so she took her mother's awl and pierced a hole in the lodge skins and, peeping through the hole, she saw a young man standing not far off.

When she had looked at him for a little while, she liked him, and determined that she would go out to see who it was. She did so, and as she walked past him he spoke to her, and she stopped. Then they talked to each other, and the girl asked him who he was, and why he had come; for she saw that he was a stranger. The young man said: "The home of my people is far from here, and I have come to get you. Come with me, and we will go to my father's lodge."

The young man spoke pleasantly, and the girl, after she had thought a little while, said to him: "Very good, I will go with you. Other young men want me, but I do not want them. I will go only with you. First, however, you must let me go back and get my awl and sinew and my quills." The girl went into the lodge and made up a bundle of her things, and then came out again and said to the young man: "Now, I am ready. Which way do you live from here? In which direction must we go?"

"I live toward the rising sun," said the young man. "There are many camps of my people there." They set out toward the east.

As they were going along, she said to him: "What is your name? What do they call out when you ask your friends to come to a feast with you?"

"My name," he said, "is Red Eye."

They traveled along for some time, and it was almost night when they came near to the camp. There were many trees where the camp was pitched, and all among the trees you could see the light shining through the lodge skins. They passed into the circle of the camp, and went up to a big lodge standing in the center, and when they got to the door, the young man and the girl stopped. Through the lodge skins they could see the shadows of many men sitting about the fire, and could hear them talking and laughing. The young man's father was speaking. He said to the others: "My son has gone far away. He has gone to get a chief's daughter to marry. He has seen her and liked her, and now he has gone to get her. After a time, if he has good luck, he will return with her." So the old man talked about his son.

At last Red Eye said to the girl, "Come, let us go in." He first went into the lodge. When his father saw him he was surprised. He said to him: "Why, my son, I did not think to see you again so soon. I hope you have had good luck."

The girl followed the young man into the lodge, and went over and sat on the women's side. She saw her father-in-law speaking to her husband, and she noticed that he had a very sharp nose; and after a time, as she looked about, she saw that all the men sitting around the lodge had sharp noses. The lodge was nicely fixed up, and the linings handsomely painted. On the beds were many nice warm buffalo robes.

At the girl's home there was great trouble. The chief's daughter had disappeared, and no one knew what had become of her. Her father and mother were crying because their daughter was lost. All the young men were out searching for her. They could not find her, nor any trace of her. When they could not find her, her father felt still worse, and said to the young men who were searching for her, "The young man who finds my daughter shall marry her."

When the girl awoke in the morning, she found that she was in a big hollow tree, and all about the tree were sitting mountain rats. The buffalo robes on which they had been lying were grass nests.

A young Cheyenne man was out looking for this girl, and as he passed a great hollow tree the girl came crawling out from it.

"Girl," he said, "where have you been? Everyone in camp is in great sorrow because you are lost. We have been searching for you everywhere."

"Friend," said the girl, "the rats stole me away, and brought me here to this tree." Then the young man took her back to her father's lodge, and afterward he married her.

That was the beginning of rats stealing things from people.

THE LITTLE GIRL AND THE GHOST

THERE was once a camp and in one of the lodges a little girl sat crying; she was angry about something. Her mother did all she could to make the child stop, but at last the mother became angry and she opened the lodge door and pushed the child out and said, "Ghost, take away this child."

The Cheyennes

A ghost must have been standing somewhere close by the door, for when the mother put the child out something picked it up. As soon as she was put out, the child stopped crying. After a time the woman went out; and when she could not find her daughter, she went about among the lodges, crying and looking for her. The one that took away the child was a young ghost, and at the place the young ghost came from there was an old ghost. The young one brought the child to the old one and said, "Here is your food."

In the morning the old ghost said to the little girl, "Go and bring in some wood." The little girl went out and gathered some dry wood. A little bird flew close to her and said, "You are getting that wood for yourself"—meaning that it was to be used to cook her. She took the wood up to the lodge and the old ghost looked at it and said, "That is not the kind I want"; and sent her to get some more. Again the little bird said to her, "You are getting that wood for yourself." She took it up to the lodge and again the old ghost found fault with it, and sent her for other wood. She went a third time and again the little bird spoke to her. She was sent back a fourth time. The bird flew close to her and said, "This is the last time; when you go back they will cook you."

The girl said: "It is useless to tell me that; the big ghost has got me and I cannot help myself. Can you help me?" The bird answered: "Yes, I can help you. Now right over here is a mountain peak. I will take you there and when you get there, you must say at the door in the rock: 'My grandfather, I have come for protection; my father, I have come for protection; my brother, I have come for protection; my husband, I have come for protection.' This must be said at the door. I will take you there. There is a big stone lying against the peak; that is the door."

The bird told her to put a hand on each of its shoulders and flying close to the ground it carried her to the peak. When they arrived the girl repeated what the bird had told her. The bird said, "Place your hand on the rock and push it to one side." She did so and went in, and saw an old man sitting there. He said, "Come in, my grandchild; I know you have come to me for protection."

When the old ghost missed the girl, he went out and followed her. He knew she had gone to the peak. As he drew near, he commenced to hoot like an owl; and when he hooted the ground shook. Four times he hooted and each time the ground shook. When the child heard the ghost, she was afraid and ran around inside the lodge, trying to hide; but her grandfather told her to keep quiet and not to be afraid. After hooting four times, the ghost came up to the rock. He stood in front of the door and said, "Bring out my meat; if you will not, I must come in after it." Four times he said that.

The old man said, "Come in and take her out." The ghost said, "Open the door that I may come in." After he had been asked four times, the old man got up and pulled the door open just far enough for the ghost to get its head in; and when the ghost had put its head in, the old man let the door fly back and cut the head off the ghost, so that it fell on the ground inside. The man picked it up and threw it outside the lodge; and said to the girl, "Get some dry wood and throw it over the head." After she had made a pile over it, the old man set it on fire; then he threw the ghost's body in the fire and handed the girl a stick and said, "Now, if anything rolls out, do not touch it with your hand, but push it back in the fire with this stick." After he had lighted the fire the head and body cracked open and pieces of flint and old-time beads rolled out. The little girl wanted to pick them up, but the old man said, "No, push them into the fire." They watched the fire until the ghost was all burned up.

When the girl was seventeen years old, the old man said she might go back to her village. He dressed her like a man; made a robe for her and painted it with Indian red paint; her leggings and moccasins were also painted red. He made her a thunder bow and put buffalo bull tails on the heels of her moccasins. Then he tied the skin of a prairie owl on her forehead. So she was dressed like a Contrary.

When she was ready to start the old man gave her a live mink and told her to put it inside her dress on her breast. He said to her: "You must pass by four villages; stop at none of them; they will call out to you, but keep on and pass by. After that, you will find a single lodge. Go in and stop there, for by that time it will be sundown. At that lodge you will find an old woman who has great power; she tries to kill everyone who comes to her lodge. When you have gone in, she will boil a kettle of brains and meal for you to eat. The brains will be those of someone she has killed. She will hand you a bowl of this with a horn spoon, but you must not eat it. Feed that to the mink. Then she will cook you some buffalo meat; eat that."

Before the girl left him the old man told her that when she stopped at this old woman's lodge she must not sleep. He said: "If you sleep, she will try to kill you; but, if you do fall asleep, keep the mink up close to your neck and it will act as a guard over you. After she thinks you are asleep, she will begin to scratch her leg and her leg will swell up; then she will use her leg as a club and will strike you on the head with it."

As the girl passed the first village she came to, on her journey, the women called out to her, "Come here, young man, and stop," but she paid no attention. When the women found that she paid no attention to them, they called out to her, "You walk like a woman." This happened at each of the four villages.

Just at sundown she got to the top of the hill and down in the valley saw a lone lodge. The old woman came out and said, "Come down, my grandchild," and took her by the hand and brought her to the lodge. She hung her thunder bow on the limb of a tree; then she went in and saw that everything in the lodge looked very fine. The old woman said, "My grandchild must be hungry; I will cook some mush for you." So she put the brains on the fire in a pot. When it was cooked she gave her a bowl full and a spoon, but the girl fed it to the mink. The old woman said, "My grandchild is still hungry," and began to boil her some buffalo meat, and the girl ate it.

After a time the old woman asked the girl if she was sleepy. She said, "Yes, I would like to go to sleep," and she lay down with the mink up close to her throat. The old woman said, "I will sit up and keep the fire burning, so that you will be warm." The girl pretended to sleep and snored, and saw the old woman get up close to the fire and begin to scratch her leg. It began to get larger and she crawled up to where the girl lay and raised her leg to strike her with, but just as she held it over her head, the girl pushed the mink out. It caught hold of the woman's leg and tore off a piece of flesh. The old woman cried out, "You have killed me," and fell over; then she began to cry and said, "You have strong spiritual power."

217

The girl jumped up and went out; and, as she did so, picked up a burning brand and set the lodge on fire. She took up her thunder bow and started off in the direction of her camp.

She traveled all that night, and next day arrived at the big village. There she stood up on the hill with her thunder bow, and all the village came out to see the strange young man. Two young men came to her and said, "Where did you come from?" She answered, "This is my village; I have been away a long time and have come back." So they took her to the center of the camp and called an old man to announce that a young man who belonged to the village had arrived. The old man called it through the village and everyone came up to look at her. No one knew who she was. Finally they asked her who her family was. She hung her head down, for it made her ashamed to remember that her mother had put her out of her lodge. She said she was the girl thrown out of the lodge by her mother and carried off by the ghost. Then they all recognized her and her people took her to their lodge.

(A Cree story contains some of these elements.)

TALES OF WIHIO

A MEDICINE MAN'S ARROWS

A MAN who possessed great power was traveling down the creek by himself. As he came to each big tree, he stopped and looked at it. If it was straight and had not many limbs, he would kick it and knock it over. He only had to kick the tree once. He knocked down all the best trees he came to.

Wihio came to meet him and said, "Why are you knocking down all the best trees, my brother?" The man did not answer him, but went along kicking down the trees. Wihio caught hold of him, saying, "You must stop this."

The man said, "I am getting my arrow sticks; soon I am going out on the warpath and I need good, straight arrows." Wihio said: "You cannot use these big trees for arrows. Stop knocking them down." The medicine man said: "Do not bother me. I told you I was getting my arrow sticks." Wihio said, "If those are your arrow sticks, shoot at me with one of them."

The medicine man said, "Go over yonder and stand." Wihio walked over a little way and stopped, but the medicine man motioned him to go on farther. Wihio stopped four times and each time was told to go farther, till he reached the top of a big hill. The man picked up one of the trees, turned the root end toward Wihio and threw it; he did not use a bow. It flew toward Wihio, and as it came the leaves made a noise like the wind.

He saw it coming, for it came slowly, and he tried to dodge it, first one side and then the other, but the tree followed him. He came to a hole and tried to creep in, but the hole was too small and he could only put in his head. The tree struck him and carried away his body, leaving his head sticking in the hole. The man walked up to where the head lay; the body was some distance away.

Wihio's head said, "Take pity on me and put me back on my body again." The man replied, "I will cure you; I only wanted to show you I could shoot with the trees," so he put the head on the shoulders of Wihio's body and he was cured.

"You are a good shot," said Wihio.

THE WOMAN'S CAMP

Wihio was traveling up the river when he came to a big camp. All the people were outside, and when he walked up to them he saw they were all women; there was not one man among them. When they saw him, they all ran toward him and began calling out, "Come with me; come to my lodge," and some caught hold of him, but he said, "No; I own another [I see another woman that I like better]," for behind him he saw a very handsome woman. Wihio said to the others, "Keep quiet now; this one first picked me out for her husband." The others let him go, so he walked up to this one and she took him to her lodge; there was only one trail by which to reach it, for the timber was growing close all around it. There were many big plum bushes there. The lodge was painted with stripes all around it and when he went in he saw on each side a nice bed, with white buffalo skins hanging over the head and backrests. The lodge lining was decorated with porcupine quills. He married this woman.

One day he told his wife he was going on a trip up the river. When he had gone a long distance, he came to another camp, but here, instead of women, all the people were men. Wihio said to them: "Come here, my friends; come around me. I have something to tell you." The men all crowded around him and he said, "Farther down the river I have found a camp in which there are only women; that will be a very good thing for all of us." The men said to one another, "That is good; take us there." Others said, "Let us go with him." They got around him and said, "Wait; you may go off and leave us, for you are a swift runner."

The news was so good they were afraid he would get away before he had showed them the village. So they tied rocks to his feet and put a robe on him and filled it with stones. After they had loaded him with stones, they said, "Where is the camp?" And when he told them, they all started to run there. Wihio's burden of stones was so heavy that he could hardly walk, so he followed behind slowly. He called to them, asking them to come back and wait for him, and when they did not stop he told them to look out for his lodge and said it was painted in stripes and that his wife was a handsome woman; they must not go there. They all answered, "Oh, no, we will not go there."

The Indians all ran to the camp and picked out the best-looking women for their wives; and one of them chose Wihio's wife for his wife. When Wihio arrived he walked up to his lodge, saying to himself, "I think everything is right, in here," but he found a man in the lodge sitting beside his wife. This man said, "I have taken your wife; you will have to go out and get another; be quick now before they are all gone." So Wihio had to go out and stand in the middle of the camp with the rocks still tied all around him. He hunted all over and finally found a little old lodge off to one side. He went in and found a very old woman sitting there. She said, "Come in, my son-in-law."

Wihio said, "I am not your son-in-law," but she still said he was, though he said again that he was not. He walked up to her and sat down beside her and said, "I want to marry you; I want you for my wife." So she agreed and he married her. She was the oldest woman in the camp.

WHERE THE MICE DANCED

ONE day the little mice were having a dance. They were dancing in an elk skull. Wihio came walking along over the prairie, and heard the singing, but could not tell from whence it came. He listened, and for a long time looked everywhere to find the singers. At last he found the place.

When he found the skull where they were dancing, he got down on his knees and looked into it. He said to the mice, "Oh, my little brothers, let me come in; I want to dance too."

"No," said the mice, "you must stay outside. You cannot come in. There is not room for you here."

Wihio kept begging them to let him come in, but they would not consent. Then he made up his mind that he would go in anyhow. It looked nice in there. A white lodge was standing there, food was being cooked, and preparations were being made for a great feast.

Wihio made himself small, so as to go in the hole at the back of the elk's skull. The hole was small, but at last, by twisting and turning, Wihio got his head in. When he did this, the mice all became frightened, and scampered out of the skull and ran away.

When Wihio saw that no one was left in the skull, he tried to get his head out of the hole, but he could not. His head was stuck fast. For a long time he tried to free himself, but he could not get the skull off his head, and at last he started to go home. He could not see where he was going, and for a long time he wandered about on the prairie, stumbling over stones and buffalo bones, and falling down into ravines, all the time crying.

At last he reached the river, and followed it down toward his camp.

His children were in swimming near the camp, and when they saw him they did not know what it was they saw and were frightened, and ran home crying. His wife came out of the lodge to see what had scared the children. She saw a person coming with an elk's skull for a head, and she did not know what to think of it. When she heard the person talking she knew her husband's voice. Then she was angry, and got an axe and tried to break the elk skull. While she was trying to break the skull off, she more than once knocked Wihio down; but at last she set him free.

HE CATCHES FISH

Once there was a man who wished to go fishing, but he had no fishing line and no bait. So he cut a strip of his skin from each side of his body, beginning at his feet and running up his leg and side, and the side of his face, until the strips almost met on his forehead, just over his nose. He threw the strips of skin down into the water, and bent down his head and waited. After a little while he felt something pulling at the strips of skin, and jerked his head back and tightened the strips, and they flew out of the water and threw the fish that had been biting at them out onto the bank. Thus he caught many fish—a big pile. He kept on down the river, fishing wherever the water looked right for it.

After a time, Wihio came along, and when he saw the man catching fish, he began to cry, and say, "O my friend, I want that power."

For a little while the man did not answer him, but at last he said, "Very well, I will give you this power; but you must not do this more than four times at each bend of the creek." The man took out his knife and said to Wihio, "Lie down." Wihio did so, and he began to cut the strips from his skin. "O friend," said Wihio, "that tickles, that hurts"; but he lay still until the man had cut the strips on both sides up to his forehead, and left them hanging. Then Wihio got up. "Now," said the man, "I have told you that you must not do this more than four times at each bend of the river." Then the man went on his way, carrying his load of fish.

Wihio was longing to try this, to see whether he could catch fish. He went down below where his friend had been, and began to fish, and when the fish took hold of the strips of skin, he threw his head back and threw the fish out, until he had a big pile. He was glad, and said, "Ah, this is the way I am going to support my wife and children." He put the fish in a sack, and started on down the river. He had gone only a little way when he began to fish again, and again caught a great many, and then went on. He said to himself, "That is once that I have done this"; he did not remember the first trial. He went a little farther, and again caught many fish. Then again he was pleased, and said, "This is good; this is twice." His sack was now nearly full.

Again he tried it, and caught many. "That is three times," he said; but really it was four times.

The next time he began to fish, something caught hold of the strips of skin, and when he threw back his head, he could not pull this thing out of the water. Instead, it began to pull him in. He caught hold of the grass and weeds and brush, to hold himself, but they all pulled up. Finally, this great fish dragged him into the water and swallowed him. Now Wihio was so large that when the fish swallowed him it choked and died, and then floated down the stream.

Wihio's camp was down the stream from where he had been fishing, and his wife and his children were there. Early the next morning his wife went down to the stream for water, and there lying on a sandbar she saw a great big fish. The woman dropped her bucket and ran back to the camp, and called out: "Oh, children, down on the sandbar is the biggest fish I ever saw! Hurry and come down!" She ran and got her knife, and they all went down to the fish. They dragged it out on the sandbar, and the woman began to cut it up.

Wihio had heard her talking, and recognized her voice, and called out: "Hold on, my wife! Be careful! Do not cut me!" When the fish was cut open, and he got out, he said to his wife, "I wish to have the choice pieces of this fish saved for me, for I caught it." Then his wife was angry, and she began to beat him, and she knocked him about on the sandbar, while the strips of skin on his forehead flew about. At last Wihio begged his wife to cut off the strips, and she did so.

A SCABBY BULL

ONE time in the spring a herd of scabby bulls were lying together on the prairie. Presently one of them rose to his feet and went up on the hill. He stood there for a time, looking about, and then turned and ran down toward the other bulls. Just before he reached them, he stopped and shook himself, and all the old hair came off his body, so that he stood there naked. Then the bull went to the herd, and lay down among them.

After a little while he rose again and went up on the hill, as before. Again he ran down to the other bulls, stopped and shook himself, and short new hairs came out all over him. Once more he lay down.

Again he got up and went to the top of the hill, and again ran down, and stopped and shook himself, and he turned into an old scabby bull again. He went over and lay down.

A fourth time he went up on the hill, and came down running as hard as he could, and shook himself, and at once he was covered with new long hair, and looked round and smooth.

Wihio came out from behind the hill, where he had been watching, and went up to the bulls, crying; "Oh," he said, "I want to be able to do that; I want to be a bull."

The bull said, "You saw what I did, and where I stopped; you do the same; do just as I did."

Wihio went up on the hill and did as the bull had done, and when he shook himself he turned into a scabby bull. He did not wait long; he went up, and then ran down again and shook himself, and was covered with new hair. The third time he turned into a scabby bull when he shook himself. The fourth time he did it he had fine long new hair. He liked this; so soon he went up again, and again ran down and shook himself, and turned into a scabby bull again.

"Ah," said his bull friend, "you are now really a bull, and you must look out for people, because they kill us. We can smell them if we get

224

to leeward of them, and if we see or smell them we must run hard." Soon all the bulls got up and went on, and Wihio with them.

Before they had gone far, Wihio called out, "Look out! I can smell them; they are coming." The other bulls turned up their noses, but could smell nothing; but Wihio was frightened, and kept thinking he could smell something.

The bulls traveled a long way, and at last were tired and lay down. Wihio was very tired and went to sleep. After a time the other bulls got up and went on, leaving Wihio sleeping there, and when he awoke he was alone. When he saw that he was alone, he thought that the people had chased the other bulls away, and he was frightened almost to death. He ran this way and that way, and fell down steep places, and into ravines, and bruised himself badly. Sometimes he would call out, "I am not a bull, I am Wihio." It sounded just like the grunting of a bull. The more he ran, the more frightened he was, and he ran until he could run no longer.

HOW HE GOT TONGUE

Wihio was living in his home, and not far away was a camp of people. One day he had nothing to eat, and no way to kill anything; so he paid a visit to one of his neighbors, hoping that he would be asked to eat with him.

When Wihio stepped into the lodge he saw that there was plenty of food there—dried meat and back-fat and tongues. Every time the man went out he killed an elk, and when he did so he took the tongue out and saved it, and tongues hung all about his lodge. Wihio longed for the tongues, but the man did not offer him any; he just gave him some dried meat. As Wihio was returning to his lodge, he saw a coyote not far off, and called to him, asking him to come in.

When the coyote had sat down, Wihio told him about what he had seen in the man's lodge, and he asked the coyote to go there with him again, so they might eat there.

The coyote thought the man would not let him come in, because everyone knows that coyotes always steal meat.

"Well," said Wihio, "let us arrange some plan by which you can come. What can we do? How can we get in?" The coyote thought for a long time, and at last he told Wihio how they might do what they wished to. The coyote said: "Do you dress up like a woman, and tie me up like a baby, and carry me there. Give me good things to eat when you get the meat."

"Ah," said Wihio, "it is good; I will give you a part of everything that is given to me." Then he began to tie up the coyote like a baby, so that he could carry him. After he had done so he took up the coyote on his arm like a baby, and went back to the lodge and said to the man, "My child is crying for food." Wihio whispered to the coyote to cry for tongue, and he did so. The man asked Wihio what the baby wanted, and Wihio said, "He is crying for tongue." The man took a tongue and put it in the water and boiled it.

After the tongue was cooked the man gave it to Wihio, who began to eat, and gave the coyote only just a taste of it. Wihio ate all he could, for he was hungry. The coyote kept whispering to him, "Give me some too; I am hungry"; but Wihio continued to eat, and just dipped his fingers in the soup and let the coyote lick them. At last the coyote grew angry and said, "I am going to tell him about you, that you have dressed me up like a baby in order to get some tongue."

Wihio kept on eating very fast, and gave the coyote none of the tongue, and at last went out of the lodge, carrying the baby. He went to the river, and said to the coyote: "You were going to tell of me, were you? You ought to keep quiet when I am eating; you trouble me too much." Then he threw the coyote, all tied up, into the river, and he floated down the stream.

THE WONDERFUL SACK

A LONG time ago a man was living in a lodge by himself. He had no wife nor family, but about his lodge much meat was hanging on the branches and the drying scaffolds, and he had many hides and robes.

One day Wihio came that way, and entered the lodge and spoke to the man, saying: "I am glad that I have found you, my brother; I have been looking for you for a long time, and have asked everyone where you were. At last I got sure news about you, and learned where your lodge was; so I came straight to you."

After Wihio had said this the man began to cook food for him; and while he was cooking, Wihio was sitting there looking about the lodge. Tied up to a lodge pole at the back of the lodge was a great sack. Wihio could not think what might be in this sack, and kept wondering what it contained. The longer he looked at it the more curious he grew.

After he had eaten, Wihio said to the man, "My brother, may I sleep here tonight with you?" The man said, "Yes, yes; stay if you wish."

When night came they made up the beds to sleep. The man had been watching Wihio, and had seen him looking at the sack, and thought that Wihio wished to take it; so he took a cupful of water and put it on the ground at the back side of the fire, in front of the sack.

Soon they went to bed, and the man fell asleep; but Wihio did not sleep; he lay there watching and listening.

When the man was sleeping, Wihio arose, and reached up and untied the sack from the lodge pole, and put it on his back and started out of the lodge, carrying it.

Before he had gone far he suddenly came to the shores of a big lake, and started to go around it, running fast so that the man should not overtake him. He ran until nearly morning along the shores of this lake, which seemed to have no end. By this time he was very tired and sleepy; so he lay down to rest a little, the sack being still on his back so that he could start again just as soon as he awoke.

In the morning when the man awoke, he saw Wihio lying there with his head on the sack, and said to him, "My brother, what are you doing with my sack?" Wihio awoke, and was very much astonished to find himself still in the lodge. He did not know how to answer the man, but at last he said, "My brother, you have treated me so nicely that I was going to offer to carry your sack for you when you moved." The man took the sack and tied it to the lodge pole, where it belonged.

After they had eaten, they sat there talking, and Wihio said to the man, "My brother, what are you afraid of?" The man replied, "My brother, I am afraid of nothing except a goose."

Wihio said, "I also am afraid of that; a goose is a very dangerous bird." After a little while Wihio said to the man, "My brother, I am going," and he went out.

When night came, Wihio came back to the camp in the shape of a goose, and went behind the lodge and called loudly. The man was frightened and took his sack on his back, and rushed out of the lodge and ran away; and Wihio was glad, and went back to where he had left his wife and family. When he got to them he said: "My children, I am glad; now I have got what I have long wished for. I have driven from his lodge a person who has a good home and plenty of food. We will go there and live."

After they reached the lodge, Wihio told his wife about the sack, saying to her, "I want to find out what is in that sack, and I shall follow that man until I do so."

When they had eaten, Wihio set out to follow the tracks of the man, to see where he had gone. He followed him for a long time, but at last he found him, and again called out like a goose, and frightened the man. But when the man ran away he carried the sack with him. Twice more Wihio frightened him, and each time when the man ran away he took the sack; but the fourth time he left it behind him, and Wihio took it. But when the man dropped the sack he called out, saying, "I can open that sack only four times." Now Wihio put the sack on his back, and went back to the lodge, and said to his wife, "Well, I have got the thing I wished for."

After he had reached the lodge, Wihio untied the sack and opened the mouth, for he wished to see what was in it. As soon as he opened the mouth, a buffalo ran out, and the heads of other cows were seen crowding toward the mouth of the sack. Then Wihio quickly tied it up again.

"Aha," he said, "that is the way I shall do." He killed the buffalo, and they had plenty of food. When all the meat was gone he opened the sack again, and another cow ran out, and he tied up the sack and killed the cow.

When this meat was gone he let out another buffalo, and then again; but he had forgotten to keep count of the buffalo he had killed, and when he had opened the sack the fourth time he said, "That is three times."

A fifth time he opened the sack, and the moment it was opened many buffalo rushed out, and he could not close the sack. They came out in such numbers that they trampled on and killed him and all his family. Not one was left alive.

The buffalo started north and south and west and east, and spread all over the world. This is where the buffalo came from; and this is the last of Wihio.

THE COMING
OF THE WHITE MAN

THE COMING
OF THE WHITE MAN

THE COMING OF THE WHITE MAN

KNOWLEDGE of the white man came to the different tribes of the West at different times, but a century ago most of them knew little of him, and there are many tribes which have had a real intercourse with the whites for a still shorter time. Long before this the Spaniards in the southwest and on the Pacific coast had made their presence felt, but the Indians usually do not consider that Spaniards are of the same race with the people of European origin who came to them from the east, and often they have a special name for them.

Even after the Indians had learned of the existence of white people, they did not at once come into contact with them. It was often quite a long time before they even began to trade with them, and when they did so, it was in a very small way. The first articles traded for were arms, beads, blankets, and the gaudy finery that the savage loves. Horses—which transformed the Indian, which changed him from a mild and peaceful seeker after food to a warrior and a raider—were by many tribes first obtained not directly from the whites, but by barter from those of their own race.

Most tribes still preserve traditions of the time when they met the first white men, as well as of the time when they first saw horses; but in many cases this was so long ago that all details of the occurrence have been lost. It is certain that the Spaniards and their horses had worked their way up the Pacific slope into Oregon and Washington long before there was any considerable influx of white trappers into the plains country and the Rocky Mountains; and that of the western tribes, those which in miles were furthest from Mexico were the last to learn of the whites and their wonderful powers. One of these peoples was the Blackfeet, of whom I have been told by men still living in the tribe that fifty years ago no Blackfoot could count up to ten, and that a little earlier the number of horses in all three tribes of that confederation was very small. Then they had but few guns, and many of them even used still the stone arrowheads and hatchets and the bone knives of their primitive ancestors.

233

Pawnee, Blackfoot and Cheyenne

A people whose intercourse with the whites has been so short and, until recent times, so limited, ought to retain some detailed account of their earliest meeting with civilized men, and such a tradition has come to me from John Monroe, a half-breed Piegan, now nearly seventy years old. It tells of the first time the Blackfeet saw white people—a party of traders from the east, either Frenchmen from Montreal, or one of the very earliest parties of Hudson Bay men which ascended the Saskatchewan River. John Monroe first heard the narrative when a boy from a Blood Indian named Sútane, who was then an old man, and Sútane's grandfather was one of the party who met the white people. The occurrence probably took place during the latter half of the eighteenth century.

When this people lived in the north, a party of the Blackfeet started out to war. They travelled on, always going southward, until they came to a big water. While passing through a belt of timber on the north bank of this river, they came upon what they took for strange beaver work, where these animals had been cutting down the trees. But on looking closely at the cuttings, they saw that the chips were so large that it must have been an animal much bigger than a beaver that could open its mouth wide enough to cut such chips. They did not understand what this could be, for none of them had ever seen anything like it before. Each man expressed his mind about this, and at last they concluded that some great under-water animal must have done it. At one place they saw that the trunk of a tree was missing, and found the trail over the ground where it had been dragged away from the stump. They followed this trail, so as to see where the animals had taken the log, and what they had done with it, and as they went on, they found many other small trails like this one, all leading into one larger main trail. They then saw the footprints of persons, but they were prints of a foot shaped differently from theirs. There was a deep mark at the heel; the tracks were not flat like those made by people.

They followed the trail, which kept getting larger and wider as it went. Every little while, another trail joined it. When they came to where they could look through the timber, they saw before them a little open spot on the bank of the river. They looked through the underbrush, and saw what they at first thought were bears, and afterward took to be persons, lifting logs and putting them up in a large

234

pile. They crept closer, to where they could see better, and then concluded that these were not people. They were very woolly on the face. Long masses of hair hung down from their chins. They were not clothed—wore no robes. The Blackfeet said: "Why, they have nothing on! They are naked!" Some of them said, "Those are *Súye tuppi*" (water people). They stole around to another point of the timber, still nearer, where they could see better. There they came close to one of these people alone. He was gathering sticks and putting them in a pile. They saw that the skin of his hands and face was white. This one had no hair on his face. So they said: "Well, this must be a she water animal. The he ones have hair on the face, and the she ones do not."

The oldest man of the party then said: "We had better go away. Maybe they will smell us or feel us here, and perhaps they will kill us, or do something fearful. Let us go." So they went away.

When they got back to their camp, they told what they had seen; that to the south they had found animals that were very much like people—water animals. They said that these animals were naked. That some of them had red bodies, and some were black all over, except a red mark around the bodies and a fine red tail. Moreover, these people wore no robes or leggings and no breech-clouts.

This description caused a great excitement in the camp. Some thought that the strange beings were water animals, and others that they were a new people. All the men of the camp started south to see what this could be. Before they left the camp, the head man told them to be very careful in dealing with the animals, not to interfere with them nor to get in their way, and not to try to hurt them nor to anger them.

The party started, and when they reached the opening, the animals were still there at work. After they had watched them for some time the head man of the party said to the others: "All you stay here, and I will go down to them alone. If they do nothing to me you wait here, but if they attack or hurt me, you rush on them, and we will fight hard, and try not to let them capture any of us." The man started, and when he came close to the corner of the houses he stood still. One of the men, who was working near by, walked up to him, looked him straight in the face, and stretched out his arm. The Indian looked at him, and did not know what he wanted. Some more of the men came up to him, and the Indian saw that all of them were persons like himself, except that they were of a different colour and had a different voice. The hair on their faces was fair.

When the other Indians saw that no harm had been done to their leader, some of them went down to him, one by one, and by twos and threes, but most of the party remained hidden in the timber. They were still afraid of these strange new beings.

The whites spoke to them, and asked them to come into the house, making motions to them, but the Indians did not understand what was meant by these signs. The whites would walk away, and then come back and take hold of the Indians' robes and pull them. At last some of the Blackfeet followed the white men into the house. Those who had gone in came back and told the others strange stories of the wonderful things they had seen in this house. As they gained confidence, many others went in, while still others would not go in, nor would they go close to the new people.

The whites showed them a long and curious-looking piece of wood. They did not know of what kind of stone one part of it was made. It was hard and black. The white man took down from the wall a white cow's horn and poured out some black sand into his hand, and poured it down into a hole in this long stick. Then he took a little bunch of grass and pushed this into the hole with another stick, then measured with his fingers the length of the stick left out of the hole. Then he took a round thing out of a bag, and put it into the hole, and put down some more fine grass. Then he poured out some more of the black sand into the side of the stick. The Indians stood around, taking great interest in the way the man was handling this stick. The white man now began to make all kinds of signs to the Indians, which they did not understand. Sometimes he would make a big sound with his mouth, and then point to the stick. He would put the stick to his shoulder, holding it out in front of him, and make a great many motions. Then he gave it to one of the Indians. He showed him the under parts, and put his finger there. The Indian touched the under part and the stick went off in the air and made a thundering sound, a terrible crash. The Indian staggered back, and the others were very much scared. Some dropped to the ground, while all the whites laughed and shook their heads at them.

All laughed, and made many signs to the Blackfeet, none of which they understood. The white man took down the horn of black sand, and again did these things to the stick, but this time the Indians all stood back. They were afraid. When he had finished the motions, the white man invited them out of doors. Then he sat down, and took aim at a log lying on the ground. The same great thunder sounded. He walked up to the log, showed the bullet hole, and pushed a little stick into it; then he loaded the gun again.

By this time the Indians were beginning to understand the power of the stick. After the white man had loaded it, he handed the gun to the Indian, took him close to the log, showed him how to aim the gun and how to pull the trigger. The Indian fired and hit the log.

The white men showed these Blackfeet their knives, whittling sticks with them, and showing them how well they could cut. The Indians were very much delighted with the power of these knives. Then they saw a big, woolly white man standing out in front of the house, and he with his axe would cut a big log in two in only a short time. All these things were very strange to them. The white men looked closely at the Blackfoot war dresses and arms and wanted them, and gave their visitors some knives and copper cups for their dresses and the skins that they wore. The visitors stayed with the white men some days, camping near by. They kept wondering at these people, at how they looked, the things which they had, and what they did. The white men kept making signs to them, but they understood nothing of it all.

After a time the Blackfeet returned to their camp. Afterward, many others visited the whites, and this was the beginning of a friendly inter-course between the two peoples. After a time they came to understand each other a little, and trade relations were opened. The Indians learned that they could get the white man's things in exchange for the skins of small animals, and they began to trade and to get guns. It was when they got these arms that they first began to take courage, and to go out of the timber on to the prairie toward the mountains. In those old days the Hudson Bay traders used to tell the Indians to bring in the hair from the skins of buffalo, to put it in sacks and bring it in to trade. They did so, but all of a sudden the traders would take no more buffalo hair.

Pawnee, Blackfoot and Cheyenne

This probably refers to the attempt made during the last century in the Selkirk settlement to establish a corporation for making cloth from buffalo hair.

Of the special articles brought by the white men, the first to exercise an important influence on the people were horses. The possession of these animals greatly increased their liberty, stimulated them to wars with their neighbours, and in fact wrought a most important change in the character of the people. The knowledge of the horse advanced from the south northward, and these animals spread northward up the Pacific coast more rapidly than on the east side of the mountains. The tribes of the southern plains—Comanches, Kiowas, Wichitas, Arapahoes, Navajoes, and others—obtained horses very early. The Pawnees and various tribes of the Dakotas later. The Utes, Snakes, and Kutenais had horses early; and the last of the plains tribes to obtain them were the Blackfeet, Assiniboines, and Plains Crees. In the case of tribes that have long had horses, it is impossible to even approximate the date at which they were obtained—it happened too long ago—but with the more northern tribes, which have had horses for a short time only, I have been more successful in my inquiries, and from several old men among the Piegans I have accounts of the first coming of horses.

As I have said, many myths exist to account for the coming of the horse, but this Piegan testimony is that of an eye-witness. Wolf Calf is probably over one hundred years old. He well remembers when the first white men passed through the country, and old men of seventy years or thereabouts tell me that he was a proved warrior when they were little boys. He believes that he was born in 1793. From him I have definite and detailed accounts of the ways of the Piegans in days before they had been at all influenced by civilized man. I believe his statements to be as worthy of credence as any can be which depend solely on memory. The account which follows is a translation of his narrative, taken down from his own lips some years ago. He said:

"Long ago, when I was young, just getting big enough to use a bow, we used arrowpoints of stone. Then the knives were made of flint. Not long after this, arrowpoints of sheet iron began to come into use. After we used the stone knives, we began to get white men's knives. The first of these that we had were made of a strip of tin. This was set into a bone, so that only a narrow edge of the tin protruded, and this was sharpened and used for skinning.

"Before that time the Piegans had no horses. When they moved their camp they packed their lodges on dogs.

"The first horses we ever saw came from west of the mountains. A band of the Piegans were camped on Belly River, at a place that we call 'Smash the Heads,' where we jumped buffalo. They had been driving buffalo over the cliff here, so that they had plenty of meat.

"There had come over the mountains to hunt buffalo a Kutenai who had some horses, and he was running buffalo; but for some reason he had no luck. He could kill nothing. He had seen from far off the Piegan camp, but he did not go near it, for the Piegans and the Kutenais were enemies.

"This Kutenai could not kill anything, and he and his family had nothing to eat and were starving. At last he made up his mind that he would go into the camp of his enemies and give himself up, for he said, 'I might as well be killed at once as die of hunger.' So with his wife and children he rode away from his camp up in the mountains, leaving his lodge standing and his horses feeding about it, all except those which his woman and his three children were riding, and started for the camp of the Piegans.

"They had just made a big drive, and had run a great lot of buffalo over the cliff. There were many dead in the pískun, and the men were killing those that were left alive, when suddenly the Kutenai, on his horse, followed by his wife and children on theirs, rode over a hill near by. When they saw him, all the Piegans were astonished and wondered what this could be. None of them had ever seen anything like it, and they were afraid. They thought it was something mysterious. The chief of the Piegans called out to his people: 'This is something very strange. I have heard of wonderful things that have happened from the earliest times until now, but I never heard of anything like this. This thing must have come from above (i. e., from the sun), or else it must have come out of the hill (i. e., from the earth). Do not do anything to it; be still and wait. If we try to hurt it, may be it will ride into that hill again, or may be something bad will happen. Let us wait.'

"As it drew nearer, they could see that it was a man coming, and that he was on some strange animal. The Piegans wanted their chief to go toward him and speak to him. The chief did not wish to do this; he was afraid; but at last he started to go to meet the Kutenai, who was coming. When he got near to him, the Kutenai made signs that he was friendly, and patted his horse on his neck and made signs to the chief. 'I give you this animal.' The chief made signs that he was friendly, and the Kutenais rode into the camp and were received as friends, and food was given them and they ate, and their hunger was satisfied.

"The Kutenai stayed with these Piegans for some time, and the Kutenai man told the chief that he had more horses at his camp up in the mountains, and that beyond the mountains there were plenty of horses. The Piegan said, 'I have never heard of a man riding an animal like this.' He asked the Kutenai to bring in the rest of his horses; and one night he started out, and the next day came back driving all his horses before him, and they came to the camp, and all the people saw them and looked at them and wondered.

"Some time after this the Kutenai said to the Piegan chief: 'My friend, why not come across the mountains to my country and visit me? I should like to have you see my country. Bring with you those of your people who wish to come. My people will give you many horses.'

"Then the Piegan chief said: 'It is good. I will go with you and visit you.' He told his people that he was going with this Kutenai, and that any of them who wished to do so might go with him. Many of the Piegans packed their dogs with their lodges and with dried meat and started with the Kutenai, and those who had no dogs packed dried meat in their parfleches and carried it on their backs.

"In those days the Piegans did not take women to sit beside them until they were near middle life—about thirty-five or forty years old; but among those who went across the mountains was a young man less than thirty years old, who had taken a wife. Many of the people did not like this, and some made fun of him because he had taken a wife so young.

"The party had not travelled many days when they got across the mountains, and near to where the Kutenai camp was. When they had come near it, the Kutenai man went on ahead, and when he had reached his village, he told the chief that he had with him visitors, Piegans who lived on the prairie, and that they had no horses, but had plenty of buffalo meat. The Kutenai chief told the man to bring these Piegans into the camp. He did so, and they were well received and were given presents of horses, and they traded their buffalo meat for more horses. The young man with the wife had four parfleches of dried meat, and for each one of these he received a horse, and all four were mares.

"The Piegans, stayed with the Kutenais a long time, but at length they returned over the mountains to their own country, taking their horses with them. When the other bands of the Piegans saw these horses and heard what had happened, they began to make peace with the Kutenais, and to trade with them for more horses. The young man who had a wife kept the four mares, and took them about with him wherever he went. He said to his wife: 'We will not give away any of these horses. They are all mares and all young. They will breed and soon we will have more.' The mares bred, and the young man, as he grew older, proved to be a good warrior. He began to go to war against the Snakes, and to take horses from them, and after a time he had a great herd of horses.

"This young man, though once everybody had laughed at him, finally became head chief of the Piegans. His name at first was Dog, and afterward Sits in the Middle, and at last Many Horses. He had so many horses he could not keep track of them all. After he had so many horses, he would select ten boys out of each band of the Piegans to care for his horses. Many Horses had more horses than all the rest of the tribe. Many Horses died a good many years ago. These were the first horses the Piegans saw.

"When they first got horses the people did not know what they fed on. They would offer the animals pieces of dried meat, or would take a piece of backfat and rub their noses with it, to try to get them to eat it. Then the horses would turn away and put down their heads, and begin to eat the grass of the prairie."

The date first mentioned by Wolf Calf would be—if we assume his age to be given correctly—about 1804–1806, or when he was from ten to twelve years of age, and I presume that their first horses may have come into the hands of the Blackfeet about that time, or in the very earliest years of the present century. This would agree fairly well with the statement of Mr. Hugh Monroe, who says that in 1813, when he first came among this people, they had possessed horses for a short time only, and had recently begun to make war excursions to the south on a large scale for the purpose of securing more horses from their enemies. Hugh Monroe's wife, who was born about 1796–1798, used to say that when she was a little girl the Piegans had no horses, dogs being their only beasts of burden, and all the evidence that I can gather in this tribe seems to point to the date given as that at which they obtained their first horses. We know that the chief Many Horses was killed in the great battle of the Cypress Hills in the autumn of 1867, and he is always spoken of as a very old man at that time.

Wolf Calf also gave the following account of the first visit of white traders to a Piegan camp. He said: "White people had begun to come into this country, and Many Horses' young men wanted ropes and iron arrowpoints and saddle blankets, and the people were beginning to kill furs and skins to trade. Many Horses began to trade with his own people for these things. He would ask the young men of the tribe to kill skins for him, and they would bring them to him and he would give them a horse or two in exchange. Then he would send his relations in to the Hudson Bay post to trade, but he would never go himself. The white men wanted to see him, and sent word to him to come in, but he would never do so.

"At length, one winter, these white men packed their dog sledges with goods and started to see Many Horses. They took with them guns. The Piegans heard that the whites were coming, and Many Horses sent word to all the people to come together and meet him at a certain place, where the whites were coming. When these came to the camp, they asked where Many Horses' lodge was, and the people pointed out to them the Crow painted lodge. The whites went to this lodge and began to unpack their things—guns, clothing, knives, and goods of all kinds.

"Many Horses sent two men to go in different directions through the camp and ask all the principal men, young and old, to come together to his lodge. They all came. Some went in and some sat outside. Then these white men began to distribute the guns, and with each gun they gave a bundle of powder and ball. At this same time, the young men received white blankets and the old men black coats. Then we first got knives, and the white men showed us how to use knives;

to split down the legs and rip up the belly—to skin for trade. There were not knives enough for each to have one, and it was then that knives with tin edges were made.

"The whites showed us many things. They had flint, steel, and punk, and showed the Indians how to use them. A white man held the flint and struck it with the steel and lighted the punk. Then he gave them to an Indian and told him to do the same. He did so, but when he saw the spark burning the tinder, he was frightened and dropped it.

"Before that, fire was made with firesticks, the twirling stick, being made of greasewood, was hard, and in the hollow which received the point, finely powdered dry grass was put, which caught the fire. This was transferred to tinder and blown into a flame."

As I have said elsewhere, the possession of guns and horses transformed the Blackfeet from a more or less stationary people dwelling in the timber, and devoting all their energies to hunting and the food supply, to a tribe whose chief ambition was the acquiring of glory and riches by warlike pursuits. Now they began to go to war, and in a few years they had conquered from their enemies on the south a great territory, and had begun to make themselves rich in horses. Inhabiting a country abounding in buffalo, it was easy for them to procure robes to supply to the traders who at length penetrated their country, and so to provide themselves with all the goods that the white men offered. But fast in the wake of the white men followed disease, and smallpox and measles and scarlet fever breaking out in their camps, swept off thousands upon thousands of the race. The white men learned that Indians liked liquor and began to use this in trade, and liquor killed more than disease.

Any tribe of Indians who had obtained possessions of any sort from the white man had manifestly a tremendous advantage over any other tribe who still had only their primitive equipment, and we are told by Cheyenne tradition that that brave and warlike people during their migration toward the southwest were utterly routed and put to flight by the Assiniboines, who had recently obtained guns from the white traders.

As a rule, the early intercourse between Indians and whites in the West was friendly, and their relations pleasant. Yet among the more warlike tribes, stranger and enemy were synonymous terms, so that the horses of white men were often stolen. Of course, when this occurred, efforts were made to kill the thieves, and thus active war was very often brought about. A man or two killed on either side would for some time to come insure reprisals and fighting at all subsequent meetings of parties of whites and Indians belonging to the tribe engaged, and each battle would make others more probable. Sometimes a peace would be made which was lasting, and there are some tribes which have never engaged in any wars with the whites, while others, in the face of shameful injury and ill treatment, have always been their faithful allies in their wars with other tribes.

BENT'S FORT

I

WHEN BEAVER SKINS WERE MONEY

Whenever the history of the Southwest shall be written, more than one long and interesting chapter must be devoted to the first permanent settlement on its plains and the first permanent settler there. In the accounts of that wide territory through which the old Santa Fé trail passed, William Bent and Bent's Old Fort have frequent mention.

Who were the Bents and whence did they come?

Silas Bent was born in the Colony of Massachusetts in 1768. His father is said to have been one of those who attended the famous "Boston Tea Party." Silas was educated for the bar, and came to St. Louis in 1804 at the time the government of Louisiana was turned over to the American authorities. Here he served as a judge of the Superior Court, and here he resided until his death, in 1827.

Of his seven sons, John was educated for the bar and became a well-known attorney of St. Louis. The youngest son, Silas, as flag-lieutenant of the flag-ship "Mississippi," was with Perry in Japan, and wrote a report on the Japan current for an American scientific society. He delivered addresses on meteorology in St. Louis in 1879, and on climate as affecting cattle-breeding in the year 1884. Four other sons—Charles, William W., and later George and Robert—were prominent in the Indian trade on the upper Arkansas and elsewhere between 1820 and 1850, and remained trading in that region until they died.

The leading spirit in this family of Indian traders was William W. Bent. Early in life Charles and William Bent had been up on the Missouri River working for the American Fur Company. Colonel Bent stated to his son George that he went up there in the year 1816, when very young. Very likely he was then a small boy only ten or twelve years old. It was there that Charles and William Bent became acquainted with Robert Campbell, of St. Louis, who remained a firm friend of the brothers throughout his life. William Bent could speak the Sioux language fluently and the Sioux had called him Wa-sĭ'cha-chischĭ'-la, meaning Little White Man, a name which confirms the statement that he entered the trade very young, and seems to warrant the belief that his work for the fur company was at some post in the Sioux country.

In his testimony before the joint commission which inquired into Indian affairs on the plains in 1865, William Bent stated that he had first come to the upper Arkansas and settled near the Purgatoire, just below the present city of Pueblo, Colorado, in 1824; that is to say, two years before he and his brother began to erect their first trading establishment on the Arkansas. Previous to this time William Bent had been trapping in the mountains near there, and may very well have done some individual trading with the Indians.

William Bent was undoubtedly the first permanent white settler in what is now Colorado, and for a very long time he was not only its first settler, but remained its most important white citizen.

By his fair and open dealings, by his fearless conduct, and by his love of justice, William Bent soon won the respect and confidence of the Indians with whom he had to do. Among the rough fraternity of mountain trappers he was also very popular, his reputation for courage being remarkable even among that class of daring men. He was tirelessly active in prosecuting the aims of his trade, making frequent trips to the camps of the various tribes with which he, and later his company, had dealings, and to the Mexican settlements in the valley of Taos and to Santa Fé. Every year, probably from 1824 to 1864, he made at least one journey from the fort on the Arkansas, across the plains of Colorado, Kansas, and Missouri, to the settlements on the Missouri frontier.

About 1835 William Bent married Owl Woman, the daughter of White Thunder, an important man among the Cheyennes, then the keeper of the medicine arrows. Bent's Fort was his home, and there his children were born, the oldest, Mary, about 1836, Robert in 1839 —his own statement made in 1865 says 1841—George in July, 1843, and Julia in 1847. Owl Woman died at the fort in 1847 in giving birth to Julia, and her husband afterward married her sister, Yellow Woman. Charles Bent was the child of his second marriage.

William Bent appears to have been the first of the brothers to go into the Southwestern country to trade for fur, but Charles is said to have gone to Santa Fé as early as 1819, and a little later must have joined William. The two, with Ceran St. Vrain and one of the Chouteaus, established the early trading post near the Arkansas. After occupying this stockade for two years or more, they moved down below Pueblo and built another stockade on the Arkansas. Two years later they began to build the more ambitious post afterward known as Bent's, or Fort William, or Bent's Old Fort. George and Robert Bent apparently did not come out to the fort until after it was completed—perhaps after it had been for some time in operation. Benito Vasquez was at one time a partner in the company.

It was in 1828 that the Bent brothers, with St. Vrain, began this large fort, fifteen miles above the mouth of Purgatoire River. It was not completed until 1832. Four years seems a long time to be spent in the construction of such a post, even though it was built of adobe brick, but there were reasons for the delay. Charles Bent was determined that the fort should be built of adobes in order to make it fire-proof, so that under no circumstances could it be burned by the Indians. Besides that, adobes were much more durable and more comfortable—cool in summer, warm in winter—than logs would have been. When the question of how the fort should be built had been decided, Charles Bent went to New Mexico, and from Taos and Santa Fé sent over a number of Mexicans to make adobe brick. With them he sent some wagon-loads of Mexican wool to mix with the clay of the bricks, thus greatly lengthening the life of the adobes.

Only a short time, however, after the laborers had reached the intended site of the fort, smallpox broke out among them, and it was necessary to send away those not attacked. William Bent, St. Vrain, Kit Carson, and other white men who were there caught the smallpox from the Mexicans, and though none died they were so badly marked by it that some of the Indians who had known them well in the early years of the trading did not recognize them when they met again.

During the prevalence of the smallpox at the post William Bent sent a runner, Francisco, one of his Mexican herders, north, to warn the Cheyennes not to come near the post. Francisco set out for the Black Hills, and on his way encountered a large war-party of Cheyennes on their way to the fort. He told them of what had happened, and warned them to return north and not to come near the post until sent for. The Cheyennes obeyed, and it was not until some time later, when all at Fort William had recovered and when the temporary stockade with all the infected material that it contained had been burned, that Bent and St. Vrain, with a few pack-mules, started north for the Black Hills to find the Cheyennes and invite them to return to the post. The year of this journey has been given me as 1831. Perhaps it may have been a year earlier.

After the smallpox had ceased, more Mexican laborers were sent for, and work on the fort was resumed. Not long before his death, Kit Carson stated that at one time more than a hundred and fifty Mexicans were at work on the construction of the post.

Accounts of the dimensions of the fort differ, but on certain points all agree: that it was of adobes, set square with the points of the compass, and on the north bank of the Arkansas River. Garrard says that the post was a hundred feet square and the walls thirty feet in height. Another account says that the walls ran a hundred and fifty feet east and west and a hundred feet north and south, and that they were seventeen feet high. J. T. Hughes, however, in his *Doniphan's Expedition*, printed in Cincinnati in 1848, says:

"Fort Bent is situated on the north bank of the Arkansas, 650 miles west of Fort Leavenworth, in latitude 38° 2' north, and longitude

103° 3′ west from Greenwich. The exterior walls of this fort, whose figure is that of an oblong square, are fifteen feet high and four feet thick. It is 180 feet long and 135 feet wide and is divided into various compartments, the whole built of adobes or sun-dried bricks."

At the southwest and northeast corners of these walls were bastions, or round towers, thirty feet in height and ten feet in diameter inside, with loopholes for muskets and openings for cannon. Garrard speaks of the bastions as hexagonal in form.

Around the walls in the second stories of the bastions hung sabres and great heavy lances with long, sharp blades. These were intended for use in case an attempt were made to take the fort by means of ladders put up against the wall. Besides these cutting and piercing implements, the walls were hung with flint-lock muskets and pistols.

In the east wall of the fort was a wide gateway formed by two immense swinging doors made of heavy planks. These doors were studded with heavy nails and plated with sheet-iron, so that they could never be burned by the Indians. The same was true of the gateway which entered the corral, to be described later.

Over the main gate of the fort was a square watch tower surmounted by a belfry, from the top of which rose a flagstaff. The watch tower contained a single room with windows on all sides, and in the room was an old-fashioned long telescope, or spy-glass, mounted on a pivot. Here certain members of the garrison, relieving each other at stated intervals, were constantly on the lookout. There was a chair for the watchman to sit in and a bed for his sleeping. If the watchman, through his glass, noticed anything unusual—for example, if he saw a great dust rising over the prairie—he notified the people below. If a suspicious-looking party of Indians was seen approaching, the watchman signalled to the herder to bring in the horses, for the stock was never turned loose, but was always on herd.

In the belfry, under a little roof which rose above the watch tower, hung the bell of the fort, which sounded the hours for meals. Two tame white-headed eagles kept at the fort were sometimes confined within this belfry, or at others were allowed to fly about free, returning of their own accord to sleep in the belfry. One of these eagles finally disappeared, and for a long time it was not known what had become of it. Then it was learned that it had been killed for its feathers by a young Indian at some distance from the fort.

At the back of the fort over the gate, which opened into the corral, was a second-story room rising high above the walls, as the watch tower did in front. This room—an extraordinary luxury for the time —was used as a billiard-room during the later years of the post. It was long enough to accommodate a large billiard-table, and across one end of the room ran a counter, or bar, over which drinkables were served. These luxuries were brought out by Robert and George Bent, young men who did not come out to the fort until some time after it had been constructed, and who, being city-dwellers—for I have no record of their having any early experience of frontier life—no doubt felt that they required city amusements.

The watch tower and billiard-room were supported on heavy adobe walls running at right angles to the main enclosing walls of the fort, and these supporting walls formed the ends of the rooms on either side of the gates in the outer walls.

The stores, warehouses, and living-rooms of the post were ranged around the walls, and opened into the patio, or courtyard—the hollow square within. In some of the books dealing with these old times it is said that when the Indians entered the fort to trade, cannon were loaded and sentries patrolled the walls with loaded guns. This may have been true of the early days of the fort, but it was not true of the latter part of the decade between 1840 and 1850. At that time the Indians, or at least the Cheyenne Indians, had free run of the post and were allowed to go upstairs, on the walls, and into the watch tower. The various rooms about the courtyard received light and air from the doors and windows opening out into this courtyard, which was gravelled. The floors of the rooms were of beaten clay, as was commonly the case in Mexican houses, and the roofs were built in the same fashion that long prevailed in the West. Poles were laid from the front wall to the rear, slightly inclined toward the front. Over these poles twigs or brush were laid, and over the brush clay was spread, tramped hard, and gravel thrown over this. These roofs were used as a promenade by the men of the fort and their families in the evenings. The top of the fort walls reached about four feet above these roofs, or breast-high of a man, and these walls were pierced with loopholes through which to shoot in case of attack.

Hughes in his *Doniphan's Expedition* says: "The march upon Santa Fé was resumed Aug. 2, 1846, after a respite of three days in the neighborhood of Fort Bent. As we passed the fort the American flag was raised in compliment to our troops and in concert with our own streamed most animatingly on the gale that swept from the desert, while the tops of the houses were crowded with Mexican girls and Indian squaws, beholding the American Army."

On the west side of the fort and outside the walls was the horse corral. It was as wide as the fort and deep enough to contain a large herd. The walls were about eight feet high and three feet thick at the top. The gate was on the south side of the corral, and so faced the river. It was of wood, but was completely plated with sheet-iron. More than that, to prevent any one from climbing in by night, the tops of the walls had been thickly planted with cactus—a large variety which grows about a foot high and has great fleshy leaves closely covered with many and sharp thorns. This grew so luxuriantly that in some places the leaves hung down over the walls, both within and without, and gave most efficient protection against any living thing that might wish to surmount the wall.

Through the west wall of the fort a door was cut, leading from the stockade into the corral, permitting people to go through and get horses without going outside the fort and opening the main gate of the corral. This door was wide and arched at the top. It was made large enough, so that in case of necessity—if by chance an attacking party seemed likely to capture the horses and mules in the corral—the door could be opened and the herd run inside the main stockade.

About two hundred yards to the south of the fort, and so toward the river bank, on a little mound, stood a large ice-house built of adobes or sun-dried bricks. In winter when the river was frozen this ice-house was filled, and in it during the summer was kept all the surplus fresh meat—buffalo tongues, antelope, dried meat and tongues —and also all the bacon. At times the ice-house was hung thick with fresh food.

On hot days, with the other little children, young George Bent used to go down to the ice-house and get in it to cool off, and his father's negro cook used to come down and send them away, warning them not to go in there from the hot sun, as it was too cold and they might get sick. This negro cook, Andrew Green by name, a slave owned by Governor Charles Bent, was with him when he was killed in Taos, and afterward came to the fort and was there for many years, but was at last taken back to St. Louis and there set free. He had a brother "Dick," often mentioned in the old books.

Besides Bent's Fort, Bent and St. Vrain owned Fort St. Vrain, on the South Platte, opposite the mouth of St. Vrain's Fork, and Fort Adobe, on the Canadian. Both these posts were built of adobe brick. Fort St. Vrain was built to trade with the Northern Indians; that is, with the Sioux and Northern Cheyennes, who seldom got down south as far as the Arkansas River, and so would not often come to Fort William. The Fort Adobe on the Canadian was built by request of the chiefs of the Kiowa, Comanches, and Apache to trade with these people. The chiefs who made this request were To′hau sen (Little Mountain) and Eagle-Tail Feathers, speaking for the Kiowa, Shaved Head for the Comanche, and Poor (Lean) Bear for the Apache.

These in their day were men of importance. Shaved Head was a great friend of the whites and a man of much influence with his own people and with neighboring tribes. He wore the left side of his head shaved close, while the hair on the right side was long, hanging down to his waist or below. His left ear was perforated with many holes made by a blunt awl heated red-hot, and was adorned with many little brass rings. Before peace was made between the Kiowas, Comanches, and Apaches in the year 1840, the last three tribes were more or less afraid to visit Fort William, lest they should there meet a large camp of their enemies, and Colonel Bent and the traders were also especially anxious to avoid any collision at the fort. Each tribe would expect the trader to take his part, and this he could not do without incurring the enmity of the other tribes. The wish of the trader was to be on good terms with all tribes, and this William Bent accomplished with singular discretion. Although he had a Cheyenne wife, he was on excellent terms, and always remained so, with the enemies of the Cheyennes.

Both Fort St. Vrain and Fort Adobe, being built of adobes, lasted for a long time, and their ruins have been seen until quite recently. Near the ruins of Fort Adobe two important fights have taken place, to be referred to later.

In the business of the fort William Bent had the direction of the trade with the Indians, while his brother Charles seems to have had more to do with affairs in the Mexican settlements, until his death there, at the hands of the Mexicans and Pueblos, in the year 1847. It is not certain when St. Vrain, Lee, and Benito Vasquez became partners in the business, nor how long they were interested in it. George and Robert Bent, who came out from St. Louis, certainly later than the two elder brothers, may have been partners, but there is nothing to show that they were so. Robert died in 1847.

Some time before this George Bent went to Mexico and there married a Mexican girl, by whom he had two children, a son and a daughter. The son, Robert, went to school in St. Louis. He died at Dodge City, Kan., in 1875. George Bent was a great friend of Frank P. Blair, whom he appointed guardian for his children. He died at the fort about 1848 of consumption, and was buried near his brother Robert in the graveyard which lay a short distance northeast of the northeast bastion of the fort. The old tailor, a Frenchman, afterward planted cactus over George Bent's grave to protect it from the wolves and coyotes. Their remains were later removed to St. Louis.

After the death of Charles Bent, in 1847, William Bent continued his work. Perhaps St. Vrain may have remained a partner for a time. Fitzpatrick speaks of "Messrs. Bent and St. Vrain's post" in 1850. Bent was an active man and interested in many other projects besides the fort and trade with the Indians. He bought sheep and mules in New Mexico and drove them across the plains to the Missouri market. In the forties, in company with several other men, he secured a large land grant from the Mexican government in the Arkansas valley above the fort and attempted to found a colony there. Mexican settlers were established on the lands. The colonists were inert, the Indians were hostile, and from these and other causes the project proved a failure. In 1847 William Bent and St. Vrain drove a large herd of Mexican cattle to the Arkansas and wintered them in the valley near the fort, thus making the first step toward establishing the cattle industry, which many years later so flourished on the plains.

Besides his lands near the fort, Bent had a fine farm at Westport (now Kansas City), in Missouri, and a ranch south of the Arkansas in the Mexican territory. In 1846 he guided Colonel Price's Missouri regiment across the plains to New Mexico, and was so popular among the volunteer officers that they gave him the brevet of colonel, a title which stuck to him until the day of his death.

II

GOVERNOR CHARLES BENT

CHARLES BENT was a close rival to his brother William in the esteem of his fellow traders and the trappers and Indians of the Arkansas. He seems from the first, however, to have taken the most active part in the Santa Fé trade of the company, leaving the Indian trade to the other partners. Among the traders and teamsters of the Santa Fé caravans he was as much liked as William Bent was among the trappers and Indians; indeed, on more than one occasion, he was elected captain of the caravan and conducted it safely to Santa Fé. These caravans of Missouri traders were richly laden for those days. The outfit of 1832 brought back from New Mexico $100,000 in specie and $90,000 in other property, including large numbers of Mexican mules. In 1833 the caravan with Bent as captain assembled at Diamond Springs, on the Missouri frontier. There were 184 men, with ninety-three large wagons loaded with goods. They brought back $100,000 in money and much other property.

Charles Bent married a Mexican woman and made his home at San Fernando, a small town in the valley of Taos. He was popular among his Mexican and Pueblo neighbors until he was appointed governor of the territory by General Kearny, who marched into New Mexico with his little army in the fall. Having put Governor Bent and his civil government in control of affairs, the general left a few troops in and about Santa Fé, and with the rest of his forces marched for California. Hardly had he gone when rumors of a revolt of the Mexican and Indian population against American rule began to be heard, and late in December evidence of such a plot was unearthed. These events are set forth in the following letter from Governor Bent to the Hon. James Buchanan, secretary of state:

"Santa Fé, N. M., Dec. 26, 1846.—Sir: I have been informed indirectly that Col. A. W. Doniphan, who, in October last, marched with his regiment against the Navajo Indians, has made treaty of peace with them. Not having been officially notified of this treaty, I am not able to state the terms upon which it has been concluded; but, so far as I am able to learn, I have but little ground to hope that it will be permanent.

"On the 17th inst. I received information from a Mexican friendly to our Government that a conspiracy was on foot among the native Mexicans, having for its object the expulsion of the United States troops and the civil authorities from the territory. I immediately brought into requisition every means in my power to ascertain who were the movers in the rebellion, and have succeeded in securing seven of the secondary conspirators. The military and civil officers are now both in pursuit of the two leaders and prime movers of the rebellion; but as several days have elapsed, I am apprehensive that they will have made their escape from the territory.

"So far as I am informed this conspiracy is confined to the four northern counties of the territory, and the men considered as leaders in the affair cannot be said to be men of much standing.

"After obtaining the necessary information to designate and secure the persons of the participators in the conspiracy, I thought it advisable to turn them over to the military authorities in order that these persons might be dealt with more summarily and expeditiously than they could have been by the civil authorities.

"The occurrence of this conspiracy at this early period of the occupation of the territory will, I think, conclusively convince our Government of the necessity of maintaining here, for several years to come, an efficient military force."

Having taken measures for the arrest of the leaders of the conspiracy, Governor Bent set out from Santa Fé early in January for a few days' visit to his family at San Fernando, near the pueblo of Taos, inhabited by civilized Pueblo Indians. Three Pueblo thieves had been arrested and locked up in the calabozo at San Fernando some time before Governor Bent's arrival. On the 19th of January a mob of

Pueblos entered the town and attempted to force the American sheriff, Lee, to give up these three prisoners. Lee, being helpless to resist the Indians' demands, was on the point of releasing his prisoners when the prefect of the town, Vigil, a Mexican who had taken office under the American Government, appeared among the Indians and, calling out to them in a fury that they were all thieves and scoundrels, ordered Lee to hold the three prisoners. Enraged at the prefect's harsh words, the Pueblos rushed upon him, killed him, cut his body into small pieces, and then, being joined by a number of Mexicans, set out to kill every American in the settlement.

Governor Bent's house was the first they visited. He was still in bed when aroused by his wife on the approach of the mob, and he at once sprang up and ran to a window, through which he called to a Mexican neighbor to help him get through into his house and conceal him. The Mexican refused his aid and replied that he must die. Seeing that all ways of escape were blocked, the governor quietly left the window and returned to his family. "He withdrew into his room," writes Mr. Dunn, "and the Indians began tearing up the roof. With all the calmness of a noble soul he stood awaiting his doom. His wife brought him his pistols and told him to fight, to avenge himself, even if he must die. The Indians were exposed to his aim, but he replied, 'No, I will not kill any one of them; for the sake of you, my wife, and you, my children. At present my death is all these people wish.' As the savages poured into the room he appealed to their manhood and honor, but in vain. They laughed at his plea. They told him they were about to kill every American in New Mexico and would begin with him. An arrow followed the word, another and another, but the mode was not swift enough. One, more impatient, sent a bullet through his heart. As he fell, Tomas, a chief, stepped forward, snatched one of his pistols, and shot him in the face. They took his scalp, stretched it on a board with brass nails, and carried it through the streets in triumph."

Garrard, who was at Taos in the days immediately following the massacre, tells of Governor Bent's death in the following words:

"While here in Fernandez (San Fernandez) with his family he was one morning early aroused from sleep by the populace, who, with the aid of the Pueblos de Taos, were collected in front of his dwelling, striving to gain admittance. While they were effecting an entrance, he, with an axe, cut through an adobe wall into another house. The wife of the occupant, a clever, though thriftless, Canadian, heard him, and with all her strength rendered him assistance, though she was a Mexican. He retreated to a room, but seeing no way of escaping from the infuriated assailants who fired upon him through a window, he spoke to his weeping wife and trembling children clinging to him with all the tenacity of love and despair, and taking a paper from his pocket endeavored to write, but fast losing strength he commended them to God and his brothers, and fell pierced by a Pueblo's ball. Rushing in and tearing off the gray-haired scalp, the Indians bore it away in triumph."

Among the people killed were Stephen Lee, Narcisse Beaubien, and others.

When the news of Governor Bent's death reached the plains it created great excitement, for Charles Bent was exceedingly popular with white people and Indians alike. The Cheyennes proposed to send a war-party to Taos and to kill all the Mexicans, but William Bent would not permit it. A party from Bent's Fort set out for Taos, but on the road were met by messengers announcing that Colonel Price had marched into Taos at the head of two hundred and fifty men and had had a fight with Mexicans and Indians in which two hundred were killed, and had then bombarded the town and knocked down its walls. A neighboring town was razed and a large amount of property destroyed.

The killing of the people at Turley's Ranch, on the Arroyo Hondo, was a costly triumph to the Pueblos. Here were shut up men who fought well for their lives.

Ruxton tells of the battle in graphic language:

"The massacre of Turley and his people, and the destruction of his mill, were not consummated without considerable loss to the barbarous and cowardly assailants. There were in the house, at the time of the attack, eight white men, including Americans, French-Canadians, and one or two Englishmen, with plenty of arms and ammunition. Turley had been warned of the intended insurrection, but had treated the report with indifference and neglect, until one morning a man named Otterbees, in the employ of Turley, and who had been dispatched to Santa Fé with several mule-loads of whiskey a few days before, made his appearance at the gate on horseback, and hastily informing the inmates of the mill that the New Mexicans had risen and massacred Governor Bent and other Americans, galloped off. Even then Turley felt assured that he would not be molested, but, at the solicitations of his men, agreed to close the gate of the yard round which were the buildings of a mill and distillery, and make preparations for defence.

"A few hours after, a large crowd of Mexicans and Pueblo Indians made their appearance, all armed with guns and bows and arrows, and advancing with a white flag summoned Turley to surrender his house and the Americans in it, guaranteeing that his own life should be saved, but that every other American in the valley of Taos had to be destroyed; that the Governor and all the Americans at Fernandez and the rancho had been killed, and that not one was to be left alive in all New Mexico.

"To this summons Turley answered that he would never surrender his house nor his men, and that, if they wanted it or them, 'they must take them.'

"The enemy then drew off, and, after a short consultation, commenced the attack. The first day they numbered about 500, but the crowd was hourly augmented by the arrival of parties of Indians from the more distant pueblos, and of New Mexicans from Fernandez, La Cañada, and other places.

"The building lay at the foot of a gradual slope in the sierra, which was covered with cedar-bushes. In front ran the stream of the Arroyo Hondo, about twenty yards from one side of the square, and on the other side was broken ground, which rose abruptly and formed the bank of the ravine. In rear and behind the still-house was some garden-ground, inclosed by a small fence, and into which a small wicket-gate opened from the corral.

"As soon as the attack was determined upon, the assailants broke, and, scattering, concealed themselves under the cover of the rocks and bushes that surrounded the house.

"From these they kept up an incessant fire upon every exposed portion of the building where they saw the Americans preparing for defence.

"They, on their parts, were not idle; not a man but was an old mountaineer, and each had his trusty rifle with good store of ammunition. Wherever one of the assailants exposed a hand's breadth of his person there whistled a ball from an unerring barrel. The windows had been blockaded, loop-holes being left to fire through, and through these a lively fire was maintained. Already several of the enemy had bitten the dust, and parties were constantly seen bearing off the wounded up the banks of the Cañada. Darkness came on, and during the night a continual fire was kept up on the mill, while its defenders, reserving their ammunition, kept their posts with stern and silent determination. The night was spent in running balls, cutting patches, and completing the defences of the building. In the morning the fight was renewed, and it was found that the Mexicans had effected a lodgment in a part of the stables, which were separated from the other portions of the building, and between which was an open space of a few feet. The assailants, during the night, had sought to break down the wall, and thus enter the main building, but the strength of the adobes and logs of which it was composed resisted effectually all their attempts.

"Those in the stable seemed anxious to regain the outside, for their position was unavailable as a means of annoyance to the besieged, and several had darted across the narrow space which divided it from the other part of the building, and which slightly projected, and behind which they were out of the line of fire. As soon, however, as the attention of the defenders was called to this point, the first man who attempted to cross, and who happened to be a Pueblo chief, was dropped on the instant and fell dead in the center of the intervening space. It appeared an object to recover the body, for an Indian immediately dashed out to the fallen chief and attempted to drag him within the cover of the wall. The rifle which covered the spot again poured forth its deadly contents, and the Indian, springing into the air, fell over the body of his chief, struck to the heart. Another and another met with a similar fate, and at last three rushed at once to the spot, and, seizing the body by the legs and head, had already lifted it from the ground, when three puffs of smoke blew from the barricaded window, followed by the sharp cracks of as many rifles, and the three daring Indians added their number to the pile of corpses which now covered the body of the dead chief.

"As yet the besieged had met with no casualties; but after the fall of the seven Indians, in the manner above described, the whole body of assailants, with a shout of rage, poured in a rattling volley, and two of the defenders of the mill fell mortally wounded. One, shot through the loins, suffered great agony, and was removed to the still-house, where he was laid upon a large pile of grain, as being the softest bed to be found.

"In the middle of the day the assailants renewed the attack more fiercely than before, their baffled attempts adding to their furious rage. The little garrison bravely stood to the defence of the mill, never throwing away a shot, but firing coolly, and only when a fair mark was presented to their unerring aim. Their ammunition, however, was fast failing, and to add to the danger of their situation the enemy set fire to the mill, which blazed fiercely and threatened destruction of the whole building. Twice they succeeded in overcoming the flames, and, taking advantage of their being thus occupied, the Mexicans and Indians charged into the corral, which was full of hogs and sheep, and vented their cowardly rage upon the animals, spearing and shooting all that came in their way. No sooner, however, were the flames extinguished in one place, than they broke out more fiercely in another; and as a successful defence was perfectly hopeless, and the numbers of the assailants increased every moment, a council of war was held by the survivors of the little garrison, when it was determined, as soon as night approached, that everyone should attempt to escape as best he might, and in the meantime the defence of the mill was to be continued.

"Just at dusk, Albert and another man ran to the wicket-gate, which opened into a kind of inclosed space, and in which was a number of armed Mexicans. They both rushed out at the same moment, discharging their rifles full in the faces of the crowd. Albert in the confusion threw himself under the fence, whence he saw his companion shot down immediately, and heard his cries for mercy, mingled with shrieks of pain and anguish, as the cowards pierced him with knives and lances. Lying without motion under the fence, as soon as it was quite dark he crept over the logs and ran up the mountain, traveled day and night, and, scarcely stopping or resting, reached the Greenhorn, almost dead with hunger and fatigue. Turley himself succeeded in escaping from the mill and in reaching the mountain unseen. Here he met a Mexican, mounted on a horse, who had been a most intimate friend of the unfortunate man for many years. To this man Turley offered his watch (which was treble its worth) for the use of his horse, but was refused. The inhuman wretch, however, affected pity and commiseration for the fugitive, and advised him to go to a certain place where he would bring or send him assistance; but on reaching the mill, which was now a mass of fire, he immediately informed the Mexicans of his place of concealment, whither a large party instantly proceeded and shot him to death.

"Two others escaped and reached Santa Fé in safety. The mill and Turley's house were sacked and gutted, and all his hard-earned savings, which were considerable, and concealed in gold about the house, were discovered, and of course, seized upon, by the victorious Mexicans.

"The Indians, however, met a few days after with a severe retribution. The troops marched out of Santa Fé, attacked their pueblo, and levelled it to the ground, killing many hundreds of its defenders, and taking many prisoners, most of whom were hanged."

The death of Charles Bent, of his brother Robert later in the same year, and of George Bent in 1848, left only Colonel William Bent to carry on the business of Bent's Fort, and the trade with Mexico, together with all the other operations in which he was engaged. From this time forth William Bent worked alone.

Charles Bent had one son and two daughters. Alfred, the son, died some years ago. One of the daughters is said to be still living (1909) in Mexico, very old. Tom Boggs married the other daughter. She had one son, Charles Boggs. He and his mother are both believed to be dead.

III

FORT ST. VRAIN AND FORT ADOBE

In its best days Bent's Fort did a business surpassed in volume by only one company in the United States—John Jacob Astor's great American Fur Company. As already stated, besides Bent's Fort the Bent partners had a post on the South Platte at the mouth of St. Vrain's Fork, and one on the Canadian River, called the Fort Adobe, for trade with tribes of Indians hostile to the Cheyennes—trade which Colonel Bent, of course, wished to hold.

St. Vrain's Fork runs into the South Platte from the north and west, a few miles south or southwest of Greeley, Colo.

The site of the fort, known later and now as Adobe Walls, was the scene of two hard battles between white men and Indians. The first of these took place in 1864, and was fought between the Kiowas, Apaches, and Comanches, with a few Cheyennes and Arapahoes, who were present chiefly as onlookers, and a detachment of troops under the command of Kit Carson, who then bore a commission in the United States army. Carson had with him a number of Ute scouts. The fight was a severe one, and Carson, after burning one of the Kiowa villages, was obliged to retreat. In that battle the Indians fought bravely, and one of them possessed a cavalry bugle and knew the various calls. Carson and his officers generally acknowledged that they were beaten by the Indians, and Carson finally withdrew, the Indians saving most of their property, though they lost a number of men. Among the Kiowas killed was a young man who wore a coat of mail.

At this fight a spring-wagon was found in the possession of the Indians, and its presence in the Kiowa camp has often been wondered at. At that time wagons were never used by plains Indians, whose only vehicle was the travois, which consisted of two long poles tied together over the horses' withers, and dragging on the ground behind. Across these poles, behind the horses' hocks, was lashed a platform, on which a considerable burden might be transported.

The late Robert M. Peck, of Los Angeles, Cal., who was a soldier, serving under Major Sedgwick, then in command of troops along the Arkansas, not long before his death told the story of an ambulance presented to one of the Kiowa chiefs by the quartermaster of the troops under Major Sedgwick, which may have been this one. Mr. Peck said:

"That was before the Kiowa war broke out in 1859. To' hau sen was always friendly to the whites, and tried to keep the Kiowas peaceable. A small party of them, his immediate following, kept out of that war. These were mostly the old warriors, but the younger men, who constituted a majority of the tribe, went on the warpath after Lieut. George D. Bayard, of our regiment killed one of the Kiowa chiefs, called Pawnee, near Peacock's ranch, on Walnut Creek.

"That summer (1859) we had been camping along the Arkansas River, moving camp occasionally up or down the river, trying to keep Satank and his turbulent followers from beginning another outbreak. Old To' hau sen used frequently to come to our camp. Lieut. McIntyre wanted to get rid of this old ambulance, which he had long had on his hands and which in some of its parts was nearly worn out. After inducing Major Sedgwick to have it condemned as unfit for service, Lieut. McIntyre had his blacksmith fix it up a little and presented it to the old chief. McIntyre fitted a couple of sets of old harness to a pair of To' hau sen's ponies and had some of the soldiers break the animals to work in the ambulance. But when To' hau sen tried to drive the team, he could not learn to handle the lines. He took the reins off the harness and had a couple of Indian boys ride the horses, and they generally went at a gallop. The old chief seemed very proud of the ambulance."

The second battle of the Adobe Walls took place in June, 1874, when the Kiowas, Comanches, and Cheyennes made an attack on some buffalo-hunters, who had built themselves houses in the shelter of the Adobe Walls. The attack on the buffalo-hunters was made in the endeavor to drive these hide-hunters out of the buffalo country, in order to save the buffalo for themselves. The hunters finally drove off the Indians with much loss, but soon afterward abandoned their camp.

St. Vrain's Fort and the Adobe Fort were abandoned between 1840 and 1850, when the fur business began to decline. By this time the beaver had begun to get scarce, having been pretty thoroughly trapped out of many of the mountain streams, and besides that the silk hat had been invented, and was rapidly taking the place of the old beaver hat, and the demand for beaver skins was greatly reduced. Now, the mountains were full of idle trappers, and a colony of these settled some miles above Bent's Fort, on the site of the present city of Pueblo, Col., where they did a little farming and a great deal of smuggling of liquor from Mexico to the plains country. The stagnation in the beaver trade, of course, affected the business of William Bent, who, since the death of his brother Charles, had not lessened his activities in trading. At this time his chief business was in buffalo robes and in horses. The establishment at the fort was now reduced, and in the early fifties Bent tried to sell it to the government for a military post, but failing to receive what he considered a fair price for his property, in 1852 he laid large charges of gunpowder in the buildings and blew the old fort into the air.

In the winter of 1852–53 he had two trading houses of logs among the Cheyennes at the Big Timbers, and in the autumn of 1853 began to build his new fort of stone on the north side of the Arkansas River, about thirty-eight miles below old Fort William, and finished it the same year. This was the winter camp of the Cheyennes. At that time the Big Timbers extended up the river beyond the fort, and within three miles of the mouth of Purgatoire River, but by 1865 practically all the timber had been cut down, leaving the fort in the midst of a treeless prairie.

In 1858 gold was discovered in the country northwest of the new fort. There was a rush of gold-seekers to the country the following year, and for some reason William Bent decided to lease his post to the War Department. This he did. A garrison was sent there. It was at first intended to call the new fort Fort Fauntleroy, after the colonel of the old Second Dragoons, but finally the place was rechristened Fort Wise, in honor of the Governor of Virginia. The following summer, 1860, the troops built a stockade half a mile above Bent's old stone buildings. When the Civil War began in 1861 and Governor Wise joined the Confederates, the post was again renamed; this time Fort Lyon, in honor of General Lyon, who had been killed not long before at Wilson's Creek, Mo. In 1866 the river threatened to carry away the post, and it was moved twenty miles up the river.

Meanwhile William Bent had built a new stockade on the north side of the river, in the valley of Purgatoire Creek, and lived there, continuing to trade with the Indians. Kit Carson lived on the same side of the river, and not far from the Bent stockade. Carson died at Fort Lyon, May 23, 1868, and his friend William Bent, at his home, May

19, 1869. Ceran St. Vrain died October 29, 1870. The last year of his life was spent at Taos, N. M., but he died at the home of his son Felix, in Mora, N. M.

In 1839 Mr. Farnham visited Bent's Fort, and met two of the Bent brothers, whose names he does not give. They were clad like trappers, in splendid deerskin hunting-shirts and leggings, with long fringes on the outer seams of the arms and legs, the shirts decorated with designs worked in colored porcupine quills, and on their feet moccasins covered with quill work and beading.

This great establishment, standing alone in the midst of a wilderness, much impressed the traveller, who not long before had left a region where men, if not crowded together, were at least seen frequently, for he had recently come from Peoria, Ill. He spoke of it as a solitary abode of men seeking wealth in the face of hardship and danger, and declared that it reared "its towers over the uncultivated wastes of nature like an old baronial castle that has withstood the wars and desolations of centuries." To him the Indian women, walking swiftly about the courtyard and on the roofs of the houses, clad in long deerskin dresses and bright moccasins, were full of interest; while the naked children, with perfect forms and the red of the Saxon blood showing through the darker hue of the mother race, excited his enthusiasm. He wondered at the novel manners and customs that he saw, at the grave bourgeois and their clerks and traders, who, in time of leisure, sat cross-legged under a shade, smoking the long-stemmed Indian stone pipe, which they deliberately passed from hand to hand, until it was smoked out; at the simple food—dried buffalo meat and bread made from the unbolted wheaten meal from Taos, repasts which lacked sweets and condiments.

Here, as it seemed to him, were gathered people from the ends of the earth: old trappers whose faces were lined and leathery from long exposure to the snows of winter and the burning heats of summer; Indians, some of whom were clad in civilized clothing, but retained the reserve and silence of their race; Mexican servants, hardly more civilized than the Indians; and all these seated on the ground, gathered around a great dish of dried meat, which constituted their only food. The prairie men who talked narrated their adventures in the North, the West, the South, and among the mountains, while others, less given to conversation, nodded or grunted in assent or comment. The talk was of where the buffalo had been, or would be; of the danger from hostile tribes; of past fights, when men had been wounded and killed; and of attacks by Indians on hunters or traders who were passing through the country.

He describes the opening of the gates on the winter's morning, the cautious sliding in and out of the Indians, whose tents stood around the fort, till the court was full of people with long, hanging black locks and dark, flashing watchful eyes; the traders and clerks busy at their work; the patrols walking the battlements with loaded muskets; the guards in the bastion, standing with burning matches by the carronades; and when the sun set, the Indians retiring again to their camp outside, to talk over their newly purchased blankets and beads, and to sing and drink and dance; and finally the night sentinel on the fort that treads his weary watch away. "This," he says, "presents a tolerable view of this post in the season of business."

Soon after the construction of the fort a brass cannon had been purchased in St. Louis and brought out for the purpose of impressing the Indians. It was used there for many years, but in 1846, when General Kearny passed by, some enthusiastic employee charged it with too great a load of powder, and in saluting the General it burst. Some time after that an iron cannon was brought from Santa Fé, and during the day always stood outside the big gate of the fort, and was often fired in honor of some great Indian chief when he came into the post with his camp. The old brass cannon lay about the post for some time, and is mentioned by Garrard.

The passage of General Kearny's little army on its march into Mexico made a gala day at Bent's Fort. The army had encamped nine miles below the post to complete its organization, for it had come straggling across the plains from Missouri in small detachments. On the morning of August 2 the fort was filled to overflowing with people: soldiers and officers, white trappers, Indian trappers, Mexicans, Cheyennes, Arapahoes, Kiowas, and Indian women, the wives of trappers from the far away Columbia and St. Lawrence. Every one was busy talking—a babel of tongues and jargons. The employees, with their wives and children, had gathered on the flat roofs to witness the wonderful spectacle, while in a securely hidden nook Charles Bent was rejoicing the souls of a few of his army friends with the icy contents of "a pitcher covered with the dew of promise."

A cloud of dust moving up the valley "at the rate of a horse walking fast" at length announced the approach of the troops. At the head of the column rode General Kearny, behind him a company of the old First United States Dragoons, behind the dragoons a regiment of Missouri volunteer cavalry and two batteries of volunteer artillery, and of infantry but two companies. It was an army of 1,700 men, and yet to the Indians assembled at the fort it must have seemed indeed an army, for perhaps few of them had ever dreamed that there were half as many men in the whole "white tribe." The column drew near the fort, swinging to the left, forded the river to the Mexican bank, turned again up the valley, and went on its way, a part to the city of Mexico, a part to California, and a part only to Santa Fé, whence but a few months later they would march to avenge the murder of Charles Bent, now doling out mint-juleps to the loitering officers in the little room upstairs in the fort.

IV

KIT CARSON, HUNTER

THERE were two or three employees at the fort whose labors never ceased. These were the hunters who were obliged constantly to provide meat for the employees. Though the number of these varied, there might be from sixty to a hundred men employed at the fort, and many of these had families, so that the population was considerable.

For a number of years the principal hunter for the fort was Kit Carson, who was often assisted by a Mexican or two, though in times when work was slack many of the traders, trappers, employees, and teamsters devoted themselves to hunting. Often game could be killed within sight of the post, but at other times it was necessary for the hunter to take with him a wagon or pack-animals, for he might be obliged to go several days' journey before securing the necessary food. It was the duty of Carson and his assistants to provide meat for the whole post. It was here that in 1843 Carson was married to a Mexican girl.

Though, as already suggested, difficulties sometimes occurred with the Indians, these troubles were very rare; yet the vigilance of the garrison, drilled into them from earliest times by William Bent, never relaxed.

The animals belonging to the fort were a constant temptation to the Indians. The fort stood on the open plain by the riverside, and there was an abundance of good grass close at hand, so that the herd could be grazed within sight of the walls. Even so, however, the Indians occasionally swept off the stock, as in 1839, when a party of Comanches hid in the bushes on the river-bank, ran off every hoof of stock belonging to the post, and killed the Mexican herder.

Farnham while there heard this account of the event:

"About the middle of June, 1839, a band of sixty of them [Comanches] under cover of night crossed the river and concealed themselves among the bushes that grow thickly on the bank near the place where the animals of the establishment feed during the day. No sentinel being on duty at the time, their presence was unobserved: and when morning came the Mexican horse guard mounted his horse, and with the noise and shouting usual with that class of servants when so employed, rushed his charge out of the fort; and riding rapidly from side to side of the rear of the band, urged them on and soon had them nibbling the short dry grass in a little vale within grape shot distance of the guns of the bastion. It is customary for a guard of animals about these trading-posts to take his station beyond his charge; and if they stray from each other, or attempt to stroll too far, he drives them together, and thus keeps them in the best possible situation to be driven hastily to the corral, should the Indians, or other evil persons, swoop down upon them. And as there is constant danger of this, his horse is held by a long rope, and grazes around him, that he may be mounted quickly at the first alarm for a retreat within the walls. The faithful guard at Bent's, on the morning of the disaster I am relating, had dismounted after driving out his animals, and sat upon the ground, watching with the greatest fidelity for every call of duty; when these 50 or 60 Indians sprang from their hiding places, ran upon the animals, yelling horribly, and attempted to drive them across the river. The guard, however, nothing daunted, mounted quickly, and drove his horse at full speed among them. The mules and horses hearing his voice amidst the frightening yells of the savages, immediately started at a lively pace for the fort; but the Indians were on all sides, and bewildered them. The guard still pressed them onward, and called for help; and on they rushed, despite the efforts of the Indians to the contrary. The battlements were covered with men. They shouted encouragement to the brave guard—'Onward, onward,' and the injunction was obeyed. He spurred his horse to his greatest speed from side to side and whipped the hindermost of the band with his leading rope. He had saved every animal: he was within 20 yards of the open gate: he fell: three arrows from the bows of the Comanches had cloven his heart, and, relieved of him, the lords of the quiver gathered their prey, and drove them to the borders of Texas, without injury to life or limb. I saw this faithful guard's grave. He had been buried a few days. The wolves had been digging into it. Thus 40 or 50 mules and horses and their best servant's life were lost to the Messrs. Bents in a single day."

Long before this, in 1831, when the fort was still unfinished, Carson with twelve white employees went down the river to the Big Timbers to cut logs for use in the construction work. He had all the horses and mules belonging to the post with him, and while he and his men were at work, a party of sixty Crows crept up close to them, and coming out of the brush and timber drove off the herd. Carson and his men, all on foot, followed the Crows across the open prairie. With them were two mounted Cheyenne warriors, who had been visiting the camp when the Crows made their attack, but who luckily had both their ponies by them, and thus saved them. The Crows had not gone many miles before they halted, and camped in a thicket on the margin of a little stream, thinking that a party of twelve men would not dare to follow them on foot; therefore, when they beheld Carson and his men coming on their trail they were greatly astonished. They left the stolen animals behind them, and came boldly out on the open prairie to annihilate the venturesome white men, but all of Carson's party had excellent rifles and one or two pistols apiece. Carson used to tell how surprised those Crows were when they charged down upon his men and were met by a stunning volley. They turned and made for the thicket, the whites following them at a run. Into the thicket went the Crows and in after them tumbled Carson and his men. Some spirited bushwhacking ensued, then out at the far edge of the thicket came the Crows, with Carson and his men still after them. Meantime, when the Crows had come out to charge the whites, the two mounted Cheyennes had quietly slipped round in the rear and run off all the captured horses, so now Carson's men mounted and rode exultingly back to their camp, while the discomfited Crows plodded on homeward, nursing their wounds.

In the years before the great peace was made between the Kiowas and Comanches, and the Cheyennes and Arapahoes, the home country of the Southern Cheyennes lay chiefly between the Arkansas and the South Platte Rivers. In August many of them used to go east as far as the valley of the Republican, for the purpose of gathering winter supplies of choke-cherries and plums. In the autumn the Suhtai and the Hill people—Hǐs'sǐ-o-mē'ta-nē—went up west into the foot-hills of the mountains to kill mule-deer, which were plenty there, and at that season fat. All the different bands of Cheyennes used to make annual trips to the mountains for the purpose of securing lodge-poles. A cedar which grew there was also much employed in the manufacture of bows.

At this time the range of the Kiowas was from the Cimaron south to the Red River of Texas, on the ridge of the Staked Plains. They kept south in order to avoid, so far as possible, the raiding parties of Cheyennes and Arapahoes, who were constantly trying to take horses from them. In those days—and still earlier—the Kiowas used to make frequent trips north to visit their old friends and neighbors, the Crows, but when they did this they kept away to the westward, close to the mountains, in order to avoid the camps of the Cheyennes. Nevertheless, such travelling parties were occasionally met by the Cheyennes or Arapahoes, and fights occurred. It was in such a fight that an old woman, now (1912) known as White Cow Woman, or the Kiowa Woman, was captured. She was a white child, taken from the whites by the Kiowas when two or three years of age, and a year or two later captured from the Kiowas as stated by the Cheyennes. She is now supposed to be seventy-six or seventy-seven years old. The fight when she was captured took place in 1835, or three years before the great fight on Wolf Creek.

Before the Mexican War the Arkansas was the boundary between the United States and Mexico, and Bent's Fort was, therefore, on the extreme border of the United States. In those days the Indians used to make raids into Mexican territory, sweeping off great herds of horses and mules. They also captured many Mexicans, and many a Comanche and Kiowa warrior owned two or three peons, whom he kept to herd his horses for him.

These peons were often badly treated by their Mexican masters, and after they had been for a short time with the Indians, they liked the new life so well that they would not return to their old masters, even if they had the opportunity. Many of these men led the warriors in raids into Mexico. They kept in communication with peons in the Mexican settlements, and from them learned just which places were unguarded, where the best herds and most plunder were to be secured, and where the Mexican troops were stationed. The peon then led his war-party to the locality selected, and they ran off the herds, burned ranches, and carried off plunder and peon women and men. Some of the peons captured became chiefs in the tribes that had taken them. In the old days, Colonel Bent sometimes purchased these Mexican peons from the Kiowas. In 1908 one of these peons was still living at the Kiowa Agency, eighty-two years old.

Carson was employed by the Bents as hunter for many years. Sometimes he remained at the fort, supplying the table with meat, at other times he went with the wagon-train to Missouri, acting as hunter for the outfit. The following advertisement from the Missouri *Intelligencer* marked Carson's first appearance on the page of history:

"NOTICE: To whom it may concern: That Christopher Carson, a boy about sixteen years, small of his age, but thickset, light hair, ran away from the subscriber, living in Franklin, Howard Co., Mo., to whom he had been bound to learn the saddler's trade, on or about the first day of September last. He is supposed to have made his way toward the upper part of the State. All persons are notified not to harbor, support or subsist said boy under penalty of the law. One cent reward will be given to any person who will bring back said boy.

DAVID WORKMAN.

"Franklin, Oct. 6, 1826."

This runaway boy joined the Santa Fé caravan of Charles Bent, and from that time on for a number of years was employed by Bent and St. Vrain. From 1834 to 1842, he was constantly at the fort. He married a daughter of Charles Beaubien, of Taos, who, with his son, Narcisse Beaubien, was killed at the time of the Pueblo massacre in January, 1847.

During the Civil War, Carson received a commission in the militia of New Mexico or Colorado, and rose to the rank of colonel and brevet brigadier-general.

V

LIFE AT BENT'S FORT

BENT'S OLD FORT was a stopping-place for all travellers on the Santa Fé trail, and visitors often remained there for weeks at a time, for Colonel Bent kept open house. On holidays, such as Christmas and the Fourth of July, if any number of people were there, they often had balls or dances, in which trappers, travellers, Indians, Indian women, and Mexican women all took part. Employed about the post there was always a Frenchman or two who could play the violin and guitar. On one occasion Frank P. Blair, then twenty-three years old, afterward a general in the Union army, and at one time a vice-presidential candidate, played the banjo all night at a ball at the fort.

Just before each Fourth of July, a party was always sent up into the mountains on the Purgatoire River to gather wild mint for mint-juleps to be drunk in honor of the day. For the brewing of these, ice from the ice-house was used. In those days this drink was called "hail storm."

The employees at the fort were divided into classes, to each of which special duties were assigned. Certain men remained always at the post guarding it, trading with Indians and trappers, and keeping the books. These we may call clerks, or store-keepers, and mechanics. Another group took care of the live-stock, herding and caring for the horses and mules, while still others had charge of the wagon-train that hauled the furs to the States, and brought back new goods to the fort. Other men, led by veteran traders, went to trade in the Indian camps at a distance.

Excepting in summer, when the trains were absent on their way to

St. Louis, the population of the fort was large. There were traders, clerks, trappers, hunters, teamsters, herders, and laborers, and these were of as many races as there were trades. The clerks, traders, and trappers were chiefly Americans, the hunters and laborers might be white men, Mexicans, or Frenchmen. Some of the Delawares and Shawnees—of whom Black Beaver was one of the most famous— were hunters and trappers, while others of their race were teamsters, and went back and forth with the trains between Westport and Fort William. The herders were chiefly Mexicans, as were also some of the laborers, while the cook of the bourgeois was a negro. Almost all these people had taken Indian wives from one tribe or another, and the fort was plentifully peopled with women and children, as well as with men.

During the summer season matters were often very quiet about the fort. In April, just about the time that the Indians set out on their summer buffalo-hunt, the train started for St. Louis. It was under the personal conduct of Colonel Bent, but in charge of a wagon-master, who was responsible for everything. It was loaded with robes. With the train went most of the teamsters and herders, together with some of the laborers. The journey was to last nearly six months. Each heavy wagon was drawn by six yoke of oxen, driven by a teamster, who might be a white man or a Delaware or a Shawnee. With the train went great herds of horses to be sold when the settlements were reached. Agent Fitzpatrick says that the Cheyennes moved with the train as far as Pawnee Fork, and then scattered on their hunt.

Travel was slow, for the teams made but ten or twelve miles a day. On each trip they camped at about the same places, and to the men who accompanied the train the route was as well known as is the main street to the people of a small town. When camp was reached at night the wagons were corralled, the bulls freed from their yokes, and, in charge of the night herders, who during the day had been sleeping in the wagons, were driven off to the best grass and there fed and rested until morning, when they were driven back to the corral to be turned over to the teamsters. The horse herd was taken off in another direction, and held during the night by the horse night herders. Within the great corral of wagons the fires were kindled, and the mess cooks prepared the simple meal of bread, already cooked, and coffee.

The Coming of the White Man

At daylight in the morning the oxen were brought in and yoked, the blankets tied up and thrown into the wagons, and long before the sun appeared the train was in motion. Travel was kept up until ten or eleven o'clock, depending on the weather. If it was hot they stopped earlier; if cool, they travelled longer. Then camp was made, the wagons were again corralled, the herds turned out, and the principal meal of the day, which might be called breakfast or dinner, was prepared. Perhaps during the morning the hunters had killed buffalo or antelope, and this with bread satisfied the keen appetites of the men. If fresh meat had not been killed, there was always an abundance of dried meat, which every one liked. At two or three o'clock the herds were again brought in, and the train was set in motion, the journey continuing until dark or after. So the quiet routine of the march was kept up until the settlements were reached.

The whole train was in charge of the wagon-master, who was its absolute governing head. He fixed the length of the march, the time for starting and halting. If a difficult stream was to be crossed, he rode ahead of the train and directed the crossing of the first team, and then of all the others, not leaving the place until the difficulty had been wholly overcome. Besides looking after a multitude of details, such as the shoeing of the oxen, the greasing of the wagons, which took place every two or three days, and the condition of the animals in the yokes, he also issued rations to the men, and was, in fact, the fountain of all authority. With the cavalyard were always driven a number of loose work-oxen, and if an animal in the yoke was injured, or became lame or footsore, it was turned into the herd and replaced by a fresh ox.

When the axles of the wagons were to be greased, the wheels were lifted from the ground by a very long lever, on the end of which several men threw themselves to raise the wagon, so that the wheel could be taken off. If one of the teamsters became sick or disabled, it was customary for the wagon-master to drive the leading team.

The train often consisted of from twenty to thirty wagons, most of them—in later years—laden with bales of buffalo robes on the way to the settlements, and returned full of goods. The front end of the wagon inclined somewhat forward, and about half-way down the front was a box, secured by a lock, in which the teamster kept the spare keys for his ox-bows, various other tools, and some of his own small personal belongings.

Two hunters, one a white man, and the other a Mexican, or Indian, accompanied the train, and each morning, as soon as it was ready to start, they set out to kill game, and usually when the train came to the appointed camping-place, they were found there resting in the shade, with a load of meat. Sometimes, if they killed an animal close to the road, they loaded it on a horse and brought it back to the trail, so that it could be thrown into a wagon when the train passed.

The Shawnees and Delawares were great hunters, and almost always when the train stopped for noon, and their cattle had been turned out and the meal eaten, these men would be seen striding off over the prairie, each with a long rifle over his shoulder.

In the train there were several messes. Colonel Bent and any member of his family, or visitor, messed together, the white teamsters and the Mexicans also messed together, while the Delawares and Shawnees, by preference, messed by themselves. Each man had his own quart cup and plate, and carried his own knife in its sheath. Forks or spoons were not known. Each man marked his own plate and cup, usually by rudely scratching his initials or mark on it, and when he had finished using it, he washed or cleansed it himself. Each mess chose its cook from among its members. The food eaten by these travellers, though simple, was wholesome and abundant. Meat was the staple; but they also had bread and abundant coffee, and occasionally boiled dried apples and rice. Usually there was sugar, though sometimes they had to depend on the old-fashioned "long sweetening"; that is, New Orleans molasses, which was imported in hogsheads for trade with the Indians.

The train was occasionally attacked by Indians, but they were always beaten off. In 1847 the Comanches attacked the wagons at Pawnee Fork, but they were repulsed, and Red Sleeves, their chief, was killed. The fork is called by the Indians Red Sleeves' Creek, in remembrance of this affair. Charles Hallock, who made the journey with one of these trains, wrote an account of an attack by Comanches, which was printed in *Harper's Magazine*, in 1859.

After the return to the post in autumn, the cattle were turned out into the herd, wagons ranged around outside of the corral, while the yokes and chains for each bull team were cared for by the driver of the team. Usually they were carried into the fort and piled up in some shady place. The keys for the bows were tied to the yokes, and the chains lay close to them.

Rarely a few ox-bows were lost by being taken away by the Indians, who greatly coveted the hickory wood for the manufacture of bows. There was no hickory nearer than Council Grove, and if an Indian could get hold of an ox-bow, he steamed and straightened it, and from it made a useful bow.

Back at the fort only a few men were left; the clerks, a trader or two, and a few laborers and herders. There were frequent calls there by Indians, chiefly war-parties stopping to secure supplies of arms and ammunition. Hunting parties occasionally called to procure ordinary goods. Parties of white travellers came and stayed for a little while, and then went on again. During this time especial precautions were taken against trouble with the Indians. At night, the fort was closed early, and conditions sometimes arose under which admission to the fort might be refused by the trader. This watchfulness, which was never relaxed, was not caused by any special fear of Indian attacks, but was merely the carrying out of those measures of prudence which Colonel Bent had always practised, and which he had so thoroughly inculcated in his men that they had become fixed habits.

Usually the Cheyenne Indians were freely admitted to the fort, and were allowed to wander through it, more or less at will. They might go up on the roof and into the watch-tower, but were warned by the chiefs not to touch anything. They might go about and look, and, if they wished to, ask questions, but they were not to take things in their hands. Toward the close of the day, as the sun got low, a chief or principal man went through the fort, and said to the young men who were lounging here and there: "Now, soon these people will wish to close the gates of this house, and you had better now go out and return to your camps." When this was said the young men always obeyed, for in those days the chiefs had control over their young men; they listened to what was said to them and obeyed.

On one occasion a war-party of Shoshoni came down from the mountains and visited Bent's Fort, and insisted on coming in. The trader in charge, probably Murray, declined to let them in, and when they endeavored to force their way into the post, he killed one of them, when the others went away. The Indian's body was buried at some little distance from the fort, and his scalp was afterward given to a war-party of Cheyennes and Arapahoes.

In winter the scenes at the fort were very different. Now it harbored a much larger population. All the employees were there, except a few traders and teamsters and laborers, who might be out visiting the different camps, and who were constantly going and returning. The greater part of the laborers and teamsters had little or nothing to do, and spent most of the winter in idleness, lounging about the fort, or occasionally going out hunting. Besides the regular inhabitants there were many visitors, some of whom spent a long time at the fort. Hunters and trappers from the mountains, often with their families, came in to purchase goods for the next summer's journey, or to visit, and then, having supplied their wants, returned to their mountain camps. All visitors were welcome to stay as long as they pleased.

Though the fort was full of idle men, nevertheless time did not hang heavy on their hands. There were amusements of various sorts, hunting parties, games, and not infrequent dances, in which the moccasined trappers, in their fringed, beaded, or porcupine-quilled buckskin garments swung merry-faced, laughing Indian women in the rough but hearty dances of the frontier. To the employees of the fort liquor was ever dealt out with a sparing hand, and there is no memory of any trouble among the people who belonged at the post. It was a contented and cheerful family that dwelt within these four adobe walls.

Perhaps the most important persons at the fort, after the directing head who governed the whole organization, were the traders, who dealt out goods to the Indians in the post, receiving their furs in payment, and who were sent off to distant camps with loads of trade goods, to gather from them the robes which they had prepared, or to buy horses and mules.

Of these traders there were seven or eight, of whom the following are remembered: Murray, an Irishman known to the Indians as Pau-ē-sīh′, Flat Nose; Fisher, an American, Nō-mā-nī′, Fish; Hatcher, a

Kentuckian, Hē-hĭm'nĭ-hō-nāh', Freckled Hand; Thomas Boggs, a Missourian, Wŏhk' po-hŭm', White Horse; John Smith, a Missourian, Pŏ-ō-om' mats, Gray Blanket; Kit Carson, a Kentuckian, Vĭ-hiu-nĭs', Little Chief, and Charles Davis, a Missourian, Ho-nīh', Wolf.

L. Maxwell, Wō-wĭhph' pai-ĭ-sīh', Big Nostrils, was the superintendent or foreman at the fort, but had nothing to do with the trading. He looked after the herds and laborers and fort matters in general.

Murray, who was a good hunter and trapper, and a brave man, was one of the two more important men among the traders. He usually remained at the fort, and was almost always left in charge when the train went to the States. Hatcher, however, was probably the best trader, and the most valued of the seven.

Each of these traders had especial friendly relations with some particular tribe of Indians, and each was naturally sent off to the tribe that he knew best. Besides this, often when villages of Indians came and camped somewhere near the post, the chiefs would request that a particular man be sent to their village to trade. Sometimes to a very large village two or three traders would be sent, the work being more than one man could handle in a short period of time.

When it was determined that a trader should go out, he and the chief clerk talked over the trip. The trader enumerated the goods required, and these were laid out, charged to him, and then packed for transportation to the camp. If the journey were over level prairie, this transportation was by wagon, but if over rough country pack-mules were used. If on arrival at the camp the trader found that the trade was going to be large, and that he required more goods, he sent back his wagon, or some of his animals, to the post for additional supplies. When he returned from his trip and turned in his robes, he was credited with the goods that he had received. The trade for robes ended in the spring, and during the summer the traders often went to different villages to barter for horses and mules.

A certain proportion of the trade with the Indians was for spirits, but this proportion was small. The Indians demanded liquor, and though Colonel Bent was strongly opposed to giving it to them, he knew very well that unless he did something toward satisfying their demands, whiskey traders from Santa Fé or Taos might come into the territory and gratify the Indians' longing for drink, and at the same time take away the trade from the fort. Two or three times a year, therefore, after many visits from the chiefs, asking for liquor, promising to take charge of it and see to its distribution, and to be responsible that payment should be made for it, a lot of liquor would be sent out to a camp, packed in kegs of varying sizes. A trader coming into the villages would deposit his load in the lodge of the chief. The Indians wishing to trade would come to the lodge and offer what they had to trade, and each would be assigned a keg of a certain size, sufficient to pay for the robes, horses, or mules that he sold. Each Indian then tied a piece of cloth or a string to his keg, so as to mark it as his, and it remained in the chief's lodge, unopened for the present. When the trade had been completed, the trader left the village, and not until he had gone some distance did the chief permit the Indians to take their kegs of liquor. Sometimes while the traders were in a camp trading ordinary goods, a party of men from Taos or Santa Fé would come into the camp with whiskey, and then at once there would be an end of all legitimate business until the Indians had become intoxicated, drunk all the spirits, and become sober again. No trader ever wished to have whiskey in the camp where he was working.

We commonly think of the trade at one of these old forts as being wholly for furs, but at Bent's Fort this was not the case. In later times furs—that is to say, buffalo robes—were indeed a chief article of trade, and were carried back to the States to be sold there; but a great trade also went on in horses and mules, of which the Indians possessed great numbers, and of which they were always getting more. These horses and mules were taken back to the settlements and sold there, but they were also sold to any one who would buy them. The cavalyard was a part of every train which returned to the States, the animals being herded by Mexicans and being in charge of a trader, who disposed of them when they reached the settlements.

The Indians frequently paid for their goods in horses and mules, but this was not the only source from which horses came. About 1845 William Bent sent his brother, George Bent, with Tom Boggs and Hatcher, down into Mexico to trade for horses and mules. They brought back great herds, and with them a celebrated rider known at the fort, and in later years to all the Cheyennes, as One-eyed Juan, whose sole occupation was breaking horses, a vocation which he followed until he was too old to get into the saddle. It was said of him that when he wished to show off he would put a saddle on a wild horse, and placing a Mexican dollar in each one of the huge wooden stirrups, would mount the horse, and no matter what the horse might do, these dollars were always found under the soles of the rider's feet when the animal stopped bucking.

While the chief market at which the horses and mules were sold was St. Louis, yet on at least one occasion Hatcher took a herd of horses which had been bought wild from the Comanches and broken by the Mexicans at the fort over to Taos and Santa Fé, and sold them there. Occasionally they sold good broken horses to the Indians for robes.

It must be remembered that a large proportion of these horses purchased from the Indians, and especially from the Comanches, were wild horses taken by the Comanches from the great herds which ran loose on the ranches in Mexico. Practically all these horses bore Mexican brands.

After the emigration to California began, herds of horses and mules were sent up to the emigrant trail on the North Platte River, to be sold to emigrants on their way to California. On one occasion Hatcher, with a force of Mexican herders, was sent up there in charge of a great herd of horses and mules, and remained alongside the trail until he had disposed of all his animals. He carried back with him the gold and silver money received for them in leather panniers, packed on the backs of animals.

Before starting on another similar trip, Hatcher said to Colonel Bent: "It is useless to load down our animals with sugar, coffee and flour, to carry up there. We will take only enough to last us to the trail, and there we can buy all we need from the emigrants. Moreover, they have great numbers of broken-down horses, and it would be a good idea to buy these for little or nothing, and then drive them back here and let them get rested and fat, and then we can take them up there and sell them again." The wisdom of this was at once apparent, and the suggestion was followed out.

Important members of the fort household were Chipita; Andrew Green, the bourgeois's cook; the old French tailor, whose name is forgotten, and the carpenter and the blacksmith.

Chipita was the housekeeper and laundress, the principal woman at the post, and the one who, on the occasion of dances or other festivities, managed these affairs. She was a large, very good-natured, and kindly woman, and is said to have been half French and half Mexican. She spoke French readily. She was married to one of the employees of the fort.

Andrew Green, the black cook, has already been spoken of as having ultimately been set free.

The old French tailor had come up from New Orleans. He had a shop in one of the rooms of the fort, where he used to make and repair clothing for the men. Much of this clothing was of buckskin, which he himself dressed, for he was a good tanner.

In winter the teamsters and laborers usually spent their evenings in playing cards and checkers in the quarters by the light of tallow candles, the only lights they had to burn. These candles were made at the fort, Chipita doing the work. They were moulded of buffalo tallow, in old-fashioned tin moulds, perhaps a dozen in a set. The work of fixing the wicks in the moulds occupied considerable time. The tallow was then melted, the refuse skimmed from it, the fluid grease poured into the moulds, and the wicks, which hung from the top, were cut off with a pair of scissors. Then the moulds were dipped in a barrel of water standing by, to cool the candles, and presently they were quite hard, and could be removed from the moulds, ready for use.

In the winter Chipita would sometimes vary the monotony of the life by getting up a candy-pulling frolic, in which the laborers and teamsters all took part, and which was more or less a jollification. During the afternoon and evening the black New Orleans molasses, which was used in the Indian trade, was boiled, and after supper the people gathered in one of the rooms and pulled the candy. Candy such as this was a great luxury, and was eagerly eaten by those who could get it.

The work of the carpenter and blacksmith, whose shops stood at the back of the fort, was chiefly on the wagons, which they kept in good order. For them winter was the busy season, for it was their duty to have everything in good order and ready for the train to start out in April.

In the store of the fort—presumably for sale to travellers or for the use of the proprietors—were to be found such unusual luxuries as butter-crackers, Bent's water-crackers, candies of various sorts, and, most remarkable of all, great jars of preserved ginger of the kind which fifty or sixty years ago used to be brought from China. Elderly people of the present day can remember, when they were children, seeing these blue china jars, which were carried by lines of vegetable rope passed around the necks of the jars, and can remember also how delicious this ginger was when they were treated to a taste of it.

At the post were some creatures which greatly astonished the Indians. On one of his trips to St. Louis St. Vrain purchased a pair of goats, intending to have them draw a cart for some of the children. On the way across the plains, however, one of them was killed, but the one that survived lived at the fort for some years and used to clamber all over the walls and buildings. The creature was a great curiosity to the plains people, who had never before seen such an animal, and they never wearied of watching its climbing and its promenading along the walls of the fort. As it grew older it became cross, and seemed to take pleasure in scattering little groups of Indian children and chasing them about. The Southern Cheyennes went but little into the mountains at this time, and but few of them had ever seen the mountain sheep. If they had, they would not have regarded the domestic goat with so much wonder.

The post was abundantly supplied with poultry, for pigeons, chickens, and turkeys had been brought out there, and bred and did well. At one time George Bent brought out several peacocks, whose gay plumage and harsh voices astonished and more or less alarmed the Indians, who called them thunder birds, Nŭn-ūm′ā-ē-vĭ′kĭs.

There was no surgeon at the fort, Colonel Bent doing his own doctoring. He possessed an ample medicine-chest, which he replenished on his trips to St. Louis. He had also a number of medical books, and no doubt these and such practical experience as came to him with the years made him reasonably skilful in the rough medicine and surgery that he practised. With the train he carried a small medicine-chest, which occasionally came into play.

For many years Bent's Fort was the great and only gathering-place for the Indians in the Southwestern plains, and at different times there were large companies of them present there.

At one time no less than three hundred and fifty lodges of Kiowa Apaches were camping near the fort on the south side of the river, and at another, according to Thomas Boggs, six or seven thousand Cheyennes were camped there at one time. When the Kiowas, Comanches, and Apaches were camped about the fort the number of Indians was very large. It must be remembered that prior to 1849 the Indians of the Southwest had not been appreciably affected by any of the new diseases brought into the country by the whites. This was largely due to the forethought of William Bent, who, by his action in 1829, when smallpox was raging at his stockade, protected the Cheyennes and Arapahoes at least, and very likely other Indians, from the attacks of this dread disease.

Shortly after the great peace between the Cheyennes, Arapahoes, Kiowas, Comanches, and Apaches, which was made in 1840, the two great camps moved up to Bent's Fort, the Cheyennes and Arapahoes camping on the north side of the river, the Kiowas, Comanches, and Apaches on the south. It was a great gathering of Indians, and the feasting, singing, dancing, and drumming were continuous. Though peace had just been made, there was danger that some of the old ill feeling that had so long existed between the tribes yet remained. Colonel Bent, with his usual wisdom, warned his employees that to these camps no spirits whatever should be traded. He recognized that if the Indians got drunk they would very likely begin to quarrel again, and a collision between members of tribes formerly hostile might lead to the breaking of the newly made peace. This was perhaps the greatest gathering of the Indians that ever collected at Fort William. How many were there will never be known.

Such, briefly, is the story of Bent's Fort, the oldest, largest, and most important of the fur trading posts on the great plains of the United States. Unless some manuscript, the existence of which is now unknown, should hereafter be discovered, it is likely to be all that we shall ever know of the place that once held an important position in the history of our country.

Bent's Fort long ago fell to ruins, but it has not been wholly forgotten. Up to the year 1868 the buildings were occupied as a stage station, and a stopping-place for travellers, with a bar and eating-house; but soon after that, when the railroad came up the Arkansas River, and stage travel ceased, the old post was abandoned. From that time on, it rapidly disintegrated under the weather.

In the autumn of 1912 I stood on this historic spot, still bare of grass, and marked on two sides by remains of the walls, in some places a mere low mound, and in others a wall four feet high, in which the adobe bricks were still recognizable. Here and there were seen old bits of iron, the fragment of a rusted horseshoe, of a rake, and a bit of cast-iron which had been part of a stove and bore letters and figures which could be made out as portions of the words "St. Louis, 1859."

The land on which the fort stood was owned by a public-spirited citizen, Mr. A. E. Reynolds, of Denver, Col., and here within the walls of the old fort he has placed a granite stone to mark its site and to commemorate its history. He has given the land over to the care of the Daughters of the American Revolution to be used as a public park for the counties of Otero and Bent, Colo.

William Bent, whose life was devoted to the upbuilding of the Southwest, will always be remembered as the one who placed on that fertile and productive empire the stamp "settled."

THE CROWN OF THE CONTINENT

FAR away in northwestern Montana, hidden from view by clustering mountain-peaks, lies an unmapped corner—the Crown of the Continent. The water from the crusted snowdrift which caps the peak of a lofty mountain there trickles into tiny rills, which hurry along north, south, east, and west, and growing to rivers, at last pour their currents into three seas. From this mountain-peak the Pacific and the Arctic oceans and the Gulf of Mexico receive each its tribute.

Here is a land of striking scenery. From some bold headland that rises abruptly from the plain, one looks eastward over naked yellow prairie. Near at hand, the ground is undulating, rising and falling like the swell of a troubled sea, but smooth and quiet in the far distance. Away to the east rise from the level land the three sharp pinnacles of the Sweet Grass Hills. On a clear day the dark column of smoke from the coal-mines of Lethbridge is seen seventy miles to the northeast. Here and there the yellow of the plain is broken by winding green water-courses, along which grow fringes of cottonwoods and willows, and at intervals little prairie lakes gleam like silver in the sun.

If one turns his back upon the prairie and looks west and south, the view is barred by a confused series of unknown mountains. Here are cañons deeper and narrower than those of the Yellowstone, mountains higher than those of the Yosemite. Some are rounded and some square-topped, some are slender pinnacles, and others knife-edged and with jagged crests, each one a true sierra. Many are patched with snow, and the highest wear their white covering from year's end to year's end. Along their verdureless slopes slow-moving ice rivers still plow their deliberate way, relics of mightier glaciers, the stiffened streams of which in a past age fashioned the majestic scenery of to-day. These old glaciers dug out for themselves channels between the mountains, and, when the ice melted, left deep cañons, the walls of which sometimes rise vertically from three to four thousand feet above the course of the stream flowing through the valley; or, again, they stand farther back, and are faced by long steep slopes of rock fragments fallen from the heights above. Often this talus is bare, or it may be covered with a dense growth of sturdy pines up to the limit —here less than eight thousand feet—where trees will no longer grow.

The rock which composes the mass of the mountain is very ancient, probably Cambrian. It consists of some thousands of feet of heavily bedded slates and shales capped by limestone. These rocks yield easily to the weather, which has carved out the mountain-peaks in fantastic shapes, which lend a strange interest to their profiles.

This region lies just south of the United States boundary-line and on the backbone of the continent. It includes in its eastern watershed the northwest corner of the Blackfeet reservation, and on the west an unexplored portion of Missoula County, and is roughly bounded by the parallels of 49° and 48° 30′ north latitude, and the meridians of 113° and 114° west longitude. In the southern portion of this territory rise Cut Bank and Milk rivers, which flow in a generally easterly course. Northwest of the heads of Milk River, a long ridge runs out in a northeasterly direction from the point of Divide Mountain, forming a crest which separates the northern and the southern waters. This is Milk River Ridge, which on its northern and western slope drains into the St. Mary's River, six hundred feet below, and on its southern and eastern into Milk River.

This region is known throughout northern Montana as the St. Mary's Lake country. In a narrow valley running back into the mountains lie two great lakes, the upper about twelve miles long, and the lower seven. These are enlargements of the St. Mary's River, a branch of the Saskatchewan, and receive the drainage of a wide area. Here, forty-eight years ago, Hugh Monroe, a devout Catholic, assisted by a party of Kootenai Indians, set up on the shores of the lower lake a great cross made of two pine-trees, and called the lakes St. Mary's. In 1853 Mr. James Doty, of Governor Stevens's party, who visited the lakes, called them Chief Mountain Lakes, after the great mountain known as the Chief, or the King, which rises almost from the prairie in a solitary needle of rock to a height of more than ten thousand feet. Since Mr. Doty named these lakes they seem to have been unknown to geographers. The name he gave them appears on many maps, but is wrongly applied to two other lakes thirty miles west and north, which form the head of the Walterton River and are locally known as the Kootenai Lakes.

This is the Blackfeet land, and for the Indians it is historic ground. A century ago it was owned by the Snakes and the Crows. In those old times, we are told, there was no war. Members of one tribe visited the camps of others, and after friendly meetings parted in peace. But already the white man had come, and had introduced among the Indians the temptation to war, as well as the means for carrying it on. Horses brought up from the south reached the Snakes, Flatheads, and Crows, and at length became known to the Blackfeet, who were then a mountain people and lived in the timber on the heads of streams flowing into the Saskatchewan. The Blackfeet wanted horses, and knew of no way to get them except by capture from their neighbors. About this time, too, the French traders from Montreal had supplied them with guns, powder, and ball. They had learned how to use these new weapons, and so had gained confidence in themselves. Their descendants of to-day have said to me: "Then first we learned to take courage, and to venture out of the timber on to the prairie, and to make journeys to war."

In their raids for horses the Blackfeet pressed farther and farther southward, driving their enemies before them, at first beyond the St. Mary's River and then beyond the Yellowstone. The Crows retreated southward and the Snakes southwest over the mountains; yet because of the great abundance of the buffalo on the plains, hunting- and war-parties of their enemies were constantly invading the territory which the Blackfeet had conquered, and so the Chief Mountain country was always a debatable ground where Blackfeet, Crows, Snakes, Gros Ventres, Crees, Assinaboines, Flatheads, Kootenais, and Stonies came to hunt, trap, and—when they met—to fight. All the prominent landmarks have their legends, stories of religion or of mythic heroes or of adventurers of later times. The Blackfeet remained the possessors of the territory, and though bit by bit their lands have been taken from them by the whites, they still retain the country of the Chief Mountain Lakes.

It was once a great game country. Over the far-stretching prairie roamed countless thousands of buffalo, and their advancing hosts creeping up along the mountain-sides covered the foot-hills and surged up the narrow valleys, as the swelling tide overflows the reefs and fills up the estuaries on some rocky shore. Far and near the prairie was black with them, and then again, in obedience to some mysterious impulse, the mighty herds receded and left it bare. In those days deer and elk without number fed in the river-bottoms. Antelope dotted the plain. Moose, elk, and mountain bison had their homes in the thick timber, and wore deep trails through it from park to park, and down to the water, and again up to the high naked buttes, where they liked to lie in the sun. Still higher, along the faces of rock slides and cliffs, are the hard-trodden paths worn by the mountain-sheep and the white goats, which dwell above the timber-line, and only now and then pass through the forest.

The Coming of the White Man

The game is almost all gone now from mountain and plain. Buffalo and bison are extinct everywhere, but in the dense forest a few moose, elk, and deer still exist, and, as of old, bears prowl through the timber, tearing to pieces the rotten logs for worms, or turning over great stones to find the ants and beetles on which they prey. On the high lands game is more abundant. The cliffs are still climbed by the nimble sheep and the sure-footed white goats, and there is no reason why the hunter should starve. During the migrations there are swans, geese, and ducks in great numbers; five species of grouse are found on the mountains; the streams and lakes swarm with trout and white-fish; and in early autumn the hillsides are covered with huckleberries.

The region is one of great precipitation. The warm west winds, which bring their freight of vapor from the distant Pacific, are chilled when they strike the cold high peaks of the main range, and their moisture is condensed, and much of it falls as rain or snow. Looking from the summit of Mount Allen, at an elevation of about eleven thousand feet, I have seen half a dozen tall peaks which lay west of my station, all apparently smoking like so many factory chimneys. A fresh wind was blowing, and not a cloud was to be seen in all the blue arch, yet from each of these cold pinnacles of rock a long streamer of heavy mist swung off to the southeast, hanging level in the air as the smoke of a passing steamer hangs over the sea, hiding the view; and in the shadow of each streamer of cloud more or less rain and snow was falling. It is this precipitation that maintains the glaciers which still lie on the north sides of all the higher mountains of this region.

My earlier visits were hunting-trips, and my time was spent climbing the mountains near the lakes for game, or fishing in the wind-swept waters; but I soon learned that the region was unexplored, and when from the summits of peaks about the lakes I looked back into the range and saw others yet unnamed, I felt a great desire to learn something more of this unknown country. Since that time I have been to the head of unexplored tributaries of Cut Bank, up the valley of Red Eagle Creek, to the head of the Upper St. Mary's River, as well as to the head of all the branches of Swift Current and a long way up Kennedy's Creek.

No words can describe the grandeur and majesty of these mountains, and even photographs seem hopelessly to dwarf and belittle the most impressive peaks. The fact that it is altogether unknown, the beauty of its scenery, its varied and unusual fauna, and the opportunities it offers for hunting and fishing and for mountain climbing, give the region a wonderful attraction for the lover of nature.

The territory of the United States has been pretty thoroughly gone over. Parties of the United States Geological Survey have sought out regions which were unknown and have mapped them, roughly or in detail; army officers with small bodies of troops have made hasty reconnaissances into others; individual hunters and trappers have penetrated where larger parties could not go; and most persistent of all has been the prospector, who in his search for "mineral"—as he calls the precious metals—has worked his way to the head of almost every stream. A few years ago I should have said that there was no place in the United States where the white man had not been. But where man goes he leaves behind him traces that endure for a long time. He cooks his food, and the ashes of his old camp-fires and charred ends of extinguished brands remain for years; he chops wood for fuel, or hews out for himself a trail, and chips and the cut ends of the sticks tell of his passage; his horses leave their signs behind them. All these things the mountaineer notices, and each sign tells its story. Such evidences of man's passage have been wanting in most of the valleys of the Chief Mountain region that I have traversed.

Beyond the head of the lower lakes wagons cannot go, and the traveler who wishes to reach the heads of any of the streams must leave his wagon and start into the mountain with a pack-train. This means that all his possessions—his food, his bedding, and his camp furniture—must be lashed on the backs of horses or mules, and so carried through the dense forests and up the steep mountain-sides. This is a pleasant mode of traveling, though it is slow and entails much more labor than traveling in a wagon. It has, however, the great advantage that it makes one independent. With a pack-train the explorer can go almost where he pleases. Neither dense brush, close-standing timber, nor steep hills furrowed by deep ravines can stop him; wherever a man can ride, a pack-horse can follow.

A well-broken pack-train moves on through the whole day with but little attention. Each animal has its own place and will fight to keep it. The post of honor is next to the horse ridden by the leader, and is usually occupied by the best fighter in the train. The animals display remarkable intelligence in avoiding obstacles and in keeping their loads in proper shape. There is a great deal of character in horses and mules, and as a packer is obliged to handle each one of his animals several times each day, he soon becomes acquainted with the idiosyncrasies of every one of them. Some are always gentle, easily caught, intelligent enough to stand still if they feel that their loads are coming loose; others are wild, readily frightened, and always making trouble. Some, while apparently well disposed, lack sense and are constantly getting into difficulties. They get "hung up" in timber, fall over cliffs, mire down in swamps, and try to drown themselves when crossing deep rivers. For some of the animals in his train the explorer comes to have a real affection, some he dislikes, and some he holds in contempt.

Wherever it is possible, those who travel through unexplored mountains make use of old game-trails, for in its migration from place to place the game selects the easiest paths, and these wild animals have been the real road-makers in Western exploration. Mountain men have an old saying: "The deer made the first trails; the elk followed the deer, the buffalo the elk, and the Indians the buffalo; after the Indians came the trapper; then an army officer came along and discovered a pass."

In these rough mountains the most practicable routes for horses are in the stream valleys or just above them; but at best progress is slow. In a bad country accidents and delays occur continually. Animals become wedged in between trees, fall down while crossing swift-running streams, lose their footing on steep mountain-sides, and roll far down the hill. Many of these mishaps involve the repacking of the animal, and when to this is added the fact that the train is winding about to avoid obstacles, now climbing hills and again descending into valleys, it will easily be seen that, however long the day's march may be in hours, it seldom covers many miles.

On the September day in 1891 when our party of five men set out to try to reach the head of the St. Mary's River above the lakes, we were late in getting away from camp. This is always to be expected on the first day's march. Pack-saddles and "riggings" are to be fitted to the horses, provisions, cooking-utensils, and blankets to be sorted out and made up into packs; and this, with the loading of the animals, takes a great deal of time. After a day or two, when each packer knows just where every article belongs, the work is much more quickly done. At length the last rope is made fast, and the leader of the train rides off up the trail. The pack-horses fall in behind him, and the other riders, after giving a last look over the abandoned campground to see that nothing has been left behind, take their places in the line, distributing themselves along it, so that each man has in front of him one or two animals which are his special charge. He must keep them from lagging and must watch their loads.

The trail follows up the west shore of the lake, for two miles passing through dense growths of aspens, and then into a long, wide prairie which is crossed here and there by the wooded courses of little streams. To the right, or west, and little more than a mile distant, tower the cliffs of Single Shot Mountain; while across the lake, hills wooded with dense pine forests rise toward Milk River Ridge and the point of Divide Mountain. About seven miles above the end of the upper lake is the true gate of the mountains. Here two long points, from Red Eagle Mountain on one side and from Goat Mountain on the other, jut out into the lake and almost meet, forming the Lower Narrows. The northern face of the ledge from Goat Mountain is vertical and can be climbed at only one point, and there by a very steep trail. Most people prefer to ascend this on foot, leading their horses, and a little excitement is usually given to the scramble by the rocks which, loosened by the horses' hoofs, come bounding down the slope. Occasionally it happens that a pack-horse loses its footing and rolls down, hoofs over load. This is worse for those below than a fifty-pound rock, because less easily avoided.

After climbing the point of rocks, the trail winds through the green timber near the foot of Goat Mountain, and then passes out on to the steep slide-rock, which in many places extends from the lake shore, in a slope broken only by cliffs, up to the walls of rock forming the mountain's crest. Ever ascending, the trail climbs this slide-rock, following an ancient path trodden into the rock by the game, and at length passes along a narrow ledge with precipices above and below. A little alder-grown trickle of water crosses here, and this was where our party met with its first accident.

For a few yards below the crossing, the sharply sloping mountainside is overgrown with alders, and then breaks off in a cliff one hundred feet high. The trail is twelve or fifteen inches wide, but appears narrower, for the summer's growth of weeds, grass, and alder sprouts extends out over it. The man who was in advance was on foot, leading a pack-horse. After him came another loaded animal, and this was closely followed by two horsemen. When these were within a few yards of the brook crossing they heard a yell of dismay from the man in front, and then a shout: "The black mare has rolled down the hill!" Slipping off their horses and leaving them standing in the trail, they ran forward, and reached the scene of disaster just in time to see the second pack-horse spring upon a large flat rock which lay in the way, and as its four unshod feet came down on the smooth stone, it slipped, lost its footing, and rolled slowly off the trail. It had not fairly got started before the men had it by the head and had stopped its descent, holding it by the loosened hackamore. The animal made one or two struggles to regain its footing, but the brush, the slope, and its load made it impossible for it to rise, and it lay there while the three men held it. Meanwhile the black mare by a lucky chance had regained her feet before reaching the precipice, and was now making her way up the slope toward the trail.

To get the pack off the fallen beast was the first thing to be done. A man climbed down the rocks behind the horse, so as to be out of the way of its feet if it should flounder, and cut the lacing which attaches the hook to the lash cinch, thus freeing the load, which was then readily pulled aside, and with a little effort and help the horse stood on its feet and was led up to the trail, and then on to a grassy bench where there was a little level ground. The other horses were then carefully led past the dangerous point, and as it was now late in the afternoon, and the work of repairing damages would occupy an hour or two, we camped here, and after stretching ropes across the trail so that the horses could not go back, turned them loose to forage on the ledges. While supper was being cooked, a large white goat came out to the edge of the cliff three hundred yards above us, and made a leisurely inspection of the camp.

Two days later we had made some progress up the untraveled valley of the Upper St. Mary's and had camped on the edge of a narrow grassy park in the valley of the south branch of the river. This is much the larger of the two streams, and its milky water shows the presence of glaciers at its head, while the north fork is clear.

On the left of the camp towered the vertical cliffs of Citadel Mountain; the high wooded shoulder running down from Mount Reynolds was to the right, and before us, up the valley, stood the peak of Fusillade and the rounded mass of Mount Jackson.

The following day's march was very laborious. For the first few miles no obstacles more formidable than fallen timber, dense alders, and mire were met with; but after we had passed the point of Citadel and turned south, progress became very difficult and slow. Many years ago an avalanche had swept down the valley and overthrown its great trees, which now lay piled up on the ground like giant jack-straws, barring the way, and it was necessary to climb a shoulder which runs down between the valley and Citadel Mountain. The ascent of this was steep, and the ground was thickly overgrown with tough brushwood, standing shoulder-high, among which lay the rotting trunks of great trees fallen years before. The combination was very discouraging, and it was not long before the horses became so tired that they refused to face the brush, and I had to dismount and lead my animal, breaking a trail as I went. To add to our discomfort, rain began to fall about midday, and in a very short time all hands were thoroughly soaked. After an all-day struggle with brush, fallen timber, and hills, we found ourselves at night in a little grassy meadow lying between two old moraines, almost at timber-line and only a few hundred yards from the foot of the great glacier which runs down from the mountain to the south. Here we made our camp, and a few stunted spruces gave us half a dozen lodge-poles. Though wet and weary, the men, as they worked to make camp that night, carried about with them a feeling of contentment born of difficulties overcome and an object attained, and one of them referred to the little party as the "get there" brigade.

The camp stood on the east side of the valley. To the south and southeast were the moraines and ice-fingers stretching down from the great Blackfoot Glacier, and behind these the sloping mass of ice rises toward the mountain's crown. East were the vertical walls of Citadel Mountain; to the west stood Mount Jackson, and to the north was Fusillade. The Blackfoot Glacier is by far the most imposing that I have seen in the Rocky Mountains south of the Canadian boundary. From our camp in this valley we could see only a small part of its lower end, but I have looked on this mountain from two different points of view, at a distance of a dozen miles, and have seen that the glacier covers the whole northern side of the mountain. The mass of the ice lies behind (south of) Citadel Mountain and west of the great crest of rock from the eastern side of which flow waters running into Red Eagle Creek. At the foot of this main ice is a lofty cliff, and over this pour great milky streams, the volume of which seems at least one half of the water which flows into the St. Mary's Lake.

Mount Jackson, one of the highest mountains to be seen, is a rounded mass, in part ice-covered, as is also the high ridge by which it joins the shoulder of the Blackfoot Mountain. North of Jackson is a deep valley which separates it from Fusillade Mountain. At the head of this valley is a little lake, and beyond the lake a low saddle, over which a trail across the range could easily be made. On the west side of this pass is another little lake, from which a stream runs southwestward toward the Pacific Ocean. The wall of rock separating these two lakes is not more than one hundred yards in thickness, and to tunnel it would afford a passage for a railway with but slight grade.

We spent nearly two weeks in this wonderful spot, climbing the mountains and hunting goats and sheep and ptarmigan. Goats were abundant and tame, but the member of the party who had the nearest view of them was one who had never before been in the Rocky Mountains. He was laboriously working his way up some vertical cliffs, and, needing both hands to climb with, had strapped his rifle on his back. As he raised himself up over a rock he met face to face, and not forty feet away, a large goat coming toward him. The two saw each other at the same moment, and at first astonishment held each motionless. In a moment the goat recovered himself and started back up the mountain, and by the time the hunter had freed his gun, the game had disappeared behind some rocks and was not seen again.

A goat-hunting incident gave Fusillade Mountain its name. We had moved our camp to the little lake below that peak, and one morning two of the men climbed high upon its side in pursuit of a dozen or twenty goats which made it their feeding-ground. The day had passed, and we had heard no shot, and from the camp could see the goats still feeding undisturbed. Just about sunset, as we were eating supper, the report of a gun was heard far above us. Glasses were leveled, and as shot after shot rang out and echoed along the mountain-side, we saw puffs of blue smoke rising from a point far below the goats. These at first did not seem to be interested in the shooting. Very likely they had never before heard a gun. But at length, when the balls began to strike near them, they jumped about a little, and at last, looking like so many flies crawling up a wall, all slowly clambered up the mountain and passed out of sight over the top. When all had disappeared, the hunters, who had been shooting at long range and had not expected to hit anything, rose from their places of concealment and started down toward the camp. They had come but a short distance when over the top of the mountain all the goats appeared again and crawled deliberately down the seemingly vertical wall back to their feeding-ground.

We had intended to go to the head of the north fork of the river, and perhaps to take our train across from there to the head of Swift Current River, but we found so much to do on the south fork that this plan had to be postponed for another year.

The journey down the valley to the lake was rough, but was accomplished in two days. For two or three miles above the head of the upper lake there are signs of travel in this valley. Old Indian blazes are seen on the trees, and occasional choppings. But beyond this we could detect no indications that man had ever been over the ground, and it added something to our satisfaction to find that there were no camp-fires, no choppings, no signs of horses. The region seemed unvisited.

Two miles from where St. Mary's River leaves the lower lake, it is joined from the west by a large stream known as Swift Current. The valley of this river is narrow where it joins that of the St. Mary's, but above this it becomes wider. The mountains which inclose it on each hand, at first low and round-topped, gradually become bolder and higher, and at last are continuous walls two thousand feet in height, broken at intervals by "basins," each one narrow at its mouth, but often wide within, from which pour torrents fed by melting snows, or by springs high up in the rocks. Swift Current valley is straight, and as one rides along toward its head he can see the long, narrow mountain which separates its two branches, and the great mass of ice which supplies water for the southernmost of the two. Up this valley for perhaps fifteen miles, passing through the groves of aspens and the grassy parks which lie on the north of the stream, runs a well-worn Indian trail. On the south side, the heavily timbered mountains, still the home of a few moose, stand close to the river. At intervals along the stream are little lakes, and the fifth of these, counting from its mouth, receives the two main branches into which Swift Current is here divided. Just below this lake are the falls of Swift Current, two broken cataracts or steep cascades, one of fifty and the other of seventy-five feet, beautiful waterfalls, but insignificant in comparison with their surroundings.

The first day's journey up the stream usually carries one to a large grassy park below the falls, where Indian hunting-parties make their permanent camps. Once these mountains abounded in sheep and goats, and everywhere about this park may be seen the sites of old Indian camps, with rotting lodge-poles, old fireplaces, and piles of bone and hair, showing where game has been cut up and hides dressed. Above this park the trail forks, the right-hand branch following up the north arm of the river toward Mount Wilbur, and the other, which is blind and not easy to find or to follow, crossing a shoulder of Mount Allen and keeping on the south side of the south branch of the river to its head. On this arm of the stream are two glacial lakes, each a mile long, the westernmost of the two lying at the foot of the great precipice, beneath a large glacier.

When the old camp-ground is reached, the pack-animals are quickly caught and relieved of their loads, unsaddled and turned loose. Meantime one of the men has taken the ax, and stepping off among the pine timber, is felling straight, slender poles. Before long, other men go to him, and bring the lodge-poles to the camp, where they are smoothed and three of them tied together at the proper height, to make a frame for our dwelling. These having been raised and their butts spread so as to form a tripod, other poles are set up against the forks, and the top of the lodge is tied to the last pole. When this is in position, the canvas is spread over the frame. Then the front of the lodge is pinned together, the outside poles fixed in the ears, the border of the lodge pinned to the ground, and we have a comfortable house which is warm, water-tight, and wind-proof. The fire is built on the ground in the middle of the lodge; the beds are spread about the walls. Outside saddles and ropes are neatly piled up, and we are at home for a night or for a month. The evening meal is eaten about dark, and the hours before bedtime are spent about the fire. The camp is roused at dawn, and while breakfast is being cooked, some one goes out, finds the horses, and drives them close to the camp. After breakfast, while some make up the packs and tear down the lodge, others catch and saddle the animals, which are soon packed, and before long the train is strung out over the trail on the day's march.

Below the westernmost of the two lakes on the south branch of Swift Current is a little spruce-dotted meadow in which we always camp. Here there is grass enough for a dozen horses for two or three weeks. Across the lake, to south of west, is the great cliff above which lies the ice, north of the glacier, the dividing ridge between the two streams, and south, Mount Gould, a huge buttress of which, Monroe Peak, each day interrupts the sun, and, like a vast dial, from ten o'clock till two, casts its slow-moving shadow across the waters at its foot. East of Gould Mountain and the range which runs southeast from it is the narrow valley of Cataract Creek, four or five miles long. The stream rises in the divide which separates the Swift Current system from the north branch of the Upper St. Mary's River, and is fed by banks of permanent snow and ice which lie in the ravines and on the rugged shoulders of Mount Gould. On the other side of the valley is Mount Allen, one of the highest mountains on Swift Current.

On my first visit to the Swift Current Glacier I approached it by climbing up the face of the precipice at its foot. The climb was long and hard, and though we started about three o'clock in the morning, it was long after dark that night when we returned to the camp. Most of the time after we reached the ice was devoted to examining it, though we stopped long enough during the ascent to kill a great bighorn, the tracks of which we found in the new snow on the edge of the glacier. Following these footprints, which led in the direction we were going, on rounding a point of rocks we saw the sheep standing in a snow-drift on the mountain-side far above us. A quick shot was made, and with one bound he disappeared from view; but on climbing up to where he had stood, we saw from the blood and footprints in the snow that he was hard hit and could not go far. He had turned down the mountain, and one of the men followed him down the cliffs and over the snowbanks till he found him dead at the foot of a precipice. The other two men went on higher, and spent some hours upon the glacier, which was then, in November, covered with new snow.

On another occasion, some years later, I found this glacier melting rapidly in early September. It was everywhere extensively crevassed and pierced by deep wells, into which the brooks which seamed the surface of the ice poured with loud roarings. Indeed, the rush of many waters here was fairly appalling. The tinkle of the streams above, the echoing fall of the plunging torrents, and the hiss of the confined water rushing along beneath the ice, made up a volume of sound so great that ordinary conversation could not be heard. It was here and at this time that I carelessly put myself in a position of serious danger. Though unprepared for ice work, I was anxious to climb an arm of the glacier which led directly to the mountain's crest, and not realizing the steepness of the ascent, I set out. Before I had gone half a mile over the ice, I wished myself back on the rocks again, for the incline was constantly increasing. I knew that if I lost my footing and began to slide down the sloping ice I should not stop until I had fallen into one of the bottomless pits or crevasses of the main glacier; and a man who had fallen into one of these would have but a very short time in which to think over his past life. To attempt to retrace my steps would be greatly to increase the danger of making a fatal slip. There was no course except to keep on climbing. I made my way to the border of the finger of ice which was embraced by the two shoulders of the mountain; but next to the rock it had melted away, and I looked down into a deep trench there, which ran back far under the ice, and from the blackness below came up the roar of the torrent and the rumble of great rocks crashing against the stream-bed as they were hurried along by the water. Keeping near the edge of the ice, I slowly and carefully climbed higher and higher, and at length reached a place where a point of solid rock jutted out to within six feet of the edge of the ice. Here I sprang across the chasm and landed safely on the mountain-side.

About the heads of Swift Current there is abundant opportunity for a mountaineer to stretch his legs. The north branch takes its rise in two streams, one heading in an odd double glacial lake at the foot of Mount Wilbur, and the other among lower mountains to the northeast. At the foot of Wilbur, and lying against the vertical cliffs which rise without a break thousands of feet above it, is a little glacier less than half a mile square, which is constantly pushing out into the lake. The waters carried by the eddying winds against this ice undermine it, and as this goes on, sections of the glacier fall off into the water, so that the little lake is dotted with a multitude of tiny icebergs, which, driven hither and thither by the wind, glitter in the sunlight until at last they melt, the supply being kept up by other fallen masses of the glacier. So here in the Rocky Mountains we have a little iceberg factory. The basin or little valley from which this stream flows is narrow and hemmed in on three sides by marvelous rock walls. Apparently vertical, this barrier rises for thousands of feet, terminating in a serrated ridge, over which it would seem that nothing but a bird could pass. Although seemingly vertical, these precipices can at some points be scaled by an active man, and from their summits one looks down into the narrow valley of Belly River, walled in by high gray and glacier-bearing mountains.

Our work in the mountains is not all pleasure. Often we have a "spell of weather" which forbids climbing or hunting. A blizzard sweeps over the range, and deep snows and bitter cold confine us to the lodge, and we await the advent of a favoring chinook to melt the snow. At such times short excursions are made with the shot-gun for ducks or grouse, or we wade through the drifts over the lower lands and try to find the lynxes and coyotes the tracks of which are seen in the snow, or even the bears, which have not yet entered on their long winter sleep. Much of the time, however, is spent in the lodge, where, after the few books in the camp have been exhausted, we are driven to entertain one another with stories.

Men who have seen much of the wild life of the old frontier have usually a good store of interesting reminiscences, if they can be induced to talk. As a rule, however, they are rather silent; but days of confinement often lead to the discovery among the company of some man who has an unexpected fund of good stories. Many of these will treat of personal adventure or of curious observations on the habits of birds and mammals. If Indians are in the party, they will sometimes tell stories of their own—tribal traditions of the beginning of things, of the time when their gods lived upon the earth and mingled with the people, of the magic doings of powerful medicine-men, besides many tales of the prowess of ancient warriors of their tribe. Often these weather-bound story-tellings will bring out enough interesting material to fill a volume. The tales are sometimes related with great power and even beauty. Little time is wasted in word-painting; it is the action which the storytellers deal with. Terse, epigrammatic phrases and the expressive gestures of the sign-language with which they supplement their spoken words lend a wonderful force to their narrations.

A special interest attaches to the traditional stories of the Indians, of which each tribe has its own, handed down from generation to generation by word of mouth. Such a story is the Blackfoot account of how the people first received arms. "Old Man," it must be explained, is the Blackfoot Creator and chief god.

The old men say that Old Man, soon after he was born, made the people. Instead of giving them long fingers, he made their hands like those of the bear, and they dug roots and ate berries for food.

In those days the buffalo used to eat people. It was a long time before Old Man found this out, but one day he came along and saw them feasting on a woman they had just killed. Then Old Man felt very badly; he sat down on a rock and cried, and tore out his hair, and tried to think what he could do to save the people. "Hai-yah!" he cried, "I have not made these people right. They cannot defend themselves." He sat a long time thinking what to do, and at last he knew; so he went to where there were some people, and split their hands, making long fingers instead of short claws. Then he made some bows, arrows, and knives, and taught the people how to use them. He made their right arms the strongest, so that they could bend the bow with great force.

"Now, people," he said, "you will survive; now you can defend yourself. Kill plenty of the buffalo next time they come. The meat is good to eat, and the robes will make you warm clothing."

By and by the buffalo came again, and the people did as the Old Man had told them. The first arrow struck a buffalo in the side.

"Oh, my brothers," he cried, "a great fly bites me!" and he fell down and died.

The people killed many more buffalo, and at last those still alive saw that the people were shooting them. "You people, you people," they cried out, "do not kill any more of us! We will never eat any of you again."

Then Old Man, who was sitting on a rock looking on, said to them: "Hold on! We will gamble to see which shall be eaten." He called all the animals to help the people, and they all came.

First the elk played against the buffalo and lost. The different animals in turn gambled against the buffalo and lost. On the third day, all had played except the mouse. His turn was now come. He took the bones in his little paws, and all the people and animals shouted: "Take courage, little mouse! Take courage, little mouse!" The mouse took courage, and made his paws go so fast that the buffalo could not tell which one held the bone with the black mark. They guessed the wrong one and lost. Then every one shouted, they were so glad. The people strung their bows and killed many fat cows, enough to give all the animals a feast.

Afterward Old Man gave the buffalo skulls to the mice. Even to this day you will see that they make their homes in them. This is how Old Man paid them for saving the people.

The Chief Mountain region has a real value to this country, and this consists in its being a reservoir for the storage of the great amount of moisture precipitated here. For eight or nine months of the year this moisture takes the form of snow, and supplies the annual waste caused by the melting of the glaciers. Without these glaciers and the far-reaching fields of snow which lie on many of the mountains, the lakes and the rivers would soon go dry. At present all the watercourses are full at all seasons of the year, and the winter's snows, protected by dense pine forests, are still slowly melting in June and July. The St. Mary's River is a very large stream, and south of it, until we come to the Missouri River, there is none carrying an equal volume of water flowing out of the Rocky Mountains to the eastward. A plan is already on foot to divert the St. Mary's from its present course and turn it into Milk River. If this should be done it would render irrigable many hundreds of square miles in northern Montana which are now quite without value from lack of water. But if the forests of the Chief Mountain region should be swept away by fire or the ax, its value as a reservoir would be gone. Large tracts of forest on Swift Current have been burned over by hunting-parties of Canadian Indians, and this danger is ever-present.

Persons who have given intelligent study to the problems of forestry and the needs of the arid West appreciate the importance of protecting the sources of rivers flowing from the Rocky Mountains over the plains east and west, and it is obvious that the greater the number of settlers who establish themselves on these dry plains the more water will be used and so the more needed. The question of water-supply is the most important that to-day confronts the States which border the Rocky Mountains. Already many of these States are feeling in the lessened volume of their streams the evil effect of the wasteful destruction of their forests. Great rivers like the Platte, the Arkansas, and the Rio Grande receive in a short time the quickly melting snows which lie on the naked sides of the mountains in which they rise, and when this flood is over, they fall at once to their summer level. Besides this, they are tapped all along their courses by flumes and ditches, which carry off the water and spread it over the ground. The result is that even these large rivers dwindle in midsummer and autumn to mere trickles of water, or become wholly dry. Their waters have been used up.

Happily, in 1897, by the official initiative of the United States Forest Commission, of which Professor Charles S. Sargent was chairman, a large section of this mountain country was made into a forest reserve, including Upper St. Mary's Lake. Under faithful and intelligent supervision, the dangers above spoken of will in large part be obviated, and in due time Montana will rejoice, as California is now doing, that so large a source of her water-supply has thus been preserved for her people.